THE INTERNATIONAL MARKET
IN FILM AND TELEVISION PROGRAMS

THE INTERNATIONAL MARKET
IN FILM AND TELEVISION PROGRAMS

edited by

Eli M. Noam

Joel C. Millonzi

ABLEX PUBLISHING CORPORATION
NORWOOD, NEW JERSEY

Printed in the United States of America

Library of Congress Cataloging-in-Publication Data

The international market in film and television programs / edited by
Eli M. Noam and Joel C. Millonzi.
    p.   cm. — (Communication and information science)
    Includes bibliographical references and indexes.
    ISBN 0-89391-545-9
    1. Motion pictures—Marketing. 2. Television programs—Marketing.
  I. Noam, Eli M. II. Millonzi, Joel Carl. III. Series.
  PN1995.9.M29I58 1991
  791.43 '068 '8—dc20   91-25338
                                                 CIP

Ablex Publishing Corporation
355 Chestnut Street
Norwood, New Jersey 07648

Contents

About the Authors

Jonathan B. Baker teaches economics at Dartmouth's Amos Tuck School of Business Administration. He has been an Attorney Advisor to the Acting Chairman of the Federal Trade Commission, and has been associated with the law firm of Foley & Lardner. His fields of specialization include industrial organization economics, antitrust law, and economic regulation. His scholarly publications have appeared in economics journals and law reviews. He has received a Ph.D. in economics from Stanford University, a J.D. from Harvard Law School, and an A.B. from Harvard College.

Richard Collins is Principal Lecturer in Communication Studies at the Royal Melbourne Institute of Technology, Melbourne, Australia. He is a member of the editorial board of *Critical Studies in Mass Communications*. He has published extensively in academic and broadcasting trade journals in the U.K., U.S., Canada, West Germany, and the Netherlands and is the author of *Culture Communication and National Identity* (forthcoming).

Eli M. Noam is a Professor of Economics and Finance at the Columbia University Graduate School of Business and Director of the Columbia Institute for Tele-Information. From 1987 to 1990 he served as a Commissioner on the New York Public Service Commission. He has also taught at Princeton University. His recent work includes the volumes *Television in Europe* and *Telecommunications in Europe,* and various other books on US and international telecommunications. He received an A.B., M.A. and Ph.D. in economics, and a J.D. law degree from Harvard University.

Jean-Luc Renaud is currently at Logica Consultancy Ltd. in London and is a contributing editor to *Television Business International.* He was a Visiting Assistant Professor at the University of Minnesota's School of Journalism and Mass Communication and co-authored a book on the European media industry while a research fellow at the University of Manchester's European Institute for the Media. His main research interest is in international communication policy. After studying at the Universities of Lausanne and Geneva in Switzerland, his native country, he received an M.A. from Southern Illinois University, Carbondale and a Ph.D. in mass communication from Michigan State University.

Stephen E. Siwek is Director of Financial Analysis for the research and consulting firm of Economists Incorporated, Washington, D.C. He is co-author of *International Trade in Films and Television Programs*. He has lectured on issues of international trade in media products in the United States, London, and Geneva, Switzerland. Mr. Siwek is a member of the Institute of Business Appraisers. He holds a M.B.A. from George Washington University and a B.A. in economics from Boston College.

Professor Michael Tracey is Director of the Center for Mass Media Research at the University of Colorado at Boulder. Prior to that he had been head of the Broadcasting Research Unit in London, England, a leading non-commercial center for research on broadcast-related issues. Tracey himself has published widely on numerous aspects of communications policy.

Jack Valenti is President and Chief Executive Officer of the Motion Picture Association of America. He had formerly been a Special Assistant to President Lyndon Johnson. Mr. Valenti received an M.B.A. from Harvard Business School.

Tapio Varis is currently Reader in journalism and mass communication and a senior researcher at the University of Tampere, Finland, and also at the University of Helsinki. Previously, he was the Rector at the University for Peace, created by the United Nations, in Costa Rica, from 1986 to 1989. From 1979 to 1984, he was the Director of the Tampere Peace Research Institute. He has also been researcher at the Finnish Institute of International Affairs and the Academy of Finland. His publications include approximately 100 contributions in scientific and professional journals.

David Waterman is currently Assistant Professor at the Annenberg School of Communications at the University of Southern California. Previously he was President of Waterman & Associates, a consulting firm specializing in economic and market research for government and private industry clients in the communications field. His primary field of specialization is the economics of information industries. Dr. Waterman earned his B.A. from University of Southern California and received his M.A. and Ph.D. in economics from Stanford University.

Steven S. Wildman is an Associate Professor in the Department of Communication Studies and Director of the Program in Telecommunications Science, Management and Policy at Northwestern University. Past positions include Senior Economist at Economists Incorporated, Assistant Professor of Economics at UCLA, and consultant to the Rand Corporation. Dr. Wildman has published numerous articles on media and telecommunications topics and is the co-author with Stephen E. Siwek of *International Trade in Films and Television Programs*. He holds a Ph.D. and M.A. in economics from Stanford University and a B.A. in economics from Wabash College.

Introduction

The worldwide expansion of television and other video media has vastly increased the demand for programs and encouraged their international trade. Information flows have become major economic transactions and as such they deserve economists' attention. This is the purpose of the chapters in this book. They seek to examine the economic forces in film and TV trade, looking at their impact on distribution channels, program mix, national policies, and prices. The chapters also address questions relating to global trade barriers: To what extent is the international market competitive? Do American producers enjoy a distinct competitive advantage, and if so, why? How is the market environment affected by various national policies? What are the effects of local content requirements, import quotas, and earning restrictions? What benefits are accrued to local producers by such policies? To what extent do language and culture affect economic factors?

This is, of course, not the first treatment of international media flows. But the other discussions of the subject have primarily focused on cultural, sociological, and political issues. Cultural dominance, or "media imperialism," was a major theme of that debate, especially in the light of New World Information Order concerns of Unesco. The analytical framework of this work, however, has not been adequately complemented by economic studies. To remedy this absence, this book seeks to establish a better understanding of the issues by adding to the culturally oriented literature analyses of trade, industrial organization, market structure, and program choice. Such work is overdue, since the trade in information goods has far outgrown the analytical tools applied to its understanding.

It must be clarified that the emphasis on neoclassical economics in this volume does not imply a rejection of other disciplinary or methodological approaches. Indeed, a number of noneconomists are included in the book. The editors do not consider media programs as simple commodities; there are clearly special considerations and complexities involved, particularly with respect to smaller, less-developed countries and their cultures. The assumptions, and hence the conclusions, of any academic methodology are by necessity limiting. This is an obvious point, yet one that is frequently lost in the often heated climate of academic discussions of international media. Economists are fairly used to objects of their analysis denying that economic principles apply to themselves; on media issues, the introduction of economics is frequently considered a political act, and a degradation of culture to the level of a commodity; it is often resisted with affirmation of national traditions against Hollywood-type commercialism. It is easy to caricature a mainstream economic analysis of the structure of media and its transactions as a mark of cultural insensitivity or devoid of some political context. But it would be more helpful to the continuing development of media studies as an intellectual discipline if one could deal with the arguments of various paradigms in a more relaxed fashion.

In selecting authors and topics, the editors did not seek to prove any particular position; however, the choice of mainstream economic reasoning tends to frame the discussion in a way that is different from those of other approaches. It should be emphasized in this context that the project received no financial or intellectual support from any commercial or governmental organization.

The book has two sections. The first deals with the empirical setting and with analysis of trade issues, primarily for television programming. Tapio Varis, of the University of Tampere, Finland, and author of an earlier detailed study of media flows for Unesco which played an important role in the debate, examines the trends in global television trade patterns. Comparing traffic statistics in 1973 to those in 1983, Varis examines the origins of imported programming and trends in interregional exchange. While overall patterns of trade in traditional broadcast media established in 1973 continue to persist, the effect of the video cassettes and broadcast satellites has made such patterns less distinct.

Steven Wildman of Northwestern University and Stephen Siwek, a consulting economist in Washington D.C., contribute an analysis entitled "The Economics of Trade in Recorded Media Products in a Multilingual World: Implications for National Media Policy." Their study, a continuation of work for the American Enterprise Institute, models trade in information products and focuses on the various barriers that impede product flow. It also evaluates the differentiating impact that national trade policies have on the supply and demand for programs. Based on a two-stage model of production decisions, Wildman and Siwek argue that the United States and other English language countries benefit from what they term "domestic opportunity advantage," which accounts for the flow of recorded media products from major producing countries like the U.S. They conclude that this flow is not subject to a shift in direction, but may change in magnitude and the degree to which it may affect the importing countries' national media suppliers.

Eli Noam's chapter, "Media Americanization, National Culture and Forces of Integration," takes issue with the assumption of the inevitability of U.S. producer dominance in international trade, especially among developed countries. Noam, of Columbia University and formerly a Commissioner on the New York Public Service Commission, argues that the notion of an "iron law" of U.S. inherent export advantages is based on flawed economic reasoning, and it requires a more careful evaluation than is often supplied. He then discusses the reasons for the global success of U.S. media productions, and for the emergence of multinational integrated media firms.

David Waterman's study of "World Television Trade" presents a model which examines the effects of privatization and new technologies on program trade. Waterman, of the Annenberg School of Communications at the University of Southern California, predicts that the commercial video media infrastructures (especially pay-TV and video cassettes) currently developing in some countries will eventually benefit domestic producers more than foreign ones, leading to a proportional increase in domestically produced programs. In presenting his analysis, Waterman considers the relationship between commercial incentives, the social objectives of domestic media policies, and the effects of economic constraints such as import quotas, licensing, and subsidies. Finally, he poses the dilemma of survival for public television in a largely private commercial environment.

The subject of the second section of the book is media production outside of the United States. In addressing the "gray market" in video cassettes, Jonathan Baker of Dartmouth's Amos Tuck School of Business Administration focuses on a subject of growing controversy, continuing earlier work as a litigation expert. Citing figures which suggest that unauthorized video cassettes account for virtually the entire market in some countries, Baker presents a theory of gray markets, and applies it to a cost-benefit analysis of video piracy. He examines the policy tradeoff between lower consumer prices resulting from the "allowance" of unauthorized distribution of media goods and the loss of investment by producers in countries with a significant gray market. The analysis suggests that, in spite of a world tilting toward a gray market, the long-run loss to consumers from deterring local investment usually outweighs the benefits in terms of lower prices. This chapter may make for slow reading by non-economists, but it suggests the way in which a formalized model can be used to structure an analysis of media production decisions.

Richard Collins of the Royal Melbourne Institute of Technology offers a discussion of media imperialism which argues that the rise of dominance in the international market cannot be adequately explained by conventional paradigms. The comparative advantage paradigm has flaws in its economic analysis, and it woefully neglects political, linguistic, and cultural criteria. The media imperialism paradigm, on the other hand, is inadequate because it fails to recognize the fact that imported programs may be useful sources of diversity and quality in the programming schedules. Citing the diminishing hold on the market of the network oligopoly in the United States, Collins points out that media market structures are changing. Such shifts to alternative distribution channels, in his view, is likely to create opportunities, especially for non-U.S. producers. This will lead to a revenue pool shared by a greater number of participants, a phenomenon which Collins argues will pave the way for an increased demand for low to mid-cost programming often marketed by foreign producers.

Jack Valenti, President of the Motion Picture Association of America, advocates the perspective of Hollywood producers, attributing the resurgence in cinema attendance worldwide to the larger number of desirable films available. If this trend is to continue, Valenti argues, competitive conditions must be maintained in the international market, piracy must be stopped, and trade barriers must be removed.

Jean-Luc Renaud's chapter responds to the claim that it is inherently desirable to deregulate the international media market. While acknowledging that a "protective" regime has a pejorative connotation, Renaud, of Logica Consultancy Ltd., and formerly at the European Institute for the Media, University of Manchester, argues that those who advocate wholesale abandonment of protectionist policies are either naive or insensitive to the realities of the marketplace. Deregulation may take some of the government bureaucracy out of the marketplace, but it still leaves the communications industry subject to the political motivations which underlie free market slogans. Renaud critiques the traditional economic arguments used to justify U.S. economic dominance; that it occurred naturally in a competitive environment, that import quotas deny consumers their choice, that deregulated markets combined with new distribution technologies (in particular, DBS) will meet consumer needs by fostering a local audiovisual industry, and that an undisturbed marketplace can cater better to cultural needs than public sponsored media.

In the concluding chapter, Michael Tracey of the U.K.'s Broadcasting Research Unit, and more recently of the Center for Mass Media Research at the University of Colorado, addresses some of the noneconomic issues affecting the international market. He rejects the notion that U.S. economic dominance of the international marketplace will implicitly lead to cultural hegemony. Tracey argues that studies which conclude that media exports result in wholesale cultural exploitation are conceptually inadequate and methodologically untested. In questioning the assumptions underlying such studies, Tracey casts doubt on the implication that television and film programs can override other societal institutions. He also emphasizes that such studies underestimate the growing influence of a pluralistic market structure of production and distribution currently emerging on a regional and inter-regional basis. Tracey believes that the new distribution technologies will not simply pour their wares over the populations of the world; nor will they necessarily cause the collapse of local broadcasters and producers. Rather than a "seamless (cultural) robe, woven in Hollywood," the international and local markets will resemble patchwork quilts.

All the chapters contained in this book are based on a project and a conference sponsored by the Columbia Institute for Telecommunication of Columbia University's Graduate School of Business, a research center independent of outside economic interests.

This book is part of a larger set of volumes on international communications authored or co-authored by Eli Noam, including the 1989 or forthcoming: *The Law of International Telecommunications in the United States; Television in Europe; Telecommunications in Europe; Telecommunications in the Pacific Basin;* and *Asymmetric Deregulation: The Dynamics of Telecommunications Policies in Europe and The United States.*

The editors wish to acknowledge the contributions of the Institute in the preparations of this book. We are particularly grateful to Douglas Conn, who supervised the production of this book, to Richard Kramer, Christopher Dorman, Olivier Cheng, Elizabeth Ehrenfeld, Rachel Thompson, and to our spouses—Nadine Strossen and Kate Millonzi.

Eli M. Noam
Joel C. Millonzi

1

Trends in the Global Traffic of Television Programs

Tapio Varis

The present debates on international communication have had different dimensions. At the global level, issues such as the transnational concentration of information production and dissemination, reflected in the debate on the new international order in the field of information, have been on the agenda. On the regional level, international cooperation and integration have been discussed among the poor countries as well as in areas such as Europe. Furthermore, the present international political climate has brought certain ideological elements to the debate.

In this chapter, an empirical analysis of the amount and nature of the present international flow of television programs, as part of these processes, is presented. The data are from a two-week period in 1983, and the results can be compared with respective figures from 1973. In both of these years I was in charge of gathering the empirical data for Unesco from more than 50 countries throughout the world.

The basic information on the general amount of foreign versus domestically produced material in percentages, shows that the global average of imported programs is approximately one-third of the total time programming. When compared with the 1973 figures, the 1983 situation is not radically different, although there are interesting regional developments.

Although international communication and world television can be discussed as a global phenomenon, now reaching an audience of more than one billion viewers, the transmitters and receivers world wide are strongly concentrated in a few regional centers. To be more precise, almost half of the world television audience is in the United States and the Soviet Union.

Among the 10 largest television audiences, covering three-fourths of the world audience, there is only one country from the developing world: Brazil. The basic global flow of television programming is among eight rich countries which have most of the receivers and the largest audiences. These countries are the United States, United Kingdom, Canada, Japan, Australia, Germany, France, and Brazil.

This chapter begins with an analysis of the two big television countries, the United States and the Soviet Union, which can be expected to be rather self-supportive in their programming. This is followed by a look at Western and Eastern Europe, where regional cooperation is rather advanced and efforts towards unification are strong. Finally, different regions of the developing world are reviewed briefly.

UNITED STATES

Among all other nations of the world the United States is a particular case in international television program flow, for several reasons. One, the domestic market for television programs in the United States is without equal in any other country. Two, U.S. producers and companies are the largest program exporters in the world; and three, in relation to total output, U.S. television networks import fewer foreign programs than any other country. One might even claim that foreign programs are not shown at all in the United States.

In truth, imported programs account for approximately 2% of all programming in the United States. If commercials were included in the calculations, the figure would be even lower. Furthermore, the sources of these imports are very narrow: two nations, Mexico and England, account for almost half of U.S. imports. Entertainment and culture are the dominant categories of programming purchased by the U.S.

SOVIET UNION

The data on Soviet television are from the two national networks broadcasting in Russian. Only programs that have been imported from outside the Soviet Union have been classified as foreign. However, the Soviet television also has some characteristics that deserve special attention; in particular, its multinational character. In addition to the two all-union networks, 120 regional or local stations are in operation, broadcasting programs in most of the languages of peoples living in the country.

When compared with the 1973 data, the total share of imported programs has increased from 5% to 8%, and to 18% in prime time. In contrast, that of the U.S. television has remained about the same. Approximately one-third of Soviet foreign programs originate in eastern European socialist countries, and more than two-third elsewhere, primarily in the Federal Republic of Germany, France, and the United States. Imported programs appear mainly in entertainment, children's programs, and cultural programs. There are also coproductions with other countries.

WESTERN EUROPE

Western Europe is here defined as the area encompassed by the European Broadcasting Union, which means, for example, that Yugoslavia is included in the aggregate total of Western Europe. It should be emphasized that European cable systems are not included in these calculations, which most probably means that the present figures are too low with respect to imports rather than too high. There are some case studies from Italy, for example, which show that as much as 80% to 85% of the total broadcast time of the private stations consist of imported material, mainly from the United States.

With these qualifications, the data demonstrate that approximately one-third of Western European programs are imported. Here the category "imported" refers to programs from other Western European countries in addition to those from other regions. In Britain, for example, where the International Broadcast Authority (IBA) strictly limits material from countries other than Britain, programs from other EEC countries are not classified as foreign. There are special rules for programs from other Commonwealth countries, too. In the present study, however, all imported programs are classified as foreign.

Almost half of imported programs in Western Europe originate in the United States (44%). More than 10% of total Western European broadcasting time is composed of American programs. Other major sources of imports are the United Kingdom, the Federal Republic of Germany, and France. When compared with the 1973 figures, the U.S. share has decreased slightly, although it may have increased in the private cable systems not included in the present analysis. Eastern Europe, including the USSR, provides approximately 3% of Western European imported material. It is shown in a few countries only, mainly in France, the Federal Republic of Germany, England, Finland, and on the Basque television system in Spain. There are no changes in imports from Eastern Europe when compared with the situation 10 years earlier. In general, imported programs are mainly entertainment, but there are notable differences between individual European countries (see Table 1).

EASTERN EUROPE

The figures for the Eastern European region, excluding the Soviet Union, show that the share of imported programs in Eastern European countries

Table 1. Percentage of Imported Television Programs in 1973, 1983, and Prime-time 1983 (measured in programming hours).

	% of Programming Imported		
Country and Broadcasting Institution	1973	1983	1983 Prime Time
UNITED STATES			
United States/comm.	1	2	2
United States/educ.	2		
SOVIET UNION	5	8	18
WESTERN EUROPE			
Austria	—	43	61
Belgium/BRT	—	28	33
Belgium/RTBF	—	29	28
Denmark	—	46	32
Federal Republic of Germany:			
ARD	23	13	7
ZDF	30	23	23
Regional	—	24	—
Finland	40	37	37
France	9	17	17
Greece	—	39	—
Iceland	67	66	66
Ireland	54	57	58
Italy	13	18	19
Netherlands	23	25	24
Norway	39	30	28
Portugal	35	39	—
Spain	—	33	35
Spain/EIT B Regional	—	74	—
Sweden	33	35	28
Turkey	—	36	49
United Kingdom:			
BBC	12	15	21
ITV	13	14	20
Channel 4	—	26	15
Yugoslavia	27	29	22
EASTERN EUROPE			
Bulgaria	45	27	21
German Dem. Rep.	26	30	39
Czechoslovakia	—	24	25
Hungary	24	26	35
CANADA			
Canada/CBC	34	32	24
Canada/RC	46	38	31
LATIN AMERICA			
Argentina/Canal 9	10	49	53
Brazil	—	30	23
Cuba	—	24	9
Ecuador	—	66	70
Mexico	39	34	44
Venezuela	—	38	42

4

Table 1.   (Continued).

Country and Broadcasting Institution	% of Programming Imported		
	1973	1983	1983 Prime Time
ASIA & THE PACIFIC			
Australia	57	44	46
Brunei	—	60	28
People's Rep. of China	1	8	—
Hong Kong:			
Asia TV Chinese	31	24	16
Asia TV English	40	64	72
Asia TV Ltd.	—	27	9
India/Calcutta	—	3	6
India/Delhi	—	11	10
Republic of Korea/Munhwa TV	—	16	0
Malaysia	71	54	31
New Zealand/one	75	72	64
New Zealand/two	75	75	66
Pakistan	35	16	12
Philippines	29	12	20
Philippines/Metro Manila	—	40	—
Singapore:			
Channel 8	78	55	70
Channel 5	78	70	66
Sri Lanka	—	24	22
Vietnam	—	34	—

Source: Varis, Tapio, "The International Flow of Television Programs," *Journal of Communications*, Winter, 1984.

has increased during the 1973–1983 period, with the exception of Bulgaria, which has been explained as a statistical chance. The share of imported programs in Eastern Europe is roughly the same as in Western Europe, approximately one-third. The sources, however, seem to be more diversified. For example, the Soviet programs do not have as dominant a role in Eastern Europe as American programs in Western Europe. Only 6% of Eastern European broadcasting time is made up of Soviet programs whereas, for example, 12% are from Western Europe and another 6% from other Eastern European countries. Of the total Eastern European imports, Soviet programs make up approximately one-quarter, whereas almost half originate in Western Europe. Imported programs appear in several categories, mainly entertainment, children's programs, and cultural and educational programs.

CANADA

The data for Canada are not included in figures for Western Europe, although Canada is taking part in the European process of security and cooperation.

Neither are they included in the U.S. figures, although due to the geographical location of the country, the availability of American broadcasting is significant. Research data from the Montreal area, which is regarded as a representative area for most of the country, confirm that the United States accounts for the vast majority of imported programming, on private and public, French and English networks, except in the case of the educational network, Radio-Quebec. Approximately 40% of Canadian programs are imported, and almost a third of all programming is made up of U.S. material. As much as 70% of all imported progamming originates in the United States, with the rest coming mainly from France, the United Kingdom, and Italy. The movie and entertainment categories comprise the highest proportion of imports.

LATIN AMERICA

The Latin American region is represented in the present study by Argentina, Brazil, Cuba, Ecuador, Mexico, and Venezuela. The amount of imported program material varies from one-fourth (Cuba) to two-thirds (Ecuador) of the total volume of programming. On average, approximately half of the programs broadcast in the region are imported. During prime time, the share of imported programs is higher than average.

The entertainment category is predominant in all Latin American countries analyzed in this study: Approximately half of the total transmission time is devoted to entertainment, with the exception of Cuba where the figure is one-third. Most of the imported materials are entertainment. The sources of foreign programs in Latin American countries are the following: the United States (together with production by the multinational corporations) dominates with three-quarters of the imported material. Programs from Latin American countries themselves make up 12% of the imported material. Western European programs represent a few percent of the total imported materials.

There are considerable differences among the individual countries of the Latin American region. In Argentina 38 television channels were studied. Four of these were located in the Federal capital and 24 in the provinces. Of the imported programs, 73% came directly from the United States and another 16% were multinational in character. In 1973, the percentage of American imports was estimated to be 75%. Mexico was the origin of less than 10%. Western European imports, which in 1973 were 5–6%, accounted in 1983 for approximately 2% of the total imports (see Table 2).

In Brazil, six television channels were analyzed. Of the imported programs, 93% came from the United States. Mexico produced 2% and the balance was mainly from Western Europe.

Table 2. Distribution of Programming by Region and Category, 1983.

	U.S.		Canada		Latin America		Western Europe	
	all %	imp. %	all %	imp. %	all %	imp. %	all %	imp. %
Informative	19	1	35	—	16	20	29	5
Educational	7	0	8	—	7	13	9	10
Cultural	6	9	8	24	2	14	6	12
Religious	3	—	2	28	1	18	1	11
Entertainment	40	2	36	72	44	71	35	53
Sports	4	2	3	—	5	18	8	36
Other (ads, children's, unclassified)	25	0	8	35	25	17	12	30
Total %	104		100		100		100	

	U.S.S.R.		E. Europe		Asia	
	all %	imp %	all %	imp. %	all %	imp. %
Informative	30	2	20	7	15	30
Educational	14	—	13	9	7	13
Cultural	15	4	12	21	3	6
Religious	—	—	—	—	2	9
Entertainment	27	14	36	49	48	53
Sports	9	32	10	43	10	28
Other (ads, children's, unclassified)	5	5	9	21	15	41
Total %	100		100		100		100

Note: The figures are indicative of the region as a whole as represented by the countries included in the study.
Source: Varis, Tapio, "The International Flow of Television Programs," *Journal of Communications*, Winter, 1984.

In Cuba, two channels were analyzed. The Soviet Union and the United States had almost equal shares (23 and 22% respectively), the German Democratic Republic 13%, other Socialist countries 8%, Western European countries 20%, and other countries 11%.

The data for Ecuador are based on material from nine television channels. The imported programs originated in the United States (55%), Mexico (23%), other Latin American countries (15%), Western Europe (5%) and other non-Latin countries (2%).

In Mexico, six channels were studied. The imported programs originated in the United States (74%), the United Kingdom (9%), other Latin American countries (10%), Europe and the Soviet Union. A few minutes came from Asia. In comparison with the 1973 figures, the percentage of American and British imports remains unchanged.

ASIA AND THE PACIFIC

The region of Asia and the Pacific includes countries that have great differences in the size, nature, and history of their broadcasting facilities. Among the 14 countries in the Pacific Basin, there are two fairly advanced television broadcasters, Australia and New Zealand. The inclusion of data from these are included here in the countries with the aggregate total for the region, thus introducing some distortion as far as developing countries are concerned. Japan is not included in the present data.

Certain general aspects of television in this region are important for an understanding of the data. For instance, in Asia, television has largely remained concentrated in urban areas, especially in countries such as India, Malaysia, Pakistan, the Philippines, and Thailand. Also, there are a limited number of transmitters, limited transmission time and exorbitant costs for television receivers in some of the countries. Finally, many countries are home to several languages, dialects, and cultures.

On the average, the Asian audience has access to about 10 hours of television broadcasting every day. The lowest is approximately three hours (Vietnam) and the highest, 20 hours (New Zealand). It can be concluded that the share of imported programming increases dramatically with the increase in transmission hours. Television is primarily used for entertainment and information in the region; these two categories constitute approximately three-fourths of total transmission time, and considerably more during prime time.

The volume of imports is largest among children's programs, followed by entertainment. Information, educational, cultural, and religious programs, however, are largely produced domestically. The situation varies from station to station and country to country. Comparisons with the 1973 situation are not always possible because new countries have since initiated television broadcasts in the region. The People's Republic of China had very few imported programs in 1973 (1% mainly from Northern Korea, Albania, and Rumania), but now shows 8% imported programs. This increase is partly attributable to the growing impact of educational material and information programs from the United Kingdom. The Philippines has 72 television stations throughout the country and, in 1973, imported two-thirds of its foreign programs from the United States and the rest mainly from the United Kingdom. In 1983, the U.S. share of imports is close to 90%.

Television in the Philippines is primarily an entertainment medium: 62% of the prime time and half of the total time are allotted to entertainment programs. The U.S. share has also been high in countries such as the Republic of Korea, Hong Kong and Malaysia.

It should be noted that individual broadcast stations often reveal very stark contrasts in content. In India, for example, one Calcutta station is concentrating on domestic produtions and imports very little, whereas the Delhi station has more foreign programming.

ARAB STATES

As to the Arab countries, certain specific characteristics concerning television broadcasting in this region also deserve consideration. Although television activity began in the region in the 1950s, most of the stations started in the 1960s. Exchanges between Arab countries have recently been intensified by the initiation of their own regional satellite system, Arabsat. The language of broadcasting plays a special importance in this region, as there are classic Arab, local Arab dialect, and foreign languages.

The results of this study confirm that there is a clear tendency to use the classic Arab language for broadcasting. On average, slightly more than 40% of total programs are imported, a figure which includes programs from other Arab countries. Compared with the 1973 figures, the share of imported material appears to have decreased in the region. Foreign policy changes obviously influence foreign television programming. In Egypt, for example, almost one-fifth of the imported material was from the socialist countries in 1973; 10 years later they are not visible in the statistics at all.

U.S. programs are still dominant in most of the Arab countries, comprising one-third of all of the imported programs. In the People's Democratic Republic of Yemen, their share has decreased from one-quarter of imported material in 1973 to 8% in 1983. In Syria, U.S. programs make up 23% of imported programs, while Soviet television programs account for 17%. Arab countries import relatively more from the socialist countries than Latin American, Asian, or African countries. Obviously, French imports dominate in several Arab countries, especially in Algeria, Tunis, and Lebanon. Imported programs are dominated by the categories of television plays and documentaries. Inter-Arab exchanges seem to have developed well.

AFRICA

Africa is another region where generalizations about program flows threaten to be misleading. For example, there are 46 broadcasting organizations in sub-Sahara countries, but almost one-half of the television stations are in

Nigeria. The Nigerian television stations broadcast a little over half of Africa's total. Moreover, as in other developing regions of the world, television sets are concentrated in urban areas, and the cost of a receiver puts it beyond the means of the average income earner.

Due to Nigeria's dominant role, the present statistics were calculated first including, then excluding, Nigeria. When Nigeria is included, the share of imported programs is 36%; when it is excluded, the figure is 60%. U.S. programs make up about one-half of all imported material, and one-fifth of total output. Another major source of imports is the United Kingdom. In contrast, programs from the socialist countries very rarely get time in African broadcasting. Instead, the international news film agencies and international organizations are a major source of program material in African countries. No inter-African television exchanges exist.

Although American and British programs dominate English-speaking Africa, the French have a strong influence in Francophone Africa. In Senegal, for example, 60% of imported programs originate in France and only 5% in the United States. Imported programs are mainly entertainment or information programs.

CONCLUSIONS

The trends discovered in the 1973 study seem to persist in 1983: one-way traffic from the big exporting countries to the rest of the world, and a dominance of entertainment material in the flow. However, there are also important regional developments in various parts of the world. World television remains strongly influenced by the United States. This is especially true of the poorer regions of the world, but also of Western Europe. In Europe, however, the regional process of integration has strengthened arguments for improving inter- and intra-European exchanges and program production. This has been especially true in the plans for direct broadcast satellites, first in Nordic countries and more recently in the European community. Consequently, serious discussions about quota systems for foreign programming have been activated in Europe. The problems of cultural identity, however, have been discussed more and earlier in countries like Canada that have been under strong foreign domination in the field of communication.

European discussions have also addressed East-West program exchange. According to the 1984 figures, there are still more western programs in the East than vice versa, although there seems to be a slight increase in the number of eastern programs on West German television. The eastern broadcasters, however, have slightly increased their share of western programming. In assessing these exchange figures, one has to remember that there are a number of practical problems such as financing, and that not all of the differences have ideological or political roots. Austrian and Hungarian broadcasters have discussed improving their cooperation in this field. One recent European plan is to extend the German-Swiss -Austrian satellite broadcasts to Hungary, to be received there by cable. In most Third World countries, television remains a medium found in urban centers and available to a relatively wealthy segment of the population. Furthermore, foreign programming originates almost exclusively in the major western countries and tends to have a dominant role in the program content of individual countries. The increase in regional exchanges is particularly notable among the Arab countries and in Latin America. In the Arab countries, approximately one-third of the imported programs originate within the region. Throughout Latin America, the figure is around 10%. From a global perspective, there remain great regional differences in the amount and origin of the flow between nations and regions.

This descriptive analysis reports on program flows today in the traditional broadcast television media. However, due to technological development, a rapid change in the traditional flow pattern is taking place in the new markets of video cassettes and other nonbroadcast media. The pattern of the international flow in these markets is largely unknown, but it may be even more concentrated than traditional patterns. Video cassettes may also open up new alternatives to minorities and foreigners in other countries.

Under the present economic conditions, it is difficult to predict how rapidly the deployment of the new communication technologies will take place. It has been estimated that direct broadcast satellite channels will soon be flooding western Europe with television programming. According to one estimate, most households in Europe should be able to receive at least a dozen different satellite-delivered channels by the end of this decade, while many densely populated areas, with extra equipment, could have doubled this number.

So far the introduction of satellites has not changed the basic patterns of the flow of television programs and news. Although they have contributed to the improvement of regional exchanges in some cases, there is a trend toward transnational concentration. The new communication technologies may offer some alternatives for the future. But it may also be that the rapid development in communication technologies and services, including all kinds of data offerings, only increases the gap between those who have access to information and the means to use it to influence others, and those who do not have this capability.

REFERENCES

Varis, T. (1985). *International flow of television programmes, reports and papers on mass communication.* Paris: Unesco.

Varis, T. (1984, Winter). The international flow of television programs. *Journal of Communications.*

2

The Economics of Trade in Recorded Media Products in a Multilingual World: Implications for National Media Policies

Steven S. Wildman and Stephen E. Siwek

INTRODUCTION

Complaints that U.S. media products dominate foreign markets have been commonplace in discussions of trade in the recorded media of films, television programs, and music recordings for some time.[1] While these claims are sometimes exaggerated, it is clear that motion pictures, television programs, and popular music created and produced by American companies and performers are a significant, sometimes pervasive, presence in the media markets of many countries. By contrast, foreign (especially non-English) films, programs, and music have achieved only limited penetration in the United States.[2] The success of American productions has given rise to charges of unfair competition and the erection of various forms of subsidies and trade barriers intended to protect and encourage domestic producers and artists.

---

[1] In popular music the complaints are sometimes directed at Anglo-American recordings, not just American recordings.

[2] British popular music has traditionally done very well in the United States, and this is becoming increasingly true for Australian and Canadian music as well. Films from the United Kingdom and Australia have also enjoyed commercial success in the United States, although not in as spectacular a fashion as popular music.

Recent work on the political economy of trade restraints has shown that the political/regulatory process generally works to protect domestic industries in which a country has a comparative disadvantage relative to its trading partners (Brock & Magee, 1978; Hillman, 1982; Pincus, 1975). We argue below that in the recorded entertainment media, the United States, and, to a large extent, other English-language countries, benefit from a particular kind of trade advantage which we refer to as a domestic opportunity advantage (DOA). The effect of a DOA is similar to a comparative advantage of the more traditional sort—products flow from countries with a comparative advantage to countries with a comparative disadvantage. The nearly unidirectional flow of recorded media products from the U.S. to other countries suggests that the American DOA is large in these industries. Therefore, it is not surprising that the export efforts of American media firms are hindered by barriers raised by the national governments of other nations. Still, comparison with other industries of similar size or larger clearly indicates that in most countries, the intensity of the debate over the fates of national media industries exceeds considerably what might be warranted by economic considerations alone.

National media industries are defended passionately because media products are more than just objects of commerce. They are also vehicles of communication and embodiments of national culture. From this perspective, a strong foreign presence is seen as a threat to national autonomy and an unwelcome challenge to cultural uniqueness.

Given the strength of the passions aroused by trade in media products, surprisingly little work has been done on the economic determinants of trade flows and factors that affect the economic health of domestic media industries. In Wildman and Siwek (1988) we present an economic model of international trade in films and television programs which explains observed trade patterns for these media products. In this chapter we provide additional evidence in support of that model and elaborate on the applications of the model to trade policy issues. Important similarities between sound recordings and the two video media, which will become clearer to the reader as we proceed, lead us to expand this discussion to include popular music, although with a lesser emphasis.

The remainder of this chapter is organized as follows. In the next section we provide a brief overview of available data on trade flows in the three recorded media, focusing on broad patterns in these flows. In Section III we examine linguistic and cultural correlates of the media trade flows documented in Section II. An economic model of trade in recorded media products, which explains the observed patterns of trade and identifies the roles of linguistic and cultural variation is presented in Section IV. In Section V, we look at recent experiences with liberalizing media policies in countries besides the United States in an attempt to provide a rough assessment of the strength of the economic tendencies identified in the trade model. We use the analytical perspective developed in the previous two sections to evaluate various options available to national media policy makers in Section VI.

TRADE FLOWS

Our objective in this section is not to provide exhaustive documentation of world trading relationships. More complete descriptions of individual media are available through other sources (Guback, 1969; Katz & Wedell, 1977; Tunstall, 1977; Varis, 1983; Vans & Nordenstreng, 1974; Wildman & Siwek, 1974). Rather, our intention is to familiarize the reader with the empirical character of the relationships we describe. In describing trade flows in media products, we make use of a variety of types of data. For example, in examining trade in films, we consider financial measures of trade, audience share data for domestic and imported films, and statistics on numbers of titles imported. Similarly, we look at financial totals, hours of programming, and audience measures in describing trade in television programs. The use of a variety of such measures makes for less tidy descriptions of trade flows, but a combination of factors make this approach unavoidable.

First, there are significant gaps in the data available of each type. Thus, the use of different types of data provides a more complete picture of trading relationships. Second, each type of data has its advantages for the consideration of particular policy issues. Financial magnitudes are important if policy makers are concerned with the impact of media trade on the trade balance, but measures of audience share are more relevant if the topic is the effect of imported entertainment on domestic media industries or the extent to which a country's citizens rely on foreign sources for information and entertainment. If the range of choices available to a country's citizenry is the issue, the number of titles imported would be important.

In addition, the need to use different measures is a consequence of the importance of the public good characteristics of media products.[3] In the absence of government intervention, free trade will ensure a single international price (after allowing for transportation costs) in traded commodities. This follows from the exclusive nature of commodity consumption. A unit of steel used to produce Fords in the United States cannot also be used to produce Toyotas in Japan. With competitive markets and free trade, steel prices in two countries cannot differ by more than the cost of transporting it from the lower-priced country to the higher-priced country. A higher price differential would cause steel users in the higher-priced country to increase their imports of steel from the lower-priced country until the price in the former had fallen and/or the price in the latter had risen enough to make a larger flow unprofitable. The tendency of trade to equalize prices for goods

---

[3] A public good is a product or service for which consumption by any one economic agent does not reduce the amount available for others in the community.

also means that there will be a fairly close correlation between monetary measures and physical measures of trade. Trade does not lead to a similar equalization of prices in films, television programs, and recordings. The performances, which bulk so large in the costs of these media products, can be enjoyed simultaneously by millions of consumers around the world. Therefore, a film shown to New York audiences can also be viewed in Tokyo and, depending on local market conditions, admission prices and film rental fees may vary significantly between the two cities. Thus the close correlation between physical and financial measures that will be observed for traded goods is attenuated considerably for film and television programs, and to a somewhat lesser degree, recordings.[4]

Regardless of the type of measure employed, two relationships stand out: (1) Anglo-American product, primarily American, dominates trade flows; and (b) Countries with large populations and/or large GNPs are the most imported suppliers of films and programs imported by other countries.

Films

Unesco's annual survey of films produced and imported by member countries is by far the best, and most comprehensive, source of data on numbers of films (titles) traded. Table 1 is based on a data set constructed from 1984 and 1985 Unesco statistics.[5] The nine countries listed in this table are the countries identified by Unesco as the most important sources of films created by Unesco member countries. (While Hong Kong is a British colony, we will continue to refer to film or program exporting nations for expositional convenience.) Unesco does not identify other countries separately as sources of film imports. The number of countries in which a particular country's films are distributed and the fraction of total imports accounted for by that country's films are two measures of a country's importance as a source of traded films. The importance of the United States as a supplier of imported titles is clear from both measures. U.S. films were distributed in 79 of the 87 countries for which Unesco reported imported statistics. France, Italy, and the United Kingdom followed with 68, 71, and 69, respectively. The percentage of imported titles column shows that, in terms of number of titles supplied, there is no close second to the United States. The U.S. accounted for an average of 34.8% of imported titles in the countries to which it exports films. This is four times the corresponding figure for Italy, which ranks second by this measure.

The comprehensiveness of the Unesco figures cannot be duplicated with statistics on theatrical attendance and box office shares. However, for those

---

[4] The cost of the physical medium, vinyl, tape, CD, and so on, is a much larger fraction of total cost for recordings.
[5] This data set is presented in Appendix A of Wildman and Siwek (1974).

Table 1.   Distribution of Films from Major Film Exporting Nations

Exporting Country	# Countries Distributed in	Average % of Imported Titles Supplied
U.S.	79	34.8
France	68	8.1
Italy	71	8.7
India	42	7.5
U.S.S.R.	55	7.1
U.K.	69	6.0
F.R. Germany	56	2.6
Japan	46	2.1
Hong Kong	53	7.7

Sources: Unesco, *Statistical Yearbook, 1984*, Table 8.2 and *Statistical Year-book, 1985*, Table 9.2.

Table 2.   Cinema Attendance Shares in the Combined Market of Four EC Countries*

Films From	% of Attendance
United States	47
Italy	24
France	17
United Kingdom	8
West Germany	3
Other Countries	1

* France, Italy, United Kingdom, and W. Germany.
Source: European Parliament Working Documents 1983–1984 Document 1-504/83, PE 76.975/Fin. 15 July 1983, p. 23.

countries for which such data are available, it is clear that the Unesco statistics on imported titles understate the importance of U.S. films at the box office. Statistics on attendance and theatrical rentals are most complete for Europe, as a result of a series of studies conducted by the European Parliament and the Commission of the European Communities (1984a). Table 2 reports European Parliament statistics on shares of attendance accounted for by films from the United States, France, Italy, West Germany, and the United Kingdom in the combined markets of these four large European countries. U.S. films accounted for nearly half of cinema attendance in these countries. Smaller European countries and non-European countries other than the United States were not significant factors. Of course these averages are not representative of the situations in individual countries. The same study reports shares of attendance for U.S. films in eight European countries ranging from a low of 30% (Italy) to a high of 92% (the United Kingdom). The pattern reflected in the *Variety* statistics for West Germany in Table 3 are fairly typical. Domestically produced films draw much better

Table 3.   *Variety* Estimates of Market Share in West German Film Market.

	1979	1980	1981	1982	1983
W. Germany	16.8%	9.3%	18.7%	11.7%	13.0%
U.S.	39.5	54.9	52.9	49.0	52.0
France	12.3	6.4	6.7	14.7	NA
Italy	11.4	13.8	8.4	13.8	NA
U.K.	13.0	6.9	6.6	5.1	NA
Others	7.0	8.7	6.7	5.7	NA
Total	100.0%	100.0%	100.0%	100.0%	100.0%

Source: *Variety*, March 7, 1986, p. 336.

Table 4.   Summary of Top 10 Grossing Films in Four Latin American Countries (1986).

	Brazil	Colombia	Mexico	Venezuela
No. of titles from U.S.	9 of 10	10 of 10	5 of 10	7 of 10
U.S. films' share of top 10 box office	91.8%	100.0%	56.4%	70.2%
No. of titles from Latin American countries	1 of 10	0 of 10	5 of 10	3 of 10
Latin American films' share of top 10 box office	8.2%	0.0%	43.6%	29.8%

Source: *Variety*, March 25, 1987, pp. 92, 94, 96.

within the country than elsewhere, but the important sources of imported films are those reported for the larger market.

Although comparable data on total market attendance is not available for most non-European nations,[6] statistics on top-drawing films in other countries suggests that the European pattern is repeated elsewhere with the not surprising difference that European films are considerably less important. The statistics on cinema attendance for South American countries reported in Table 4 show that films from the United States are generally the top draws, followed by native language films. This pattern appears to be fairly typical of less-developed countries.

There is very little data on the financial flows that accompany flows of films. U.S. earnings run in the neighborhood of $1.5–1.7 billion annually, with some variance due primarily to fluctuations in exchange rates. The U.S. earnings of foreign films are miniscule by comparison.[7] The trade

---

[6] Japan is an exception. In 1984, the earnings of U.S. major distributors in Japan were about 30% of the total for the Japanese market (Wildman & Siwek, 1974).

[7] For example, a study of the European film industry for the Commission of the European Communities reported that "in the first fifty of the five 'Variety' lists of Box Office Winners for 1975–1979 (that is, 250 films in all), twenty-six were national films of foreign countries. Twenty-four of these were British, all of which were distributed in the United States by American companies." (Filson, 1980).

surplus realized on these sales runs in the neighborhood of $1 billion (U.S Congress, 1986). Comparable figures for other countries are hard to come by. The 1983 export earnings of $35 million and $30 million for France and Italy, respectively, provide one basis for comparison (Commission of The European Communities, 1984b). U.S. earnings on films in that year were $1.5 billion (Goldman Sachs Research, 1985). France and Italy are probably second and third to the United States in film export earnings.

Television Programs

The most comprehensive data on flows in television programs are the product of surveys of broadcast time devoted to imported programs conducted by Varis (1983) and Varis and Nordenstreng (1974). According to the most recent Varis survey, imported programs fill an average of about 30% of broadcast time worldwide, although there is considerable variance among countries and among regions. The United States is at the very low end of the range of variation, importing only 1 to 2% of its program hours.

The Varis figures suggest that, in most countries, domestic productions play a much more important role in television than is the case for films shown in cinemas. This is no doubt due in part to the fact that governments play a much larger role in determining content for television than for films. In many countries broadcasting is programmed by the government or by an independent, noncommercial body, and in most countries there are strict limits on the percentage of air time that can be occupied by foreign programs. The countries identified as important suppliers of trade programs in the Varis surveys are among those identified as important suppliers of films above. The United States dwarfs other countries as a source of programs, but the large Western European countries and Japan are also important.

There are no studies of the audiences for domestic and imported programs that match the global sweep of the Varis surveys. However, the limited work that does permit a comparison of the importance of imported programs measured by program hours and by audience suggests that in countries with a history of commercial broadcasting, imports account for a larger share of program hours than of audience. This relationship is apparent in the Table 5 data on imported programs' shares of program hours and audiences from a recent study by Livia Antola and Everett M. Rogers (1984). The dominance of U.S. programs among imports is also apparent in this data. According to Antola and Rogers, imported programs' shares of audience are lower than their shares of program hours because domestic programs dominate the prime time hours when the audience is largest. Similar relationships have been reported for Japan and Italy.

Films are an important source of television programming in many countries. The success of American films in foreign cinemas is mirrored in sales

Table 5.   Comparison of Audiences and Program Hours of Imported Programs in Four Latin American Nations (1982).

	% of Broadcast Hours Imported	% of Audience Viewing Hours for Imported Programs	
		Total	U.S.
Argentina	40%	37%	28%
Brazil	39%	22%	19%
Mexico	50%	34%	33%
Peru	70%	66%	33%

Source: Antola & Rogers (1984), pp. 189, 191.

to foreign broadcasters. This is evident in the statistics from the *Green Paper* on the national origins of films shown on European television reported in Table 6.

The *Variety* data on Italian TV imports reported in Table 7 provide a rare glimpse of the financial figures associated with the purchases of imported programs. U.S. programs and films account for 77% of spending for imports, followed distantly by programs and films from other European nations combined at 16%. Not reflected in these figures is the recent declining trend in purchases from U.S. suppliers as their popularity with viewers has fallen relative to domestic productions.

Estimates of U.S. earnings on foreign sales of television programs vary from $500 million to as high as $1 billion. The extent to which these figures duplicate sales of motion pictures to broadcasters, which are also included in the motion picture export totals, is hard to determine.

Popular Music

Probably in part because it has not been the subject of intense policy debate, as have films and television programming, it is not possible to construct as complete a picture of patterns of trade in popular music as was the case for the other two media products. However, the 1982 and 1984 IFPI[8] data in Tables 8 and 9 on the national origins of popular music recordings sold in various, mostly European, nations suggests that the pattern of trade in popular music is similar to the patterns in films and television programs. In most countries the United States is the dominant foreign source of imported recordings. Comparison of figures for U.S. shares in Table 8 with Anglo-Saxon shares in Table 9 for the countries for which both are broken out indicates that the United Kingdom is also a very important international source of popular music.

---

[8] The International Federation of Phonogram and Videogram Producers.

Table 6. European Economic Community Origin of Films Shown on Television 1981.

Country of Showing	Country of Origin													
	Belgium		France		Germany		Italy		United Kingdom		USA		Other	
	No.	%	No.	%	No.	%	No.	%	No.	%	No.	%	No.	%
Belgium RIBF			160	48.8	15	4.3	24	6.8	12	3.4	107	30.70	17	4.9
BRI			11	6.25	7	3.98	4	2.28	24	13.64	104	59.10	26	14.17
France[1]	—	—			4	2.29	8	4.59	12	6.89	140	80.45	10	5.74
Germany[2]	—	—	48	11.79			15	3.68	26	6.38	221	54.29	93	22.85
United Kingdom[3]	—	—	6	1.14	2	0.38	6	1.14			491	93.70	20	3.81

Source: EEC Green Paper (Television without Frontiers), Annex 3, p. 334.
[1] TF, FR 3; figures broken down by country of origin not available for A2.
[2] ARD, ZDF; the ZDF figures include the first half of 1982; co-productions classified according to the first-named country of origin.
[3] BBC only.

Table 7.   Italian Film and TV Imports (1983).

Source	No. Films	Dollar Total	No. TV Episodes	Dollar Total	Grand Dollar Total
Asia	18	$ 201,500	913	$ 2,996,300	$ 3,197,800
Australia	2	14,000	8	34,500	48,500
Europe	313	6,668,200	2,345	11,974,400	18,642,600
N. America	1,082	31,508,900	8,327	59,343,588	90,852,488
U.S.A.	1,069	30,803,900	8,298	58,922,588	89,726,488
Others	13	705,000	29	421,000	1,126,000
S. America	0	0	1,127	3,048,000	3,048,000
Not classified	0	0	71	92,500	92,500
Total	1,415	38,392,600	12,791	77,489,288	115,881,888

Source: *Variety*, May 9, 1984, p. 303.

Table 8.   Breakdown of Popular Music Sales in Europe
(Percentages Based on DM Retail Values 1982).

Country	Total Pop	National	International Total	USA[1]	Other[1]
Austria	100%	29%	71%	20%	51%
Belgium/Lux	100%	9%	91%	25%	66%
Denmark	100%	30%	70%	40%	30%
France	100%	59%	41%	21%	20%
Germany	100%	52%	48%	25%	23%
Greece	100%	55%	45%	20%	25%
Ireland	100%	25%	75%	30%	45%
Italy	100%	55%	45%	27%	18%
Netherlands	100%	31%	69%	33%	36%
Norway	100%	18%	82%	45%	37%
Portugal	100%	24%	76%	26%	50%
Spain	100%	38%	62%	20%	42%
Sweden	100%	36%	64%	40%	24%
Switzerland	100%	10%	90%	25%	65%
U.K.	100%	66%	34%	25%	9%
Other Europe	100%	12%	88%	30%	58%

Source: *Statistical Profile of the Music Industry, 1983–1984*, IFPI Secretariat, London.
[1] Estimates.

It is also worth noting that the importance of foreign sales to U.S. record companies is comparable to the importance of foreign sales to the U.S. motion picture industry. In both cases sales in other countries account for about one-half of worldwide revenues, although this is a more recent pattern for the recording industry (International Marketplace, 1987).

Of course, popular music is an important component of radio programming. While we have no data on the national origins of music broadcast by radio stations, it is well known that English language songs are relied on heavily by popular music radio stations in many European countries.

Table 9.   Sales of Records and Tapes—1984,[1,2] Origin of Repertoire.

Country	National Repertoire	Anglo Saxon Repertoire	Other Foreign Repertoire
Austria	25.0%	75.0%	
France[3]	66.0%	30.0%	4.0%
Germany (FR)	35.0%	45.0%	20.0%
Hungary	96.5%	3.0%	0.5%
Italy	55.7%	44.3%	
Japan	36.0%	64.0%	
Netherlands	32.0%	68.0%	
Norway	18.0%	82.0%	
Portugal	10.0%	90.0%	
United Kingdom[4]	64.0%	34.0%	2.0%

Source: IFPI.
[1] Estimates.
[2] Excluding classical music.
[3] 1982 figures.
[4] Anglo Saxon Repertoire should be read as U.S. repertoire for the United Kingdom.

LINGUISTIC MARKETS

The proposition that differences in language and culture are the primary determinants of the natural markets for media products is virtually self-evident. Translation from one language to another, even when facilitated with dubbing or subtitles, is a burden to the consumer. Thus viewers and listeners have a natural preference for works recorded in their native tongues over material produced in other languages. Therefore, a producer of a film, television program, or musical recording in any given language starts out with an advantage over sellers of similar productions recorded in other languages in selling to consumers with the same native language. Differences in culture also impose "translation" costs on consumers since an understanding of cultural context is often a prerequisite to full appreciation of recorded entertainment. To the extent that culture varies with nationality, this would be a source of home country advantage. Of course, linguistic and cultural differences among peoples are closely correlated. Since linguistic variation is much easier to document, in what follows we focus on differences among linguistic populations on the assumption that linguistic populations constitute natural markets for recorded media products. The importance of differences among linguistic markets as determinants of trade flows is explored in the economic analysis presented in the next section.

There is no readily available metric for gauging the strength of a consumer's preference for a film, program, or recording produced in his own language over a similar piece of recorded entertainment produced in a foreign tongue. That such preferences exert a strong influence on media consumption patterns is clear from some of the data presented in the previous section

Table 10.   Linguistic Preferences in Film Imports

		Percent of Titles Imported	
Country of Origin	Language	Importing Countries with same Official Language	Other Importing Countries
United States	English	45.7	31.5
United Kingdom	English	8.2	5.4
France	French	25.7	6.5
Italy	Italian	23.6	8.4
West Germany	German	10.3	2.3

Source: *Statistical Yearbook, 1984*, Table 8.2 and *Statistical Yearbook, 1985*, Table 9.2. Paris: Unesco, 1985.

of this chapter. It is quite obvious in the two tables on popular music (Tables 8 and 9) that national repertoire sells much better in the home country than in other countries which generally have different languages. Table 3 shows German films averaging nearly 14% of German cinema attendance over a five-year period, but in Table 2 we see German films accounting for only 3% of attendance in the combined markets of Germany, Italy, France, and the United Kingdom. The importance of preferences for native language recorded entertainment, and not just native language entertainment produced in the home country, is demonstrated in Table 10. Table 10 uses Unesco data to compare five major film exporting countries' sales as a percentage of imported titles to countries with the same official languages and to countries with different official languages. The preference for same language films is quite evident.

How do the natural media markets composed of linguistic populations differ? In the next section we argue that the most important differences among markets in terms of influencing media trade flows are differences that affect spending on media products. Spending is a function of demand and the extent to which governments' policies affect financial expressions of that demand. Besides tastes, which are unobservable, the most basic determinants of demand for media products are the number of potential consumers of media products and their incomes. Table 11 reports for 12 languages the number of native speakers and the combined national income for countries for which these are official languages. The linguistic populations described are the 12 largest linguistic populations whose members are located for the most part in countries that rely significantly on market forces to organize economic activity.[9] For a variety of reasons, countries that rely on market economies tend to dominate international trade in films, television programs, and records. In addition, market economies reflect more directly the linkage between supply and demand for media products.

---

[9] The most important languages excluded by this criterion are Russian and Chinese.

Table 11.   A Comparison of Linguistic Markets

Language	Native Speakers (Millions)	1981 GNP* (Millions U.S.)
English	409	$4,230,375
Hindi/Urdu	352	209,023
Spanish	265	653,958
Arabic	163	328,547
Bengali	160	12,692
Portugese	157	303,465
Malay/Indonesian	122	237,715
Japanese	121	1,185,861
French	110	812,179
German	101	1,017,528
Punjabi	69	29,575
Italian	62	502,306

Sources: *1985 World Almanac and World Tables* (3rd ed., Vol. I). World Bank, Washington, DC.
* Totals for countries that rely on market mechanisms to a significant degree to order economic activity.

As Table 11 shows, English speakers greatly outnumber native speakers of all other languages for which market economies predominate. In addition, the relative advantage shown by English speakers, as measured by income, is still more dramatic, far surpassing the incomes of Japanese and German speakers, the second and third ranked groups. The combined GNP of the English-speaking countries is nearly four times the combined GNP's of the Japanese-speaking or German-speaking countries.

The combined GNPs associated with different languages should be viewed as rough indices of the *potentials* of the associated linguistic populations as markets for recorded video products and music. Linguistic groups differ in the extent to which their market potentials are realized. The effective size (in monetary terms) of the media market comprised of native speakers of a language may be reduced considerably below the level that its collective income would suggest. In general, the factors that most reduce the extent to which media market potential is realized can be traced directly or indirectly to the policies imposed by the governments of the countries in which the linguistic populations reside. Legal restrictions on film and program content, which are present in all nations to some extent, depress the demand for certain types of entertainment. As content censorship of this type increases, market potential is almost certainly reduced. Restrictions on film screening dates and frequency of showings have similar consequences.

Government restrictions on commercial television broadcasting probably comprise the most important factors preventing the realization of media market potential around the world. Because of the intricate ties between film and television production in most countries, television restrictions directly affect film production and vice versa. More importantly, governments in most countries tend to regulate television far more pervasively than films or record distribution. Governments, to some extent, are involved directly in the operation of broadcast stations in nearly every country in the world. Governments own or license stations, allocate broadcast frequencies, and control program content and origin in many countries. Not surprisingly, these activities can all influence media market potential in quite dramatic ways.

In general, there are considerably fewer restrictions on commercial broadcasting in English-speaking countries than in non-English speaking countries. In Western Europe, for example, television in many countries is entirely a public enterprise. Even in countries where commercial broadcasters exist, the time allowed for commercial advertising daily is much less than in the United States. The result is a significant reduction in the funds available to support programming, since, in most countries, public funding does not come close to compensating for funding lost due to commercial restrictions (Wildman & Siwek, 1987, 1988). Because most English-speaking countries impose fewer restrictions on commercial broadcasting, a greater portion of the media market potential of English-speaking peoples is realized. Accordingly, the relative difference between the actual size of the English language market and the actual sizes of other linguistic markets is probably much greater than the comparison of potentials in Table 11 would indicate.

AN ECONOMIC MODEL OF TRADE
IN RECORDED MEDIA PRODUCTS

The data presented in the previous sections revealed a pattern of trade that is similar across three recorded entertainment media. The similarity of basic trading relationships for the three media suggests that a similar economic mechanism plays an important role in trading relationships in each. In this section we present a model of trade in recorded media products which shows that trade characterized by flows of product primarily from large markets to small markets may be a straightforward consequence of the economics of competition in products with significant public good components.[10]

An understanding of the distinction between private goods and public goods is essential to the economic analysis of trade in media products. A public good is a product or service for which consumption by one individual does not reduce the amount available for consumption by other individuals. National defense is probably the most commonly used example of a public good. Each citizen of a country consumes the same amount of national

---

[10] This discussion is based on a mathematical model of trade in video products which is presented in Appendix B of Wildman and Siwek (1988).

defense, and the addition of a new citizens does not reduce the amount of defense consumed by the original citizens as long as the defense budget is not changed. By contrast, a private good, such as a candy bar, can be shared by more individuals only if it is divided into smaller portions. Exclusivity of consumption is the defining characteristic of a private good.

Media products have both public and private good components. The performances, which are preserved in physical recording media such as 35mm film, tape, vinyl, and so on, are public goods. The physical media on which the performances are recorded are private goods. It is the performances, which are the public good components of media products, that are the primary sources of value to consumers. Furthermore, expenditures on creative elements such as acting, directing, writing, and special effects which determine the consumer appeal of a performance, dominate the costs of recorded media products, especially for films and television programs. The trade model presented in this section is a model of the behavior and economic incentives of individual producers of media products for which public good elements dominate.

Critical to the financial success of a motion picture or program producer is the decision on how much to spend on creative elements such as actors, scriptwriters, directors, special effects, camera crews, props, musicians, and musical composers and arrangers. Each of these elements will have an effect on the audience appeal, and therefore the revenue generated by the production. By increasing expenditures on creative elements, the producer can increase the likely size of the box office or television sales revenues.[11] However, there are limits to how much a production budget can profitably be increased. For a single, isolated national market, which is where we begin this analysis, these limits will vary with the size of the market and with the number of competing producers in the market.

The effect of expenditures for creative elements on anticipated revenue for an individual producer's film or program is illustrated in Figure 2.1. D1 and D2 are the demand curves for the film or program with production budgets of B1 and B2, respectively.[12] Different points on the demand curves can be thought of as the amounts that purchasers (theaters or television stations) in different localities would be willing to pay to rent the film or program. The demand schedules order the locations according to willingness to pay, beginning with those willing to pay the most (presumably buyers in

---

[11] Obviously, there is no way to guarantee the popularity of a film or program. However, by spending more on talent and other creative inputs, a producer can increase the probability that his work will have popular appeal.

[12] It is assumed that the number of competing producers and their budgets are the same for D1 and for D2. That is, other producers are assumed not to respond to changes in the production budget of this particular producer by changing their own budgets or entering or leaving the market.

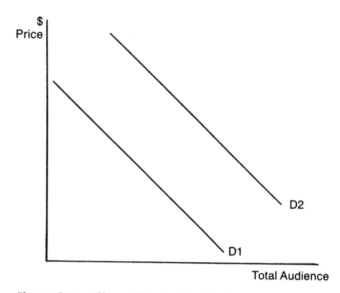

Figure 2.1. Effect of Production Budget on Demand

major metropolitan areas) on the left. B2 is assumed to be larger than B1, therefore D2 lies above D1. That is, larger rental payments can be expected with budget B2. Revenues for the two budgets will be equal to the areas under their respective demand curves. If we assume for convenience that distribution costs are negligible, profits will be higher with B2 than with B1 if the area under D2 exceeds the area under D1 by more than B2-B1.

The effect of expenditure for creative elements on producer profits is illustrated in Figure 2.2. The curve labeled R shows the relationship between revenue and production expenditures. The horizontal intercept for R is to the right of the origin to reflect the assumption that some positive level of expenditure on programming is necessary to generate even the smallest audience. R rises rapidly at first, indicating that at lower budget levels increases in expenditure on creative elements have a large effect on anticipated earnings. However, the slope of R decreases with additional expenditures, indicating that, as with other products, decreasing returns eventually set in, limiting the extent to which production expenditures can be increased profitably. Profits are equal to the vertical distance between R and the 45 degree line. Profits are maximized (the difference between revenue and production costs is greatest) at the point at which R has a slope of 1 (or is parallel to the 45 degree line drawn through the origin). The profit maximizing budget is indicated by B*.[13] One would expect that in a competitive market, entry of

---

[13] The distance from the origin to any point on the horizontal axis is equal to the vertical distance from that point to the forty-five degree line. Therefore, for any budget, profits are equal to the vertical distance between R and the forty-five degree line. This distance is maximized where R also has a forty-five degree slope.

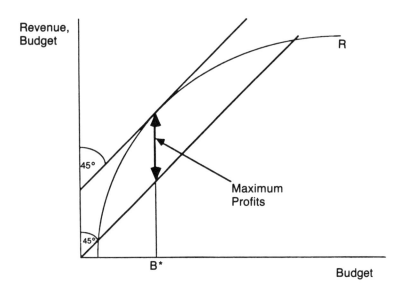

Figure 2.2.   Profits as a Function of Production Expenditures

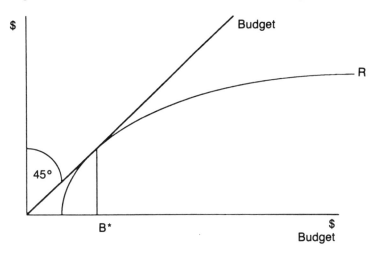

Figure 2.3.   Zero Profit Equilibrium

new firms would result in the zero expected profits situation illustrated in Figure 2.3, with R tangent to the 45 degree line through the origin.

The effect of differences in market size on production budgets in different markets is analogous to the effect of market growth on budget size within a market. The effect of market growth on production budgets is illustrated in Figure 2.4. B0* is the initial profit maximizing production budget for a representative producer in the market before growth occurs and R0 is the schedule of revenue possibilities associated with different budgets perceived by the

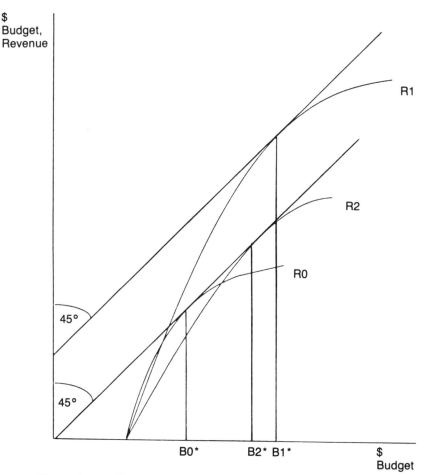

Figure 2.4.   Effect of Market Size on the Equilibrium Budget

producer for the market at its initial size. R1 and B1* represent the short run (before new producers enter the market) perceived revenue schedule and the response of an established producer following an increase in the size of the market. From the producer's point of view, each dollar spent on creative inputs now generates more dollars in revenue than when the market was smaller. Thus R1 lies above R0. Since the return to production expenditures has increased (at the margin) the producer will increase its budget. B1* is the new profit maximizing budget. Profits have clearly increased. In the longer run, however, positive profits for existing producers will attract new producers to the market. As the market is divided among an increasing number of producers, revenue per producer and revenue per production dollar will fall. The new equilibrium is represented by R2 and B2*. In the new equilibrium producers are again earning zero profits. Budgets have fallen from the short run high of B1* because the revenue generated by a production dollar has fallen as new producers have taken a share of the market. Note, however, that in the new equilibrium budgets are larger than they were before the market grew. Market growth has made possible both more diversity, in the form of more films or programs, and the higher quality (audience appeal) associated with larger budgets. Consumers, because they value both diversity and production quality, are supplied with more of both in a larger market.

The step from the analysis of competition in an isolated national market just presented, to analysis of trade between markets is straightforward. Assume that instead of representing different stages in the growth of a single market, the coordinates B0*,R0, and B2*,R2 represent equilibria in two distinct markets (the second obviously bigger than the first) which do not trade in media products. Each market has its own language. Viewers' natural preferences for films and programs produced in their own languages will be something of a barrier to trade. However, the higher production quality associated with larger budgets will, to some extent, offset the language handicap for producers in the larger market when their works are imported into the smaller market. On the other hand, films and programs produced in the smaller market will face both the language handicap and the disadvantage of smaller budgets when imported into the larger market.[14] Thus trade in films and programs between the two countries will be characterized by a larger flow from the large country to the smaller country than vice-versa.

This type of trading relationship is evident in the statistical descriptions of trade patterns and linguistic markets presented in Sections II and III of this chapter. The countries identified as major suppliers of recorded media products in Section II are countries identified by their official languages, with the important linguistic populations listed in Section III. Given its position in the large English language market, the overwhelming success of recorded media products from the United States in world markets is clearly predicted by this model, as is the relative success of recorded media products from the United Kingdom and Australia.

CASE HISTORIES

The trade barriers which many nations have erected to limit the inflow of media products from other countries can be attributed in part to the international success of Anglo-American film and television exports. These restrictions have been justified on the grounds of protecting domestic media industries, limiting foreign domination of information and entertainment,

---

[14] Trade may produce some equalization in budgets for the two markets. However, because the preference for native language productions acts as a partial barrier to trade, trade in films and programs will not eliminate complete differences in budgets among large and small nations.

and preserving the artistic expression of national culture. The model presented in Section IV, combined with the analysis of linguistic markets in Section III, suggests that the relative success of American films, television programs, and music in other countries is a consequence, at least in part, of economic factors that are fairly permanent. English speakers will continue to be more populous, and wealthier as a group, than other linguistic populations for the foreseeable future. On the other hand, as we pointed out in Section III, much of the commercial potential of the English language market is already being exploited. By comparison, potential opportunities for commercial media ventures, especially in broadcasting, remain largely undeveloped in most of the countries identified with other languages. It is also clear that, in general, public funding does not come close to replacing the financial support for programming that otherwise would be provided by commercial broadcasters. The possibility therefore remains that many countries may find policies that encourage the development of commercial television to be effective in promoting the growth of viable domestic media industries and in meeting domestic content objectives for broadcasting. The trade model presented above, in combination with what is clearly a strong preference for native language entertainment in most countries, suggests that liberalization of restrictions on media industries should produce movement toward these goals. How much movement is an empirical question. The recent histories of commercial television in Latin America and Italy, summarized briefly below, suggest that there are considerable grounds for optimism.

Case I: Latin America

Developments in Latin America are of interest for at least two reasons. First, most of the Hispanic programming currently broadcast in the United States originates in Latin America. U.S. Hispanic television networks such as Univision (formerly SIN) and Telemundo, which broadcast extensively in the United States, provide firm evidence that linguistic populations are more important than national boundaries in defining global television markets. Accordingly, the growth of these networks clearly undercuts earlier theories of programming flow which focused on political and economic hegemony rather than on language and market size (Schement, Gonzalez, Lewis, & Valencia, 1984). Latin American broadcast trends are important also because studies of Latin American broadcasting systems show that several of these countries have reduced significantly their reliance on imported U.S. programs without resorting to extensive restrictions on commercial broadcasting.

Industry characteristics. The economic organization of the production and distribution of television programs in much of Latin America is, in many ways, quite similar to the organization of production and distribution

Table 12.   Population, GNP and Television Sets in Various Latin American Nations

	Population	GNP (Billions of U.S. Dollars)	No. of Sets
Brazil	131,305,000	$267,0	16,500,000
Mexico	75,702,000	151.2	8,300,000
Argentina	29,627,000	54.2	5,910,000
Venezuela	17,993,000	66.8	2,050,000
Colombia	27,663,000	38.0	2,700,000
Chile	11,486,000	21.7	1,350,000
Peru	18,663,000	18.3	920,000

Sources: Population statistics from *World Almanac*, 1987, New York: Newspaper Enterprise Associates, Inc.; GNPs (1983) from *Statistical Abstract of the United States 1987*, 107th edition, U.S. Department of Commerce, Washington, DC: Bureau of the Census; No. of sets from *Statistics on Television Broadcasting*, 1983, Unesco, PX-23, (1983).

in the United States. For the most part, broadcasters are privately owned. While they may compete with government-controlled channels and may be required to maintain government licenses, the larger networks remain in private hands.

Another important similarity relates to commercial advertising. Private broadcasters rely primarily on advertiser support and do not derive extensive revenues from television receiver fees or other tax-based sources of income. Thus, the Latin American practice departs markedly from the prevailing model in Western Europe where receiver fees are widespread. In addition, the number of advertising minutes per day permitted in most Latin American nations seems to be much more generous than current limits on advertising in Western Europe.

Brazil and Mexico are the largest national television markets in Latin America followed by Argentina, Venezuela, Columbia, Chile, and Peru. Table 12 presents data on population, GNP, and the number of television sets in use in these countries. By way of comparison, for the same year as the data presented in Table 12, the GNP of Brazil was about the same as the GNP of Canada, while the Mexican GNP could be compared with the GNP of Australia. The economies of both nations are considerably smaller than the economies of the United Kingdom, France, West Germany, and Japan.

Trends in programming. The recent study of programming trends in six Latin American countries by Livia Antola and Everett M. Rogers (1984) is probably the most comprehensive work to date on this subject. Antola and Rogers examined trends in the percentage of program hours imported for Venezuela, Brazil, Chile, Mexico, Peru, and Argentina. They found that for the first three of these nations, imports as a percentage of total program hours declined considerably. The import percentage held steady at about

Table 13. Audience-Hours of Television Viewing in Four Latin American Nations

Country	Percent of Imported Hours			Percent Domestic
	U.S.	Latin America	Other	
Argentina	28%	9%	0	63%
Brazil	19%	2%	1%	78%
Mexico	33%	1%	0	66%
Peru	33%	25%	8%	34%

Source: Livia Antola and Everett M. Rogers, (1984). Television flows in Latin America. *Communications Research*, 11 (2), 189.

50% for Mexico, and imports' share of program hours increased in Peru and Argentina. Significantly, the traditionally commercial broadcasting systems in Peru and Argentina were placed under government control for considerable periods of time and only recently returned to private hands. For all the nations in their study, Antola and Rogers reported a general trend toward domestic productions (Straubhaar, 1984). Their comparison of program hours and audience hours (program hours weighted by audience size) for four countries showed that domestic programs' shares of audience were larger than their shares of program hours (see Table 5). Their data on audience hours for domestic and imported programs are shown in Table 13. For three of the four nations for which they were able to construct audience share statistics, domestic programs clearly dominate in terms of total audience.

The trend in Latin America toward greater reliance on domestic programs is apparently due to the increasing competitive strength of domestic program production industries. As television advertising revenues have grown in Latin American nations, more resources have been committed to producing domestic programs. Imported programs have been displaced as the production values of domestic productions have risen.

Exports to the United States. Televisa, the dominant media conglomerate in Mexico, is the primary source of Hispanic programs imported into the United States. Televisa founded the Spanish International Network (SIN) in 1961. Since then, SIN has grown rapidly to the point where it now maintains more than 400 satellite-linked broadcast and cable affiliates in the United States. In 1986, SIN was forced by the Federal Communications Commission to sell off eight UHF broadcast stations. Televisa is now the sole owner of all remaining assets of SIN (now Univision) (Lenti, 1987). During 1986, the network earned revenues of about $67,000,000 (Lenti, 1987).

The most popular type of Latin American program, both in Latin American nations and in the United States, is the "Telenovela." Telenovelas resemble American soap operas in many respects, although they seldom run beyond 120 one-hour episodes. Among its imports into the U.S., SIN has long broadcast telenovelas from several Latin American nations. In 1986, telenovelas in SIN's twelve and one-half hour, Monday to Friday, broadcast schedule included one from Venezuela, two from Puerto Rico, and three from Mexico before 6:30 p.m.; and one from Argentina and three from Mexico in prime time (Current SIN-TV Soaps, 1986).

As the U.S. Hispanic television market continues to grow (advertising revenue is now estimated at $100,000,000 per year (Hispanic TV giants, 1987)), it seems reasonable that U.S. Hispanic television imports will increase correspondingly.

Case II: Italy

Our second case history focuses on the rise of commercial, advertiser-supported television in Italy. Commercial television was initiated in Italy in 1974. By 1986, the country had five new commercial television networks (Valenti, 1986) and television advertising expenditures had grown to over $750 million annually (Privatization, 1986). While Italian commercial television, as pioneered by entrepreneurs like Silvio Berlusconi, relied initially on U.S.-made television series and motion pictures, the more recent schedules on the Berlusconi networks feature increasing numbers of Italian-made films and comedy programs. The Italian experience was undoubtably an important catalyst for the current movement toward regional privatization of the broadcasting industry in Western Europe.

Recent history. In 1974, an Italian cable entrepreneur, Peppo Sacchi, began to operate the first private cable television station in Italy. Although Sacchi's signals were limited to the small northern city of Biella, his station provided direct competition to RAI, the Italian public television monopoly, and the legality of Sacchi's service was challenged. On July 19, 1974, the Constitutional Court ruled that local, community cable TV of the type provided by Sacchi was legal. However, the Court also reconfirmed RAI's monopoly over *national* broadcasting (Werba, 1986). Following the Court's decision, Italian entrepreneurs like Berlusconi installed commercial cable systems and independent TV broadcasting stations throughout Italy. Today there are over 300 commercial television stations operating in Italy and most Italians can receive 10 or more over-the-air television signals.

By 1980, Berlusconi controlled three station groups including CANALE-5, which reached the major cities of northern Italy. He began to challenge RAI's monopoly on national broadcasting through "cassette networks" which supplied affiliated stations with common programming. He also began to air popular American programs such as *Dallas*.

By 1985, Berlusconi's station groups had grown to three commercial "networks" and his operations were called "the world's fourth biggest

Table 14. J. Walter Thompson—
Italian Advertising Budgets (Billions of Lire)

	Publitalia (Silvio Berlusconi)	RAI
1985	56	33
1984	44	21
1983	23	19
1982	13	N/A
1981	5	N/A
1980	0.8	N/A

Source: J. Walter Thompson Ad Budgets, (1986, April 23).
Variety, p. 148.

media operation after the three U.S. networks" (Werba, 1986, p. 168). While repeated court decisions still prohibited the practice of cassette networking, political support for commercial "networks" was such that various interim agreements were worked out to permit their continued operation. Berlusconi now plans to expand operations beyond Italy into all of Europe.

The importance of advertising. The growth of commercial television in Italy was supported from the beginning by the local advertising community. The Association of Advertising Companies (UPA) lobbied for commercial broadcasting in the Italian parliament and pressed for relatively generous limits on time permitted for advertising. The Italian division of the U.S. advertising agency, J. Walter Thompson, was a strong supporter of commercial television. Table 14 compares J. Walter Thompson's advertising purchases from Berlusconi with the firm's advertising placements with RAI. As the table indicates, by 1985, advertising purchases from the Berlusconi networks exceeded those from RAI by 23 billion lire.

J. Walter Thompson Italia's backing of commercial broadcasting was not surprising. RAI, with its strict advertising limits, simply could not support the large scale advertising campaigns common on U.S.-style television networks. For Berlusconi, advertiser support meant more appealing programming. In 1981, he acquired 64 episodes of *Dallas* after RAI's contract to broadcast the first 13 episodes of the popular U.S. program concluded. Subsequently, as bidding for U.S. programming drove up prices, RAI and Berlusconi both turned increasingly to Italian-made product. By 1986, the Italian Motion Picture Association (ANICA), an early opponent of Berlusconi, expressed strong support for both Silvio Berlusconi and for private television generally. ANICA president, Carmine Cianfarani set forth the Association's views:

Berlusconi has revolutionized the TV market for the members of the film industry. In the old days, public broadcaster, RAI, acquired Italian films for an average of only 6,000,000 lire ($3,750). In 1978, with the growth of commercial

**Table 15.   Italian Imports of Films for Television and TV Programs
1982 vs. 1983**

	1982	1983	1982 to 1983
Imports From All Countries			
No. of films	1,827	1,415	−412
No. of TV episodes	18,928	12,887	−6,041
Total value (U.S. dollars)	$135,568,467	$115,043,388	−$20,525,079
Imports From United States			
No. if films	1,418	1,069	−349
No. of TV episodes	12,865	8,298	−4,567
Total value (U.S. dollars)	$113,531,000	$89,726,488	−$23,804,512

Source: Imports of Films for TV and TV Programs (May 9, 1984), *Variety*, p. 303.

television, this situation changed. In the competition between private broadcasters and RAI for Italian pictures, the TV acquisition price increased. Today,
the sale of TV licensing rights brings an average of 250,000,000 lire ($150,000).
Films of classic or substantial commercial value can get much more (Italo
Motion Picture Association, 1986)

Mr. Cianfarani went on to express his group's strong support for the "Pan
European" broadcasting ambitions now espoused by Berlusconi and others.
The growing competitive strength of Italian program producers is reflected
in import statistics. Spending for imported, mainly U.S., programs and
films increased dramatically in the early years of Italian commercial broadcasting.[15] The growth in import purchases slowed as Italian producers began
to turn out more popular fare. Table 15 shows that spending on imported
programs and films for television actually declined from 1982 to 1983, as
did the numbers of programs and films imported. This trend reflects in part
a continuing movement to replace foreign series with domestic programs
during peak viewing hours. This development in Italy mirrors the similar
trend noted in Latin American nations.

CONCLUSIONS

An implication of the trade model and the data on linguistic markets presented above is that the *qualitative* nature of the media trade flows described
in Section II is not likely to change. Films, programs, and popular music
will continue to flow primarily from wealthier and more populous countries
to smaller and poorer ones, and English language productions will remain
most prominent in these flows. What is subject to change, however, is the

---

[15] Italian broadcasters spent less than $1 million for American television programs as re-
cently as 1978 (Privatization, 1986, p. 62).

magnitude of these flows and their effects on the national media and the industries that supply them in importing nations. An opinion widely held is that in the absence of restrictions on imported media products, domestic producers in most nations would be overwhelmed by competition from imports, especially imports from the United States. From this perspective, official intervention is required to ensure the survival of domestic producers and to guarantee that national media content will reflect domestic culture and other national interests.

In our opinion, the case histories of television in Italy and Latin America reviewed above convincingly refute this hypothesis. Domestic producers can survive and thrive in fairly open competition with imported programs and films. The key is adequate financial support. The general experience with public broadcasting is that the necessary financial resources will not be forthcoming from public sources alone. Commercial broadcasters appear to do much better in this regard. The lesson from the Latin American histories, in particular, is that, even in fairly small countries, advertiser-supported, commercial broadcasters exhibit distinct preferences for domestic programs and support domestic producers.[16]

The Latin American countries discussed above have long histories of commercial broadcasting. By contrast, television was a public-agency, monopoly enterprise in Italy until 1974. The Italian experience with privatization is therefore of special interest to other countries with state-controlled broadcasting systems that have begun, or are contemplating, similar privatization experiments. The private broadcasting industry grew explosively in Italy from the moment of its inception, as did advertising revenues and expenditures on programming. While foreign suppliers of programs, especially American suppliers, benefitted considerably, particularly during the early stages, from the growth of Italian television, the longer-term results seem to be especially favorable to domestic producers. Viewers have also benefitted, as the quality, quantity, and variety of programming have all increased. Furthermore, as we noted above, because broadcasters are important buyers of films, Italian filmmakers have also benefitted from the growth of commercial television.

To our minds, there is little doubt that, for most countries, policies that promote commercial television will also strengthen domestic program producers and filmmakers. Furthermore, domestic media are not likely to be dominated by foreign films and programs as a result of these policies.[17]

---

[16] Of course, producers in Latin American countries also benefit from participation in the larger Spanish-language market.

[17] Very small nations would be the exception. If the domestic market is too small, commercial revenues would not be enough to support domestic producers. The Latin American histories suggest that rather small nations can support significant program production industries through commercial revenues.

Rather, it is the state financed and controlled media that are most threatened by imports. Of course, there is no guarantee that domestic broadcasters and program producers, guided by commercial interests alone, will provide viewers with the programming that government officials want them to see. It is up to policy makers to weigh the importance of content objectives that might not be satisfiable within a commercial context against the potentially significant benefits of commercial broadcasting.

REFERENCES

Antola, L., & Rogers, E.M. (1984, April). Television flows in Latin America. *Communications Research, 11*(2), 183–202.

Brock, W.A., & Magee, S.P. (1978, May). The economics of special interest politics: The case of the tariff. *American Economic Review, 68*(2), 246–250.

Commission of the European Communities. (1984a, June). Television without frontiers: Green paper on the establishment of the common market for broadcasting, especially by satellite and cable. *Brussels COM, 84,* 300.

Commission of the European Communities. (1984b, November 16). *Promotion and development of a European programme industry: Study of an aid scheme for cinema and television co. productions* (Commission Working Paper, SEC (S4) 1798, final). Brussels.

Current SIN-TV soaps. (1986, September 24). *Variety,* p. 127.

Filson, A. (1980). *The distribution of films produced in the countries of the community.* Brussels, Belgium: Commission of the European Communities.

German speaking market at a glance. (1984, March 7). *Variety.*

Goldman Sachs Research. (1985, March). *The movie industry, the Big Picture: 1985.* New York: Goldman Sachs.

Guback, T.R. (1969). *The international film industry: Western Europe and America since 1945.* Bloomington, IN: Indiana University Press.

Hillman, A.L. (1982, December). Declining industries and political-support protectionist motives. *American Economic Review, 72*(5), 1180–1187.

Hispanic TV giants slug it out. (1987, March 25). *Variety,* p. 1.

Imports of films for TV and TV programs. (1984, May 9). *Variety,* p. 303.

International marketplace plays major role in disk biz; 50% of sales o'seas. (1987, March 25). *Variety,* p. 152.

Italo motion picture association now a Berlusconi backer. (1986, April 23). *Variety,* p. 126.

Katz, E., & Wedell, G. (1977). *Broadcasting in the Third World: Promise and performance.* Cambridge, MA: Harvard University Press.

Lenti, P. (1987, March 25). Televisa gears up for bold ventures. *Variety,* p. 118.

1985 World Almanac and World Tables (3rd ed., Vol. 1). Washington, DC: World Bank.

Pincus, J.J. (1975, August). Pressure groups and the pattern of tariffs. *Journal of Political Economy, 83*(4), 757–778.

The privatization of Europe. (1986, March 31). *Broadcasting,* pp. 61–67.

Schment, J., Gonzalez, I., Lewis, P., & Valencia, R. (1984, April). The international flow of television programs. *Communication Research, 11*(2), 163–182.

Statistical Abstract of the United States 1987 (107th ed.). (1987). Washington, DC: U.S. Department of Commerce, Bureau of the Census.

Statistics on television broadcasting. (1983). Paris: Unesco, PX-23.

Straubhaar, J.D. (1984). The decline of American influence. *Communications Research, 11*(2), 221–240.

Tunstall, J. (1977). *The media are American: Anglo-American media in the world.* New York: Columbia University Press.

Unesco. (1984). *Statistical Yearbook, 1984.* Paris: Unesco.

Unesco. (1985). *Statistical Yearbook, 1985.* Paris: Unesco.

U.S. Congress, Office of Technology Assessment. (1986, September). *Trade in services: Exports and foreign revenues special report* (OTA-1TE-316). Washington, DC: U.S. Government Printing Office.

Valenti, J. (1986, April 23). All eyes on Europe. *Variety,* p. 126.

Varis, T. (1983, Winter). The international flow of television programs. *Journal of Communication, 34*(1).

Varis, T., & Nordenstreng, K. (1974). *Television traffic: A one-way street?* Paris; Unesco.

J. Walter Thompson Ad Budgets. (1986, April 23). *Variety,* p. 148.

Werba, H. (1986, April 23). 10 years of commercial television in Italy. *Variety,* p. 143.

Wildman, S.S., & Siwek, S.E. (1987). The privatization of European television: Effects on international markets for programs. *Columbia Journal of World Business, 22*(3).

Wildman, S.S., & Siwek, S.E. (1988). *International trade in films and television programs.* Cambridge, MA: Ballinger Publishing Co.

World Almanac. (1987). New York: Newspaper Enterprise Associates, Inc.

3

Media Americanization, National Culture, and Forces of Integration

Eli M. Noam

INTRODUCTION

Critics of media liberalization frequently postulate an "iron law of television," according to which a liberalized television environment in a European country will invariably lead to its flooding by cheap American imports. Bad programs drive out good programs. This, if indeed true, could be considered to be merely a case where the demand for a product is better satisfied by foreign suppliers. However, such a conclusion would be mildly subversive, because it undercuts the legitimacy of the existing broadcast system by suggesting that its programs are watched only by the grace of some cultural protectionism. Hence, a "scientific" argument is made instead which purports to show that it is not the *content* of imported programs which undermines domestic product, but rather that some underlying *economic* logic is at work. The thesis, in a nutshell, is that a television broadcaster in a country, deciding how to fill time slots, faces a choice of either costly domestic production or importing off-the-shelf American programs which have already been produced and can therefore be obtained for marginal cost, that is, for almost nothing.

Therefore, given budget constraints or profit maximization, the cheap imports will drive away the local production, leaving American programs to predominate. To political pessimism ("The Russians are coming") and economic pessimism ("The Japanese are coming"), is added cultural pessimism

41

("The Americans are coming"). The argument has been so frequently repeated, often by respected media scholars, that hardly anyone bothers to think through its dubious logic. This argument, and a discussion of the reasoning behind it, is the subject of this chapter.

The treatment of cultural issues using economic reasoning is not likely to be persuasive to many. Most economists will consider the subject matter and its antagonists hopelessly "soft." Others, from more aesthetically oriented disciplines, view an economic analysis as a mark of philistinism and an affirmation of the adage that economists know the price of everything and the value of nothing. But economists are fairly accustomed to various industries or groups denying that economic principles apply to themselves. The author is not so politically or culturally naive as to deny the centrality of noneconomic issues in this debate. It is, however, the opponents of media liberalization who keep making pseudoeconomic arguments. Having chosen this ground, they must agree to defend it on its terms.

It should be noted at the outset that the analysis pursued in this chapter applies largely to the flow of media products between developed countries. When it comes to less developed countries, some of the notions discussed are not realistic. Where there are no active production organizations of sufficient size and technical sophistication, and where financial resources are minuscule, one cannot expect to find the same conditions as in the mature and culturally active countries of Europe.

Also, it is not the purpose of this chapter to trace the effects of modernity on traditional societies and the role of information flows in such change. This is important, but has been done by others.

EIGHT FLAWS OF THE IRON LAW

A British government White Paper outlines an economic argument that explains the potential for American programs to drive out domestic ones:

> (T)he economics of programme production [for cable] will...militate for the maximum possible use of the sort of ready-made material of which there are vast archives in the United States available at off-shelf marginal cost...an hour of original material can range from 20,000 pounds for a current affairs programme to 200,000 pounds for drama (or even more in the case of prestige product). Bought in material from the USA, where production costs have already been largely if not wholly recovered on the domestic market, can be obtained by the broadcasters for as little as 2,000 pounds an hour. (Home Office and Department of Industry, 1983, pp. 50–51)

This argument is seriously flawed.

First: It compares the marginal cost of distributing an existing product, where investments have already been sunk, to the total cost of new production. The statement, "It is cheaper to buy an already produced American program rather than to produce a program domestically" is a bit like saying, "it is cheaper to take a Chrysler taxi into the city rather than to buy a new Austin car." In other words, it compares apples and oranges; the marginal cost of rental with the total cost of production. It assumes that the American program is part of a release sequence, whereas a British program is not.

Second: It assumed that imported programming is attractive solely as a function of its low cost; however, broadcasters have a choice of programs. Why would a low quality American program have an advantage? Programs at similarly low marginal cost are available from other English-speaking nations such as Canada and Australia, as well as from the European continent, at the cost of dubbing. Large libraries of motion pictures from around the world are also available at low marginal cost. Thus, if American programs are indeed of intolerable quality, it is only necessary to pick from low-cost alternatives produced in other countries.

The exception would be if, somehow, the entire world would not offer enough programs above the U.S. quality level to fill the program requirements of one country's broadcasters, thus leading to dependence on Hollywood. But that is wildly implausible if one simply adds up the film and television productions in the various countries and then subtracts time for such domestic mainstays as news and sports. The argument further requires a simultaneous abundance of U.S. productions; otherwise prices would be bid up above marginal cost by foreign broadcasters in search of product. Finally, it also implies that of the tremendous output, past and present, of Hollywood and U.S. commercial television networks, not enough decent material can be found to satisfy the quality requirements of foreign channels.

Third: Even when imports are cheap, domestic production need not be curtailed. To demonstrate this is elementary: Suppose that there are two types of programs, F (foreign) and D (domestic), and that a programmer is indifferent between them according to a trade-off schedule that is more elastic than Albania's. This, together with the broadcaster's budget constraint, determines the distribution of foreign programs.

Assuming that foreign imports become cheaper, more resources will be freed up to support domestic production. Depending on the elasticities and prices involved, the *income effect* of the cheaper import could more than offset the *substitution effect* toward the foreign programs. Subsequently, it is possible that more rather than less domestic production will take place, unless there is a ceiling on total programs. This shift to increased domestic production is more likely where the preferences for domestic programs are high (i.e., where indifference curves are flat).

Fourth: Analysis of the "iron law" has been asymmetric. It considers the American product to be exportable to the United Kingdom at low marginal cost, without taking into account the worldwide export value of a similar

British production. Indeed, given the global prevalence of public broadcasting, one would predict an even larger international market for publicly-produced programs than for American commercial products. Furthermore, the advent of cable television systems in the United States has created channel packagers with a voracious appetite for programming. Hence, foreign producers would find a large, competitive, potential market for their productions. In one instance, the BBC switched its program offerings to the U.S. from the noncommercial Public Broadcasting System to the commercial Arts & Entertainment channel, which promised a higher compensation. And this is not surprising, since all large public broadcasters are under budget pressures.

Hence, the potential earnings of international exports should be factored into the economic analysis of whether or not to produce a program domestically. Such economic opportunities for export can become a cultural double-edged sword, since it could lead to a greater "Americanization" of the exporting country's media products to make them attractive in foreign markets. British films, for example, often cast well-known American actors since their presence provides an easier entry to U.S. audiences. The low-budget Italian "Spaghetti-Westerns" of the 1960s were an extreme case, promoting American and universal imagery to the exclusion of Italian themes; these films were an enormous financial success worldwide, and made Clint

Foreign markets, of course, include barriers to entry. For example, American audiences are accustomed to slick production quality, and are uncomfortable with subtitles, British accents, or unfamiliar sitcoms involving French families. Such barriers may fall as familiarity evolves, audience fragmentation reduces the need to appeal to vast majorities, and foreign producers learn to pitch their programs to U.S. audience tastes.

Fifth: The "Iron law" does not take into account the effect of competition for imported video products within a foreign country. If a multichannel environment existed in a European country, an attractive program from the United States would fetch no more than the marginal cost broadcasters currently pay. Under any reasonable scenario of competition among program channels, the price for the imported American show would be *above* what conventional wisdom believes is an invariably low standard rate.

At present, a number of cartel arrangements prevent such competition, making rival bidding practically nonexistent. In countries where several public channels are programmed independently, joint organizations exist for the purchase of foreign materials. In the U.K., the ITV companies purchase programs centrally, and operate an elaborate allocation mechanism if several companies are interested in the same item. A tacit arrangement of noncompetition exists between the ITV companies and the BBC. This arrangement broke down in one instance when an ITV company acquired the rights to a new season of the American soap opera *Dallas,* a highly popular BBC offering. A confrontation and much debate ensued, eventually forcing the ITV company to retreat and leaving *Dallas* with the quality-conscious BBC for another season.

Domestic arrangements are buttressed by international purchase cartels preventing competitive bidding between countries and denying program suppliers the option to hold out and seek higher prices from at least some nations, especially where cross-border broadcasting could reach many viewers. Foremost among such organizations is the European Broadcasting Union (EBU).

From the beginning, the EBU established a common bargaining position toward copyright holders such as music publishers, denying them a competitive environment to negotiate in. EBU set several standard agreements, which were entered into by the associations of copyright holders.

The EBU is the sole negotiator on behalf of its member countries for the rights to international events, and controls program distribution between member organizations. If one sells to an EBU organization in one country, one must deal with EBU members in other countries. For example, the EBU purchased the rights for Olympic games for all of its members, assessing individual costs according to a certain formula. This allows them to restrict bidding for events and squeeze out potential buyers who seek rights for one country only, thereby limiting payments to the owner of the events. In contrast, the various U.S. networks compete with each other for broadcast rights. This has led to payments that are extraordinarily higher than the ones paid by the EBU for all West European countries.

In 1975, the EBU threatened not to carry the Olympic Games rather than accept the rather modest $18 million price asked by the Montreal Olympic Organizing Committee, which, along with Canadian taxpayers, had incurred billions of dollars of expenses to stage the event. After protracted negotiations, the EBU acquired the rights for approximately $10 million. Thus, a three-week event watched intently by much of EBU's 240 million TV-population was compensated at less than one cent per day per household, while Canadian taxpayers paid huge subsidies. In 1984, the American television rights to the Los Angeles Summer Olympic Games were acquired by ABC, after competition among the three major networks, for $1.67 per household; the EBU, acquired the rights for $0.17 per household without facing competitors. (Crane, 1987)

The EBU system is, in effect, a "beggar thy neighbor's cultural and event producers" system. It is a protectionist cartel in which the interests of the broadcast institutions in receiving programs cheaply dominate the goal of encouraging cultural production. Though each country's institution is trying to minimize its program acquisition cost, they collectively depress the market for program productions. Members may even end up paying more of their share toward the cost of domestically produced programs than they otherwise would under adequate international compensation mechanisms.

Sixth: The fear of media Americanization overlooks changes in the supply of American media programs themselves. It assumes a static ideal in American production: low quality today, low quality tomorrow. Any potential for variation is overlooked by such spokesmen as the BBC's former Director General, Alistair Milne, who claimed that:

> We at the BBC already know, from years of experience and buying only the best American entertainment programmes, what an immense amount of inferior programming is being offered. To imagine that it is possible to buy additional American programs and maintain a broadcasting standard we are used to, is not to live in the real world. (Milne, 1983, p. 84)

Despite Milne's view, the American media are experiencing fundamental changes. In the past, the scarce resource of electromagnetic spectrum permitted only a tiny number of program channels, resulting in program content that attempted to serve the viewing interests of numerous groups. For the well-educated, sharing the airwaves with the less educated was generally an experience they loved to hate. In America, commercial television with its body-count economics is aimed at the peak of the bell-shaped statistical distribution, which is often—but mathematically erroneously—referred to as the "lowest common denominator." It strongly reflects popular tastes.

Commercial broadcasting has not been bad in the sense of low creativity relative to its self-defined task. It is not necessarily "easier" to successfully create popular entertainment for a huge and fickle audience. Intellectually more ambitious dramas can have their own relentless cliches and formulas just as much as a situation comedy. What one has to understand is that the outputs of a medium are defined by its structure; change the structure and the outputs will also change. There is nothing inherent in private media that produce only trash. Because they do not require an audience of 20 million households to be kept alive, as U.S. network shows do, private book and magazine publishers and filmmakers have produced high-brow as well as low-brow products. But when there are only two or three channels, profit- and audience-maximizing broadcasters will aim their product at the peak of a Gaussian distribution of viewers. When the number of channels increases, economic logic dictates that broadcasters disperse across the distribution (Noam, 1987). Some will specialize in programs for particular audience segments. This is what publishers and movie producers habitually do.

The proliferation of channels in America changes the medium's infrastructure, leading to increased production and greater differentiation of the overall fare. Fragmented audiences demand higher-quality shows (as well as lower-quality shows), presenting foreign broadcasters with much more variety to choose from than in the past.

Seventh: Another aspect of the argument of cheap American imports flooding the European television market is the assumption that American exporters do not take international program preferences into account, but view Europe as merely a dumping ground for Hollywood studios and New York networks. This, again, is flawed economics. Before making a substantial investment decision for a series, program producers calculate costs and compare them with expected revenue flows. The latter includes the probability of the series being ordered by a network and becoming an ongoing success, as well as the potential for subsequent syndication revenues in the United States and abroad. In recent years, most series have not broken even financially in their network runs, becoming profitable only through their syndication. Thus, the anticipated purchase decisions of foreign broadcasters directly affect the nature of the programs offered by the American producers. A show which clearly has no appear beyond the United States may not be produced, or offered by a U.S. network. Therefore, a view of the BBC and other European broadcasters as mere passive recipients of the hand-me-down programming decisions of American producers, who in turn dump them on the international market as an afterthought, is seriously mistaken.

In deciding on the approach, script, casting, and so on, of a film, American producers will take the foreign market into account. Let us assume that there are three "content inputs" into a film, D(domestic), F(foreign), and U(universal), and that the world consists of two countries. Domestic and foreign inputs are those that touch and illuminate familiar experiences specific to their respective societies; universal inputs touch upon both cultures. If only the domestic market is served, the producer will utilize inputs D and U up to the point where their marginal cost is equal to the expected marginal revenue they generate. Content input F is assumed to have a negative effect domestically, and will not be included. If the second country is now included, where the content input D has a negative audience effect, the producer will shift more toward universal inputs. Furthermore, there will now be inputs of F, as long as the value of the audiences gained in the second country is greater than the negative impact in the first country.

It could be argued that while this model of behavior is theoretically true, reality is quite a different matter. In particular, the argument stresses that the U.S. domestic market is so tight that a program must be a superachiever in it, or it would not be produced at all. Thus, even potential success in foreign markets would not help the survival of a program that is not a top hit with American audiences. Hence, foreign audiences play no role in shaping them. This notion of a two-stage maximization is probably empirically true at present, but only because foreign television markets are not yet profitable. Still, would an American network buy only the programs which maximized the domestic audience, without concern for follow-up foreign audiences, thus skewing the producers' choice of the mix of D, F, and U program inputs? There are two answers. First, if this is the case, it is a by-product of the rules against network syndication which are strongly defended by the

Hollywood producers. By preventing the networks from follow-up gain, they are more likely to choose programs without regard to the aftermarkets. Second, program producers can offset network preferences by proper substitution of input and budget factors. Suppose that a producer sells an episode to a network for $1 million, the network's expected advertising revenue after its own expenses and normal profit. This amount provides the cost ceiling for the episode's producer, assuming for the moment there is no follow-up syndication or aftermarket. For a $1 million total budget, the cast will not include "name" stars, special effects will be minimal, and so on. Suppose now that the foreign syndication would be introduced, and can be expected to yield another $1 million. To serve the foreign audience, the program input may have to shift relatively more toward U and F. While this mix will not be optimal for the network's domestic audience, the producers are likely to use the higher revenues to increase the overall production budget, making name stars, larger casts, and special effects affordable. In consequence, the program will be domestically more attractive than the previous one, and the network may well acquire it.

Many television executives deny that production costs affect their selection among programs; given the cost sunk into programs, this may be true. Still, the empirical fact remains that made-for-TV productions have noticeably lower budgets than theatrical films, and that theatrical films are presented as program highlights. The mechanism at work is the producer's implicit realization of upper limits on network revenues, and hence the effect of the ceiling of expected payment from the network on production decisions.

It is also true that current foreign broadcast revenues are relatively small potatoes for Hollywood television producers. But when the revenues obtained abroad increase, as they invariably will in a more varied foreign multichannel environment, the impact of global feedback on U.S. decisions will become even more important than before. Hence, the "Americanization" of foreign television environments would be accompanied by a "universalization" of Hollywood programs.

Eighth: The "Iron Law" assumes that the American head start will prevent entertainment-oriented television programs from being produced in other countries. Actually, many non-American media empires emerged as soon as foreign media were liberalized: in Italy and France, Berlusconi; in Britain, Maxwell; in Australia, Britain, and the United States, Murdoch; in Brazil, TV-Globo; in Mexico, Televisa. All have extensive international activities that go far beyond the scope of American networks, and many are also active in production. In 1986, Berlusconi's subsidiaries accounted for 62% of all Italian film production, a far greater cause for concern than American imports.

Many of the problems of large-scale American program exports result less from American media offensives than the underdeveloped state of domestic independent production in importing countries, often beholden to the monopoly broadcast institutions which are its main clients and financiers. The weak state of media financing, and the absence of profitable foreign outlets for media products also contribute to the major imperfections of domestic markets. One could argue that some "infant industry" protection would improve this situation. But to confer the status of "infant" to the cultural industries of Germany, Italy, France, or Britain is to make a mockery of that term.

THE PARADOX OF HOLLYWOOD ADVANTAGE

The success of Hollywood studios is unusual insofar as they are the high-cost producers by a wide margin. Over the years, production costs have grown steadily for a variety of reasons. Labor unions have established high compensation schedules and restrictive work rules. Name actor compensation has grown, since a known talent is usually declared necessary for a film's visibility, and talent with international recognition and appeal is scarce. The essence of a star, after all, is rarity, and rarity commands monopoly rents. In the days of the old studio systems, actors had long-term contracts with the companies; as a result, a studio reaped the benefit of early investment in an actor's reputation as it controlled subsequent compensation. Under the current system of unrelated deals, the actor is the primary beneficiary of early investments in his reputation, delineating one source of increased production cost. Another factor is the escalation of the public's expectations: sensational special effects in a new film set a standard which future audiences will want to see matched, or surpassed. Yesterday's standard may not be acceptable today, leading to ever-increasing costs. Despite occasional breaks in this escalation when some element becomes too expensive (e.g., animation, or mass battle scenes), aggregate production costs generally increase along with the number of highly specialized skills in production and distribution.

Hollywood's high-cost environment is partly offset by its advantage of economies of concentration, which are related to, but distinct from, economies of scale. These economies arise not from a single firm's size, but from an entire industry operating in close proximity. As with automobiles in Detroit, the garment industry in New York, microelectronics in Silicon Valley, silk in Lyon, cutlery in Sheffield and Solingenx and film production in Hollywood, these instances of clusters and related economic activity offer great advantages. Many examples of clustering are not dictated by the specific location of raw materials; instead they promote highly specialized firms providing special services, shorten communications flows, and provide efficient labor markets. Clusters may be the industrial form of the future, combining the control efficiency of small firms with the economies of scale of providers of specialized inputs.

Another question is whether the large size of the American domestic market permits production budgets larger than those of other countries, thus creating products of greater appeal. Market size per se cannot be the issue, or else the numerous Indian films would be more successful internationally. Even factoring in wealth, the U.S. market does not give the obvious advantage one might initially ascribe to it. The total U.S. audience is far more fragmented among the much larger number of films created in the United States than in Western European countries. According to the Motion Picture Association of America's 1987 Economic Review, there were 497 films produced in the United States compared with some 200 in the more densely populated European community. Consequently, the attention given to any U.S. film is very short lived. The domestic market may be larger only in a hypothetical sense; in reality, it is more crowded than that of most other countries. Should Hollywood producers necessarily have more money at their disposal, when Western Europe is such a rich region? Although it is linguistically diverse, each of its three major languages are spoken or understood by more than 100 million, and millions more overseas. If European film budgets are lower than in the United States, it may reflect the caution in its financial market's financing risky ventures, a problem that has similarly plagued European high technology development. By contrast, a firm such as Warner Brothers will invest one million dollars in each of 10 major projects in the hope that one will produce a significant return.

Furthermore, the American market is also accessible to foreign producers. It is again the two-stage thinking—that a film must first make money domestically, with exports only an added windfall—leading producers to consider the size of the domestic market determinative. With this kind of thinking, nobody would produce watches in Switzerland or grow Kiwi fruits in New Zealand. Ultimately, the problem is again a reflection of a country's policy of financial risk taking, that is, whether a film would be financed which requires large exports to become profitable.

If the American firms are the high-cost producers and many non-American programs are offered in the world market, what explains the global success of American products? Though it is not within the scope of this chapter to answer this question, some reasons may be suggested.

1. Hollywood programs are squarely aimed at the broad middle peak of distribution of tastes, rather than to satisfy upper culture tastes. It is thus "popular" in the way that "public" television often is not, likewise appealing to the broad audience majorities of other societies.

2. America is a country of significant ethnic and cultural diversity; thus, a program that proves popular across its population tends to have many universal themes that appeal elsewhere.

3. By force of its economic, political, scientific, and cultural influence, American themes have reached a global audience, making its own issues universal. But it is not simply the might of America that put its images forward. For nearly a century the most popular books in Germany have been the 80-plus volumes of the Karl May series, whose adventures take place on the American frontier. These books were written, well before the American political ascendancy, by an author who had never traveled across the ocean. Such a fascination with American themes is not the offspring of American power but more likely its siblings.

4. American film production has been at the technical forefront almost from its origins, creating entertainment on a highly professional level. Any visitor to Disney World must marvel at the ingenuity with which technology and imagination are harnessed into creating leisure-time experience. Entertainment is one of America's best outputs, just as food may be France's. American business has moved entertainment production from individualized, small-time operations to mass production with tremendous technical sophistication.

5. Film and television are part of the broader U.S. service economy. Throughout the developed world, manufacturing-based economies are shifting toward a service base, and this trend is most advanced in the United States. Hence, the leadership of the American film production industry is no more surprising than that of the American computer software production industry. As its manufacturing loses its primacy to Pacific Basin countries, the U.S. economy relies on such services for its present comparative advantage. From the American perspective, this makes restrictions against its own media products especially unfair: while flooded by foreign manufacturing products, its own export strength in information is stymied on grounds of cultural domination.

There are, of course, organizational reasons for the global penetration of U.S. films, most notably the distribution networks of Hollywood producers, which provide them with superior access to theaters worldwide. There is no intention here to defend certain business practices of Hollywood firms, which for decades were the target of domestic antitrust law suits. Furthermore, the acrimony of the producers' relationship with theaters is legendary, but their market power can be dealt with by other countries' own laws and regulations on unfair business practices.

Despite all the war stories, one should not overestimate the power of a distribution system. Like other forms of vertical integration, discrimination in favor of one's own product is sensible so long as that product is not inferior. It would rarely make sense for a distribution organization to push unpopular films of its own production into theaters and reject other producer's block busters. Ultimately, the market power of U.S. distributors depends on their access to U.S. programs, and not vice versa.

NATIONAL CULTURE

The question of "Americanization" of media is subtopic of the issue of "national culture," one of the ultimate sacred cows. This term needs to be discussed in order to understand why free flow of programs is controversial. To begin with, using the nation as a cultural unit is largely arbitrary. If cultural disaggregation is a central value, why not carry its logic on to units smaller than nations, such as regions and cities? Conversely, there are instances in which cultural cohesion may be stronger across borders than within a country. This can frequently occur within language groups such as the Poles, separated by boundaries for a long time.

Ethnic groups and their cultures can thus be divided into categories that are not based upon geography or language (Morgan, 1985). Class is an important dimension, as in proletarian culture, and age another, as in youth culture.

High culture in Europe was initially that of the highly internationalized nobility, who had more in common culturally with each other than with their respective subjects. During one period they spoke French; at another time clergy and scholars spoke Latin. The strong value of national culture was largely the creation of the 19th-century nation-state, part and parcel of the aggressive nationalism for which Europe eventually paid so dearly. Differences among national cultures were drawn out to absurd lengths in that era. In Germany, for instance, there was a major conflict between adherents of "sports," viewed as an alien import from England and "gymnastics" (Turnen) which was seen as genuinely German, largely because its exercises were developed during the Prussian War of liberation from Napoleon. Two separate and hostile associations existed, with the Kaiser's sympathy strongly in favor of the German form of exercises. Today, such controversies seem absurdly parochial. How many German citizens are concerned that their culture has been undermined by sports fans cheering at a soccer game rather than at a gymnastics event?

By linking culture to the nation-state, the concept of national culture was brought close to the heart of government. Its creation and distribution were typically centered in the national capital rather than the provinces or periphery. Although a certain clustering of cultural activities creates economies of scale, this is not the whole story. From the dawn of civilization, governments glorified their rule through cultural production, and hence, culture tended to flow from the center outward. Artists flocked to the place where subsidies and buyers of their services were most plentiful. To a government, influencing cultural activities was crucial as its producers were among the most articulate, well-educated, and vocal groups in society. Not only is the pen mightier than the sword, it is also cheaper. Artists of national culture could be used to articulate the state agenda, whether promoting the reduction of divisions among classes and regions, yearning for lost territories, a political spiritualism, an adventuresome and imperialistic internationalism, and so on. Those artists who opposed the state dogma were ostracized as standing apart from national culture, though when their politics ceased to be a threat, they were sometimes eulogized as national heroes for their creativity.

Underlying the question of national culture is the difficulty of enforcing group loyalty to societal norms and state control. Loyalty is easier to achieve in small group situations such as a family or a platoon. As the group grows, the incentive for "free riding" becomes larger with the ratio of contribution to direct benefit decreasing. The possibility of divergence and coalitions increases, and centrifugal forces arise. Stressing national culture is one way to establish a cohesive force, an important factor for large and heterogeneous states with strong centrifugal forces of smaller subcultures. Television plays a central role as an ideal vehicle for this patriotic culture. The nation was initially its unit of reach and of control; however, the new generation of video transmission technology has undermined the concept of a national electronic hearth. Some of the new media are highly individualistic (video cassettes); others are decidedly local (cable television and low-power television); still others are transnational (satellites). Each one fragments the national audience into more specialized groups, just as magazine publishers reach different subgroups. Hence, television becomes transformed from the medium of national culture to that of subcultures, and from a cohesive force to a differentiating one.

These observations are not made to deny that cultural activities and traditions vary from country to country, or that they are worthy of protection—for such denial would be absurd. Rather, they should instill a healthy skepticism for eager invocations of the concepts of "national culture" and "cultural identity" by governments and representatives of established and powerful institutions arguing for restrictions on media outlets. Since cultural politics are real politics, and cultural dominance is real dominance, notions of protection of national culture are not necessarily benign, but may instead mask a form of information protectionism that serves entrenched interests.

In the field of television, these groups are the state and the political parties (both governmental and opposition) controlling the programming policy, personnel hiring, and budget allocation of most existing public broadcast institutions. A third influential group are newspaper publishers, particularly medium- and small-sized operations fearing the loss of advertising revenues to commercial television. A fourth group are insider cultural influentials and journalism unionists, who have achieved links of patronage to the broadcast institutions employing or supporting many thousands of them, often under civil service-like conditions of employment and income security.

While their employment potential would be greater in a larger media land-scape, it would also be less secure and comfortable, particularly at the upper levels where political connections are vital. A program of liberalization would mostly help outsiders, a group which tends to be unorganized.

The political left is also protective, favoring the system of public broadcasting as part of a general preference for public ownership of social infrastructure, as well as for its potential for offering more sympathetic coverage than the privately owned press and its greater concern with educational and cultural values.

One would therefore expect that the political right would advocate media liberalization for symmetrical reasons. It is, however, split, because one of its major constituencies are traditionalists critical of the values of consumption and entertainment which private television promotes.

The noted American sociologist Herbert Gans describes cultural audiences as stratified into groupings of high, upper-middle, middle, and low culture. Adherents of high culture are typically those at the leading edge of cultural creation itself. Upper-middle cultural adherents are the main consumers of culture, the opera and museum attendees and supporters of the arts, including U.S. public television. In most countries, they are the culturally dominant group. Middle culture, on the other hand, is that of the best-seller novels and commercial television, representing the broad majority of tastes in industrialized countries. Lower culture is that of supermarket magazines and melodrama. Despite commercial television's alleged tendency to seek the lowest common denominator, it actually serves the low culture grouping relatively poorly. Instead, it serves broad majority of population which peaks in the middle culture range.

The different taste publics—corresponding roughly to social classes—are antagonistic toward each other's preferences; lower ones are viewed as vulgar, while higher ones are seen as snobbish. Producing a popular series is no "easier" than creating a high culture program. The quality question is one of optimal production once a target audience has been chosen; identifying quality simply by the program preferences of higher culture tastes is elitist. Control over television means control over which preferences will be fulfilled, making that control also a distributional issue of whose consumption desires are served.

The political groups in support of the present distributional allocation of television are a formidable array of forces. Moreover, they fight for a cause of undeniable merit, public broadcasting, opposed by forces of sometimes dubious standing, including entertainment entrepreneurs, fly-by-night promoters and assorted political extremists. There are few people without an axe to grind, who advocate the extension of freedom of speech to electronic media purely on principle.

Despite a formidable, a array of support groups, the traditional monopoly system is breaking up as electronic media are gradually liberalized by the entry of alternative, private distribution outlets. The process of transition is a bitter and highly polemical one. The integrity of proponents on the various sides is routinely discredited, as if the underlying two principles which must be balanced—information as a public service, and the right of free expression—are not both reasonable societal goals, regardless of the selfishness of their advocates and beneficiaries.

THE ECONOMIC FORCES OF INTEGRATION

This critique of the prevalent economic analysis of television's Americanization does not deny that strong economic forces of internationalism are at work. These forces, however, are not especially American. Perhaps the most important long-term economic force affecting media is that of *integration* in information production. Publishing, film production, television, and computer applications are overlapping and merging to form the information industry.

Integration means that alternative pathways for the delivery of information are not as neatly segregated from one another as in the past. This inevitably leads to "territorial" disputes among the various interests allied with one form of delivery or another. This, however, is not simply a dispute between the public and private sector. In America, private broadcasters opposed private cable television. In Australia, the public ABC and the private broadcasters were united in their dislike of satellite broadcasting, public or private. In Germany, the public ARD institutions opposed the creation of the public ZDF. Rather than analyzing new media issues as private versus public, a more accurate model posits newcomers versus an establishment which does not wish to share its favored position vis-á-vis audience, producers, and advertisers.

In addition to technologically interchangeable delivery channels, a key economic element promoting integration is the importance of controlling and coordinating the sequential release of a media "product" among the different nations and forms of distribution. The underlying principle is the attempt to price-discriminate between classes of viewers of different demand elasticity (Waterman, 1985). The ability to price-discriminate is crucial, since many viewers receive what economists call a "consumer's surplus," having to pay less than they would be willing to. One example is the Olympic Games, for which many viewers would be willing to pay substantial sums if they had to. The significance of new media are that they permit a refinement of price discrimination that reduces this consumer surplus—estimated in 1973 as $20 billion in the U.S. (Noll, Peck, & McGowan, 1973)—by setting up a cascading chain of distribution down to high elasticity audiences. Reducing this consumer surplus contributes to inequality, creating costly versions of formerly free products. A historical perspective is necessary to understand that the present consumer surplus is temporary rather than typical for the past, attributable to the peculiarity of conventional television, as a highly efficient distribution channel but a terrible collection mechanism for program providers. Television as an entertainment provider, in contrast to most other forms of entertainment, had become a public good. After all, few people attend movies, major sporting events, or professional live arts performances for free. The share of income devoted to movies fell considerably, from 8.7% in 1948 to 2.2% in 1972, suggesting that viewers, if forced to, would be willing to pay at least as much today for television, and probably more, given increased leisure time, higher income, greater convenience of home media, and more viewing options.

Strong economic incentives exist for a producer of a program to realize these opportunities by directly or indirectly controlling the stages of its distribution, domestic and international, thereby establishing the most profitable sequence of releases. Such incentives are not particular to private firms; without an unlimited budget public broadcasters have similar motivations.

A related economic factor favoring media integation revolves around the externalities from one stage of distribution to the next. Advertising and promotion for the book stage, for example, benefits subsequent cable and broadcasting distribution. The interests of media firms lie in representation through every phase of distribution, from books and motion picture to cable and broadcasting. This need leads to the huge, diverse, multimedia firms such as Time, Inc. in America, Bertelsmann in Germany, Murdoch (News Limited) in Australia, Maxwell in Britain and the U.S., Havas in France, and Berlusconi in Italy.

OUTLOOK

What are the implications of this growing coordination of distribution modes on media productions? First, as discussed, consumers end up paying more than in the recent past, which raises income-distributional issues.

On the positive side, it encourages the production and supply of a larger number of television programs, books, plays, and films in an effort to satiate the demand for these works by the more numerous and diverse outlets. But while some works that would not have been created at all are now being produced, not *all* media programs benefit equally. The system favors products that can be distributed through multiple stages, such as popular fiction, aiding the large integrated firms that can shepherd such works through each phase. This incentive structure extends not only into film and television production, but also into book publishing and theater, as production decisions become dependent upon further distribution stages. Similarly, these incentives render productions specific to a national culture less attractive than works of global appeal allowing for international distribution.

Moreover, this system implies that protectionism will not work in free societies to preserve a domestically-based cultural industry. Given advancing technology, information products will cross national boundaries with ever greater ease. The era when the totality of television was a tiny number of outlets, limited and controlled by the state, will prove a brief historical episode about which future generations may well shake their heads in wonder.

What, then, is the alternative? The resultant media mix will not be American, but rather will derive from a variety of large and integrated international media companies centered in several countries, in addition to numerous small producers, often arranged in clusters in many countries. If this structure does not result in enough productions of a domestic cultural type, the alternative is subsidization. Oxford University Press cannot and should not protect its circulation by preventing the publication or importation of popular books by others. Its survival should be through the quality of its output, supported by subsidies, and not through restrictions. For book or theater productions, many such subsidy mechanisms exist (to authors, authors' employees, publishers, libraries, theaters, actors, etc.). Current television productions are subsidized through the television set license fee mechanism, channelled through the public broadcasting institutions. Such a mechanism can certainly be maintained in a liberalized television environment, and further supplemented by other sources of financing and additional destinations of subsidies.

Opening one's borders to foreign cultural products need not cause one's own to disappear. The presence of Tolstoy, Dickens, and Balzac did not spell the end of German or Mexican literature. British, American, or Japanese cultures are not undermined by an enjoyment of music by Bach, Beethoven, or Mozart. Today, Latin American literature is among the world's most admired, despite (or because of) the proximity to the United States.

Ultimately, the popularity of Hollywood glitter does not negate the popularity of domestic productions. Familiar program inputs and the treatment issues close to home enhance the attractiveness of domestic programming. Audiences are not passive recipients of information and program inputs, but select, interpret, and process content selectively in light of their own values and priorities.

Thus, the "iron law of media Americanization," according to which television liberalization leaves foreign countries to be flooded by American programs, is seriously flawed in its economic analysis, at least where developed countries are concerned. More likely than Americanization is a development of increasing cultural integration in which program flow move in various directions within the developed world, while its content becomes more universal for economic reasons. These trends are reinforced by the emergence of integrated media firms controlling many stages of distribution across media and countries. But there is no evidence—theoretical or empirical—that these firms will be predominantly American.

REFERENCES

Crane, T.J. (1987). The future of sports broadcasting: An international question. *Seton Hall Legislative Journal, 10,* 201-261.
Home Office and Department of Industry. (1983). *The development of cable systems and-service* (White Paper). London: Her Majesty's Stationery Office.
Milne, A. (1983). A view from the Brits: Westward no. *Channels, 3*(2), 84.
Morgan, J. (1985). The flood of information—the age of cultural conflicts. In *Medientrends.* Hamburg: Intermedia Congress.
Noam, E. (1987). A public and private choice model of broadcasting. *Public Choice, 55,* 163-187.
Noll, R.G., Merton, J.P., & McGowan, J.J. (1973). *Economic aspects of television regulation.* Washington, DC: Brookings Institution.
Waterman, D. (1985). In E. Noam (Ed.), *Video media competition.* New York: Columbia University Press.

4

World Television Trade:
The Economic Effects of Privatization
and New Technology*

David Waterman

INTRODUCTION

The most obvious result of an Italian court's decision in 1976 to allow free entry into commercial television broadcasting has been a tremendous influx of American movies and series onto Italian television screens. Italian viewers have followed the imports. The combined audience share of the new private networks primarily featuring this programming exploded, from 6% in 1979 to 46% by May/June of 1983—nearly matching the 47% combined share of Italy's three state-owned and controlled networks, RAI1, RAI2 and RAI3 (Werba, 1986a). Prior to the 1976 decision, the well-respected RAI organization had enjoyed a virtual monopoly.

The Italian experience with commercial television has been watched with trepidation by policy makers worldwide. Sovereign nations in Europe and other parts of the world are now undergoing or anticipating the expansion and privatization of broadcast systems and the introduction of cable and other multichannel video technologies. What will be the long-term effects of this unleashing of new technology and free market forces on the program

* I owe thanks to Stan Besen, Jay Blumler, Jeffrey Nugent, Everett Rogers, Bernard Miyet, Peter Monge, and Michele Zerbib for comments. Jean Dufour and Helene Gouny provided able research assistance. Responsibility for errors remains with the author.

This chapter is a revised and expanded version of an article having the same title in the journal, *Telecommunications Policy, 12*(2), June 1988, pp. 141-151.

menus of television systems throughout the world? Will American dominance continue in Italy and be repeated elsewhere? Or will earlier expectations of de Sola Pool (1977) and others eventually materialize—that expanded broadcast capacity and new delivery systems such as cable, VCRs, and DBS will serve to increase the amount and variety of domestically produced programs?

This chapter addresses these questions from an economic perspective, focusing on the major nations of Western Europe and Japan, for which data are most accessible. Our thesis is that although increased presence of American programming worldwide is inevitable, new opportunities for domestic production within U.S. trading partner nations are being created in the process. In particular, the domestic commercial infrastructures which support television systems in those countries (e.g., their advertising industries) are rapidly developing as a result of privatization and new technology, stimulated in the short run by the demand for American-made programs. In the long term, however, development of these commercial infrastructures, especially in support of the "pay" media, such as premium channels and prerecorded videocassettes, should economically benefit these nations' domestic production industries *relatively* more than they benefit American and other imported programming. While this long-term development appears to be now underway, a significant variable in its progress remains the trade and domestic media policies of America's trading partners.

Following an introduction to the main facts about world trade in television programs that previous research has revealed, we set out in Section II an economic framework which provides a rationale for the historical dominance of program trade by the United States. In Section III we use the economic model to suggest likely effects of privatization and new technologies on program trade, and then conclude with a policy discussion in Section IV.

U.S. Dominance

A 1973 Unesco-financed study by Varis (1974) of the program menus of 50 nations documented the salient empirical fact of international trade in television programming: historical dominance of the United States as a program exporter. Varis found the United States to account for over 40% of all program hours exported worldwide, including 44% of hours imported by Western Europe. The United States had the further distinction of importing a smaller proportion of its television programming (1% to 2%) than any of the other sample countries (with exception of the People's Republic of China). In general, Varis found that relatively large and wealthy countries, such as France, the U.K., Japan, and the U.S. tend to be the major world exporters. And although these countries (including the U.S.), have also imported relatively large *absolute* numbers of programs, the *proportions* of imported program hours on their television system menus have generally been lower than those of smaller and less wealthy nations. A 1984 update by Varis showed little systematic change in world trade patterns, apart from some tendency for regional exchange of programs to replace importation from dominant exporters such as the United States. Antola and Rogers (1984) also documented an increase in regional exchanges in the case of Latin American nations.

Another consistent finding has been the prevalence of feature films, especially American films, among imported television fare (Varis, 1974; Pragnell, 1985). In this respect, television trade is closely intertwined with theatrical film industries worldwide. Notably, the export trade of movies for theatrical exhibition has also been dominated by the United States since the industry's beginnings around the turn of the century.

Previous authors have identified a number of specific cultural and institutional factors contributing to historical dominance of movie and television trade by the United States, including prevalence of the English language, ethnic diversity of the United States, postwar fascination with Hollywood, Madison Avenue exports of American products, and adoption of the U.S. model for a television system as an inducement to purchase U.S. programs (Katz & Wedell, 1977; Tunstall, 1977). Earlier authors have also recognized an economic factor: the large and wealthy domestic audience base available to U.S. producers. The simple model we set out below develops and extends this economic logic, in abstraction from other factors.[1]

AN ECONOMIC FRAMEWORK

The model's foundation is a fundamental characteristic of information products, such as television programs or motion pictures: They typically have very low marginal costs of distribution relative to the "first copy" cost of creating the product itself. The result is extraordinary economies of scale which can be realized by distributing information products to ever larger audiences. In brief, we use the model to show that, under these cost conditions, the larger and wealthier is the potential audience base for a given program, the greater is the amount of economic resources that a producer can profitably invest in that program. The larger the investment, in turn, the greater the competitive advantage of a producer in selling its programs on

---

[1] The model is conceptually similar to that employed in independently developed work by Wildman and Siwek (1988). These authors also consider audience demand to depend on a film or video product's cost and its country of origin. For related general analysis of imperfect competition between nations due to economies of scale, see, for example, Kierzkowski (1984).

the world market. Given some assumptions about audience demand for foreign programs in a free trade environment, we then show that the economic development of any one country's domestic television industry (e.g., via advertising growth or installation of "pay" media systems) helps both domestic and foreign producers, but relatively more so the former.

A Two-Country Model

In each of two countries, A and B, a single producer maximizes profit in the production of a single program. There is free trade between the countries and an advertiser-supported (or government-imposed subscriber license fee) system in both.

We define the objective functions for producers A and B as follows:

$$\Pi_A = v_A \cdot N_A \cdot R_{AA} + v_B \cdot N_B \cdot R_{AB} - C_A \tag{1}$$

$$\Pi_B = v_A \cdot N_A \cdot R_{BA} + v_B \cdot N_B \cdot R_{BB} - C_B \tag{2}$$

where:

$\Pi_{A,B}$ = profit
$v_{A,B}$ = Revenue potential per viewer
$N_{A,B}$ = TV household base
R_{AA}, R_{AB} = rating (i.e., percent of total TV households viewing) of program A in country A; rating of program A in country B, etc.
$C_{A,B}$ = production investment

The terms $v_A N_A$ and $v_B N_B$ can be thought to represent the size and efficiency of each country's economic "infrastructure" for extracting revenues from viewers; "v" itself may be interpreted as a "cost per thousand" advertising rate, or assuming it were set in a range of negligible demand elasticity, as a subscriber license fee imposed by public authority. The marginal cost of distributing the programs in both countries is assumed to be zero.

Define the audience demand functions as:

$$R_{AA} = \alpha C_A^\gamma \text{ and } R_{AB} = \alpha \delta C_A^\gamma; \tag{3}$$

$$R_{BA} = \alpha \delta C_B^\gamma \text{ and } R_{BB} = \alpha C_B^\gamma$$

where:

$0 < \gamma < 1, \ 0 < \delta < 1, \ \alpha > 0$

The parameter γ represents the elasticity of audience demand with respect to production investment. The bounds on γ reflect the assumption that other things equal, audience attractiveness of either program increases in both countries, but at a decreasing rate, as production investment in it increases. The δ parameter is a "cultural discount" factor. Its bounds represent the assumption that other things equal, foreign producers face a comparative disadvantage in attracting viewers to their programs. This disadvantage may be due, for example, to language or to general cultural differences.[2]

Each producer maximizes profit with respect to its single decision variable, production investment, yielding:

$$C_A^* = |\alpha\gamma v_A N_A + \alpha\gamma v_B N_B \delta|^{\frac{1}{1-\gamma}} \tag{4}$$

$$C_B^* = |\alpha\gamma v_A N_A \delta + \alpha\gamma v_B N_B|^{\frac{1}{1-\gamma}} \tag{5}$$

Graphically:

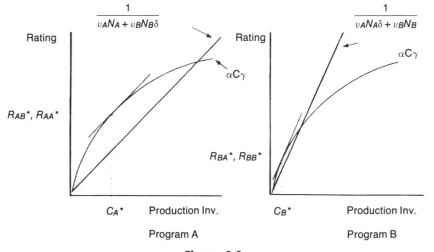

Figure 4.1.

By (3), (4), and (5), optimal investment levels C_A^* and C_B^* occur where the slopes of the respective demand functions equal those of the rays from the origin. Both C_A^* and C_B^* are increasing functions of v_A, N_A, v_B, and N_B. Because marginal costs of distribution are zero, the marginal productivity of a dollar invested increases in direct proportion to the programs

---

[2] Language differences may be partially compensated for by subtitling or dubbing, but at substantial expense. In general, domestic comparative advantage could persist if the pool of creative talent available to producers in one country cannot effectively appeal to local tastes in other countries.

total available market. Similarly from (3), $R_{AA}*$, $R_{BB}*$, $R_{AB}*$, and $R_{BA}*$ are also increasing functions of v_A, N_A, v_B, and N_B. However, if $v_A N_A > v_B N_B$, then $C_A* > C_B*$, $R_{AA}* > R_{BB}*$, and $R_{AB}* > R_{BA}*$. That is, production investments, audience sizes, total revenues, and total profits of *both* programs A and B increase with an increase in the size of the television infrastructure of either country.[3] Revenues and profits of the home country's program increase relatively more, however, as a result of its own infrastructure growth. The parameters δ and γ thus represent the "tradeoff" between the degree of audience preference for domestic programs versus the degree of audience preference for more expensive programs. A high δ and a high γ, for example, indicate a relatively stronger audience responsiveness to investment than to domestic origins. Conversely, a low δ and a low γ indicate a relative dominance of domestically-oriented content over production investment in the demand functions.

Empirical Justification

The domestic economic infrastructures which in fact support broadcast television in the United States and in five of its major trading partner countries are contrasted in Table 1 for 1984 in terms of U.S. dollars at prevailing exchange rates. While conditions are rapidly changing, as we discuss below, and cross-country comparisons are methodologically perilous, an overwhelming U.S. advantage in terms of its overall population and general economic resources is obvious from columns 1 and 2. Sizes of the combined commercial and public economic infrastructures which support broadcast television in each country are compared in columns 3–5. The American infrastructure, of course, consists almost entirely of advertiser support, the relatively small U.S. public television system receiving funds primarily from government, voluntary private contributions, and corporate underwriting of particular programs. Advertisers now support both public and private television in each of the five other countries, while "Fees, other" consists almost entirely of mandatory subscription fees levied on all owners of television sets. The ratios in columns 6, 7, and 8 of Table 1 also suggest a U.S. advantage in the relative size of its broadcasting infrastructure when adjusted for population size, or perhaps most relevant, when adjusted for the size of its general economy. In summary, Americans are not only more numerous, but spend more on a per capita basis to support broadcast television than do these comparative nations. Sketchier data for relatively small

---

[3] The model does not consider the competitive effects of higher investment in program A attracting audience away from program B in the same country, and so on. Taking account of these effects in a Cournot duopoly framework results in much more complex first-order expressions, in which the results of investment level changes are dampened but always in the same direction as those of the simple model.

Table 1. Broadcast Television Economic Infrastructures: U.S. and Major Trading Partners (1984).

	(1) G.D.P. ($ billions)	(2) Total Population (millions)	(3) Advertising ($ millions)	(4) Fees, Other ($ millions)	(5) Total ($ millions)	(6) Total TV System Revenues/ Population ($)	(7) Total TV System Revenues as % of G.D.P.	(8) TV Advertising as % of G.D.P.
U.S.	$3,635	237.0	$19,180	$ 785	$19,965	$84	.55%	.53%
France	489	54.9	538	650	1,188	21	.24	.11
U.K.	425	56.4	1,287	707	1,994	35	.47	.30
West Germany	613	61.2	470	1,125	1,595	26	.26	.08
Italy	348	57.0	777	472	1,249	21	.36	.22
Japan	1,255	120.0	3,801	1,177	4,978	41	.40	.30

Source: GDP, Population: Statistical Abstract of the U.S.; Foreign Exchange Rates: Federal Reserve Bulletin, July, 1987, Table 3.28.
Television data: U.S.: American Newspaper Publishers Association; Corporation for Public Broadcasting.
Italy, France: Dossiers de l' Audiovisuel, No. 13, May–June, 1987. Institut National de l'Audiovisuel, p. 19.
West Germany, U.K.: Committee on Financing the BBC (July, 1986). p. 9–19, 33.
Japan, NHK: Shinichi Shimizu, "Public Service Broadcasting in Japan: How NHK faces the future," Nippon HOSO Kyokai, Tokyo, n.d., p. 7ff.

Table 2.   Motion Picture Theater Infrastructures:
U.S. and Major Trading Partners (1984).

	Box Office Revenues (mil$)	Box Office Revenues as % of GDP	Total Annual Admissions (mil)	Annual Admissions per capita
U.S.	$4,030	.11%	1,199	5.7
France	455	.09	191	3.5
U.K.	119	.03	58	1.0
West Germany	285	.05	112	1.8
Italy	268	.08	131	2.3
Japan	725	.06	151	1.3

Source: Screen Digest, 1986a, p. 207–208.

countries in Western Europe, and especially for most of the Third World, provide far greater contrasts with the United States than these (Varis, 1974; Katz & Wedell, 1977; Pragnell, 1985).

Because they are responsible for producing the most widely traded television products, another important element of comparison is the relative size of domestic theatrical motion picture industries. As Table 2 shows, the United States also dominates in both absolute and relative terms with respect to theater box office receipts. These contrasts reflect rather sharp declines in theatrical film receipts throughout Europe in the past decade, while U.S. receipts have remained relatively steady in real terms.

The model suggests that U.S. producers should have responded to their more lucrative domestic infrastructure by investing greater economic resources in programming. Average production costs of American movies and television programs do appear substantially higher than those of its major trading partners when evaluated in terms of U.S. dollars at prevailing exchange rates, as shown in Table 3. One peril in such comparisons is that production costs for entertainment products partly consist of rents earned by performers who appear to charge according to the revenue base to which their product has access.[4] To a substantial degree, however, American movies and television programs unquestionably employ far more advanced production technologies and more skilled "below-the-line" labor, as well as more car crashes and spectacular special effects. Accentuating Hollywood's posi-

---

[4] More generally, cross-country comparisons in terms of exchange rates are likely to overstate the contrast. To a degree, international migration probably serves to diminish the differential that equally talented performers can command in different countries. The decline of the Italian cinema in the 1970s, for example, has been partially blamed by some on the migration to Hollywood of two of its most talented producers, Carlo Ponti and Dino DeLaurentis.

**Table 3.   Production Costs for TV Programming:
Available Data for Major Countries (1983–1986).**

	Year	Cost ($)
U.S.		
Series Drama	1985–86	$ 739,000/hr
Telefilms	1985–86	2,300,000
Theatrical Features	1985	16,800,000[1]
France		
Telefilms	1986	343,000
Theatrical Features	1986	2,040,000[2]
U.K.		
BBC Drama	1984	397,000/hr
Light Entertainment (drama)	1984	135,700/hr
Theatrical Features	1986	4,800,000
West Germany		
ARD Television Drama	1984	216,000/hr
Italy		
Theatrical Features	1983	639,000
Japan		
Television Drama	1986	175,000/hr

[1] MPAA members only.
[2] Including co-productions.
Source: U.S.: Series drama, Telefilms: *Variety*, September 24, 1985, p. 45;
                Theatrical Features: MPAA, (1985).
         France: *Variety*, February 18, 1987, p. 77.
            UK: BBC Drama, light entertainment: "BBC TV Facts & Figures," 1985,
            pp. B.4–B.8; Theatrical Features: *Variety*, January 8, 1986.
     W. Germany: ARD, *Finanzstatistik*, 1984, p. 377.
          Italy: *Cinema d'OGGI*, 11 Janvier, 1984.
       Japan: *Variety*, December 24, 1986, p. 60.

tion as an international center for entertainment production may be the great economies of scale it enjoys in drawing on thousands of different performers and craftsmen with esoteric specialties within a small geographic area. Where else could Gabby Hayes find almost continuous lifetime employment playing essentially the same minor character (a kindly, 19th century Western buffoon) in scores of different movies?

To be expected, the United States also leads most nations of the world in the volumes of television series and motion picture output, as shown in Table 3a and 3b. A larger number of programs to sell, of course, similarly enhances the American position vis-á-vis other nations in the television program trade process.

The assumption that producers have a comparative disadvantage in attracting foreign audiences to their programs is also consistent with available evidence. The evidence suggests that in spite of their higher investment levels, American programs, contrary to often held perceptions, do not overwhelm foreign audiences. Available aggregate ratings data indicate that

**Table 3a.   Comparative Production Outputs:
Domestically Produced Drama for Television
Available Data: 1982–86.**

	Hours Produced
U.S. (NBC, CBS, ABC)	4613
Belgium (BRT)	168
Denmark (DR)	222
Finland (YLE)	107
France (TF1, FR3)	415
Norway (NRK)	18
Portugal (RTP)	112
Sweden (SVT)	129
U.K. (BBC, ITV)	1208

Source: U.S. 1986 data: Estimate of the author based
on a 16-day probability sam-
ple for Jan–June, 1986.
All other: 1982 data: Pragnell (1985), p. 29.

**Table 3b.   Comparative Production Outputs:
Theatrical Features. Available Data: 1985.**

	Number of Theatrical Features Produced
U.S.	330
France	151
U.K.	31
West Germany	64
Italy	89
Japan	319
Denmark	8
Norway	10
Spain	77

Source: Screen Digest, 1987.

American programs command foreign audiences in roughly the same proportions as they occupy screen time in those countries (P. Mills, 1985). At
least in the larger European countries, the most popular individual domestic
programs consistently outperform the leading American programs.[5] One of
the most widely distributed U.S. television series export in history, *Dallas,*
reportedly earns, in many cases, smaller audiences than remakes or similar
soap operas which are produced domestically (Anatola & Rogers, 1984;

---

[5] The December, 1986 ratings report in *Eurodience,* for example, reported four American
entries among the 15 highest rated programs in Britain (ranked 11, 12, 13, and 15), one in
France (ranked 14) and three in West Germany (ranked 6, 11, and 14) (*Eurodience,* January,
1987).

Tracey, 1985). By contrast, the broadcast audiences for foreign programs in the United States are entirely overwhelmed by American products. The three commercial broadcast networks, which import essentially none of their programming, average combined prime-time audience shares 10 to 20 times greater than the 3-5% average household viewing shares earned by the imports and coproductions offered on American public television. With rare exception, the dismal performance of imported products in the United States is characteristic of both the television and theatrical film industries.

In summary, a consistent economic interpretation of the above observation then is that television viewers in other nations watch U.S. programs not because they are dazzled by American culture, but because they are "bought away" from the domestic programming they would generally prefer by the enormous production investments made by American producers. Both effects on demand, by contrast, work against foreign programs in the United States. American audiences find them not only less compatible with their cultural tastes, but also lacking in the production values to which they have become accustomed.

PRIVATIZATION AND NEW VIDEO TECHNOLOGIES

Although the economic rationale we have outlined for historical U.S. dominance of international trade in television programming is obviously crude, it provides a framework for considering our key question: How can we expect program trade flows (and thus the balance of domestic and foreign programs on national television systems) to evolve as reliance on commercial incentives increase and multichannel video delivery systems such as cable television and videocassette recorders continue to diffuse?

The main initial effect has been more lucrative markets for American and other foreign programming. The model suggests, however, that the long-term effects of these changes will be greater opportunities for domestic programming, due to a strengthening of the commercial infrastructures which support production in these countries.

Commercial Infrastructure Expansion: Traditional Broadcasting

Expanded broadcast capacity in private hands has the obvious short-term effect of providing blank program schedules which American and other foreign producers are eager to fill from existing stocks. Audiences for domestic programs decline as a result. The eventual effect of the expansion on domestic program production, however, is likely to be positive. In Europe, television advertising has historically been suppressed by low-channel capacity and direct government restrictions. But as new opportunities to advertise on television are created by new capacity and privatization, businesses can be expected to shift advertising away from other media and, to an extent, increase total advertising budgets. In this way, the domestic infrastructure for raising broadcast television revenues strengthens. If the assumption that other things being equal, audiences prefer domestic to foreign programs is correct, then domestic producers in those countries should, in the long-term, benefit from this change relatively more so than do foreign producers.[6]

These expectations must be qualified to the extent that most European television systems begin their infrastructure expansions from protectionist positions. The opening of television markets to international competition in itself induces an initial audience shift away from domestic progamming, as the Italian experience emphatically demonstrates. Moreover, a shift of audiences away from a license fee-supported system to a commercially supported system may undermine political support for the former. The overall economic effect on domestic production of a transition from public to commercial support, therefore, is not necessarily positive. But once the initial transition is complete, domestic production activity should expand at a greater rate than does foreign production activity.

Recent events in Italy suggest the effects of commercial television infrastructure development on domestic production activity. In 1983 and 1984, Italian "in-house" production activity by both the RAI and private television companies reportedly accelerated (Werba, 1986a). Berlusconi's production company, *Retitalia,* was reported by 1986 to be at the forefront of a "baby boom" in Italian cinema and has apparently become a European leader in commercial television production for both the domestic and international markets (Retitalia, 1987; Werba, 1986b). Undoubtedly a factor in this process has been the growing domestic base of Italian television advertising. Between 1974 and 1984, total television advertising in Italy increased from 55.6 billion to 1,452 billion lire, the latter accounting for 46.6% of all Italian advertising in that year (Pasquarelli, 1985). Very rapid television advertising growth has apparently continued in Italy and is reported to be occurring throughout Europe through the mid-1980s (Tully, 1987). A suggestion of these trends is that the relative advantage of the U.S. over European countries in the size of its broadcast television economic infrastructure may be diminishing.

---

[6] Note that the *absolute* benefit to imported program sellers can still be greater depending on the initial situation. Say that in a certain small country the initial condition is that 20 hours of programming are domestically produced and 80 hours imported. An expansion in that country's domestic television infrastructure might result in only 10 additional hours of domestic production compared to 20 additional hours of imports. But the domestic increase in still relatively greater, from 20 percent of the 100-hour total to about 23 percent of the 130-hour total.

Not all of the growth of Italian production, at least, can be attributed to domestic commercial infrastructure growth. There is a secondary, related factor which has certainly played a role in Italy and which should aid production industries elsewhere; this is a breakdown of buying power within U.S. trading partner nations.

Program Buying Power

Executives of American distribution companies have long complained about what they regard as excessively low license fees paid to them by Western European public television systems. Available trade reports do indicate that prices paid in the larger European countries for American programs have historically been 10 or more times lower than domestic production costs for similar programs.[7] These differences are in spite of the fact that American programs appear to attract audiences in the same ranges as those of domestically-produced programs.

These contrasts of acquisition vs. production costs serve to illustrate another potential consequence of the huge-scale economies in television program distribution. The rights to exhibit a two-hour movie produced in the United States, for example, might ordinarily sell to British television for $60,000 or more. The incremental expense of such a sale, however, essentially consists of duplicating and shipping a single videocassette, plus the administrative and marketing expenses of persuading the British to accept the program and then collecting the license fee. Even accounting for a few four-star dinners in Cannes at the Film Festival, these expenses are clearly a fraction of the $60,000 fee. A large proportion of the fee is the contribution it makes in offsetting the production cost, perhaps several million dollars, of the film itself.

Because marginal cost of distribution tends to be far below the product's value in individual countries, there tends to be a wide range of trading prices which both buyer and seller would *potentially* be willing to accept in a television program transaction. The two-country model above implicitly assumes that competition among potential buyers within both countries force the acquisition price for imported programs up to the winning bidder's reservation price—permitting the producer to reap all the excess of value over

---

[7] *Variety* reported a 1984 average price range for American series programs of $8,500 to $18,000 per hour in West Germany, compared to the $216,000 average cost per hour for domestically produced dramatic series reported in Table 4.3 for 1985. (*Variety*, 1985). The reported average cost of producing a telefilm in France in 1986 of $343,000 compares to an average price of $30,000 to $40,000 for American telefilms reported for that year (*Variety*, 1986). These comparisons reflect substantial acquisition price inflations of the early 1980s.

marginal cost of distribution. A lack of buyer competition, however, can greatly alter this situation. Imagine, for example, that an independent firm with only one program to offer were to confront a single buyer who controls all film and video product distribution in that country. This seller might then be induced to accept far less than the buyer's true reservation price (say $60,000), perhaps even only a small amount over the actual marketing and distribution expenses for that one country (perhaps a few thousand dollars). This agreement could result if the seller otherwise faces a dead loss in that market and the single buyer makes a persuasive case that this particular program can be done without. Moreover, this situation can persist if the seller has access to enough competitive markets (including its home country, for example) to still cover the production cost of a viable program.[8]

Such extreme cases are rarely encountered among buyer nations outside the Socialist Bloc.[9] In most Western European countries, however, responsibility for most television program acquisition has historically been concentrated in the hands of one or a very few buyers. The major American distributors, on the other hand, confront program buyers through the Motion Picture Export Association, a legal cartel whose members earn around 90% of U.S. theater box office revenues. At least in the television market, however, bargaining power of buyers, reinforced not only by limited channel capacity, but by quotas and other policy directives limiting the demand for imports, seems to have constrained prices to far below their potential levels.[10]

Italy provides a classic example of how buyer competition can turn the bargaining tables. Before private television was permitted, the RAI organization was virtually the only potential customer in Italy for imported programming. Silvio Berlusconi, the founder of Italy's first private network, *Canale 5,* built his business by starting a bidding war with the RAI in the

---

[8] For a formal exposition of this point, see David Waterman, "Structural Development of the Motion Picture Industry", *The American Economist,* Spring 1982. In effect, a monopsony buyer in an individual country which accounts for a small proportion of the total world market perceives a highly inelastic supply of film and video products due to their "public good" nature. The result of this monopsonist's behavior in forcing price toward marginal cost is a reduction in the supply of products available to it (in number and investment cost) from competitive sellers only in proportion to its share of the world market. Market power on the seller side may produce an intermediate result.

[9] The most extreme effects of monopsony buying power probably prevail with Eastern Bloc in their negotiations for Western-made film and television products. Though little if any data appears to be available, these countries are notorious for paying miniscule sums, relative to their size and economic resources, for the relatively few American movies and television programs they import.

[10] Often repeated arguments that U.S. distributors "dump" entertainment products in foreign markets at artificially low prices defy economic logic. U.S. distributors will seek the highest revenues they can possibly get. A not uncommon practice of the MPEA, in fact, is to restrain its members from making any sales until bids from buyers reach a certain minimum level. This was reportedly the case in Italy during the early period of private television's development (*Variety,* 1986).

late 1970s and early 1980s. Two competing private networks, *Italia I* and *Rete 4*, fueled the fires. The trade press reported "skyrocketing" prices as a result (Michie, 1984; Werba, 1986a). Between 1979 and 1985, minimum to maximum price ranges for American series programming in Italy reported by *Variety* increased from $1,800–$2,000 per half-hour to $6,000–$48,000 per half hour (Global prices, 1985). Similar but less extreme price inflations for American television products have been reported in France and other countries where privatization is occurring (Tully, 1987). These inflations are undoubtedly stimulated as well by new competition from commercially operated alternatives to standard broadcasting such as pay television networks or videocassettes—media which use many of the same programs.

Acquisition price inflation obviously benefits foreign program sellers, especially those in the United States. But another result we would expect is the creation of price umbrellas to support domestic production. As prices that foreign producers are able to charge increase, that is, the alternative of original production of domestic programs becomes relatively more attractive to television systems. *Variety* (1986a, p. 168) reported, in fact, that the acceleration in Italian domestic production activity in 1984 was undertaken "as a pressing alternative to skyward acquisition prices."

Commercial Infrastructure Expansion: The Pay Media

The economic effects of broadcast privatization and resulting competition among program buyers appear to be well underway in Italy and several other European nations. A more important element of commercial infrastructure growth to come, however, may not be that of traditional broadcasting, but of the "pay" media—cable television, premium subscription channels, and prerecorded videocassettes.[11] Conditions under which this may occur can be demonstrated by modifying the basic model so that a profit-making, "pay-per-view" pricing system replaces advertiser (or public license fee) support in country A. The system in country B remains unchanged.

We redefine the demand functions for programs A and B in country A to be:

$$R_{AA} = C_A^\gamma (\alpha - \beta P_{AA}) \qquad\qquad R_{BA} = \delta C_B^\gamma (\alpha - \beta P_{BA}) \qquad (6)$$

where P_{AA} and P_{BA} are the prices of programs A and B in country A, respectively, and $\alpha, \beta > 0$.

---

[11] The per-set annual subscriber license fee systems which prevail in most European countries are already, of course, "pay" media of a sort. The very high penetrations of television among European households, however, suggest that these fee levels are set by government authorities in highly inelastic price ranges to promote universal service.

Each producer maximizes (1) and (2) above with respect to two decision variables, "pay-per-view" price in country A and total production investment. This yields:

$$C_A^* = |\gamma \frac{\alpha^2 N_A}{4\beta} + \gamma v_B N_B \delta \alpha|^{\frac{1}{1-\gamma}} \tag{7}$$

$$C_B^* = |\gamma \frac{\alpha^2 N_A}{4\beta} + \gamma v_B N_B \delta \alpha|^{\frac{1}{1-\gamma}} \tag{8}$$

$$P_{AA}^* = \frac{\alpha}{2\beta}, \ P_{BA}^* = \frac{\alpha}{2\beta} \tag{9}$$

The necessary condition for both C_A^* and C_B^* to increase above their advertiser-support levels ((4) and (5) above) is $\alpha/4\beta > v_A$. The same condition insures that profits will be higher under direct pricing then advertiser support. That is, viewer demand for a program must be sufficiently strong to outweigh the amount of advertisers are willing to pay for the attention of viewers at $P_{AA}, P_{BA} = 0$. If this is the case, the result of a switch to pay support in country A is again that total revenues of both producers rise, but relatively more so for the producer of A.

The American experience suggests that direct pricing is, in fact, generally more effective than advertiser support as a way to extract money from television viewers.[12] If this experience holds true elsewhere, the model again suggests that the growth of those nations' commercial pay media infrastructures will further expand markets for both domestic and U.S. producers, but to relatively greater benefit of the former.[13] The process of pay media growth should be especially important because of the major role which pay media play in the financial support of theatrical features, the major imported ingredient of television menus throughout the world.

---

[12] Liberally assuming 15 commercial minutes per hour, the average 1987 "cost per thousand" network advertising rate of $8.10 (per 60 second spot) translates into a willingness of advertisers to pay approximately 12¢ per viewing household per hour (Mandese, 1987). Based on actual viewing time, the average pay cable network subscribing household paid (based on only the extra charge to cable subscribers of about $12 per household per month) approximately 28¢ per hour for that programming in 1987 (A.C. Nielsen, *Television 1987 Nielsen Report*, 1987, p. 14). A two-hour feature film generally costs $2 to $3 to rent on videocassette and $3 to $4 to view via "pay-per-view" cable networks. Significant numbers show willingness to buy videocassettes outright, generally for $20 to $90 each. While these comparisons do not consider relative transmission or delivery costs, they suggest the validity of predictions by R. Noll, M. Peck, and J. MacGowan and others that huge amounts of consumer surplus were being enjoyed by viewers of advertiser supported U.S. television (Noll, Peck, & MacGowan, 1973).

[13] This conclusion rests on the model's assumption that the price elasticity of demand in country A for both programs A and B is the same. If demand were much more price-inelastic for imported than domestic products, commercial price support in one country could help foreign producers enough for them to overcome the comparative disadvantage effect, and thus reap greater net benefit than domestic producers.

Table 4.   Pay media Infrastructures: U.S., Europe, and Japan (1985–1986).

		Basic Cable (1985)		Pay Cable (1986)		Videocassettes (1986)	
	# TV HH (mil)	% TV HH	Revenue ($Billions)	% TV HH	Revenue ($Billions)	% TV HH	Wholesale Software Revenue ($Billions)
U.S.	83	45%[a]	$4.5[a]	27%[a]	$4.0[a]	45%[b]	$2.2[b]
Western Europe	115	10–12%[c]	.4–.9[d]	2–3%[e]	.3[e]	30%[f]	.7[f]
Japan	35	11%[c]	n.a.	—	—	62%[f]	.4[f]

Source: a: Paul Kagan Associates, *Pay TV Newsletter,* June 26, 1987, p. 4.
b: Paul Kagan Associates, *VCR Newsletter,* February, 27, 1987, p. 1.
c: Wedell & Luyken, *Media in Competition.*
d: *Screen Digest,* June 87, p. 126; Patrick Whitten, "The potential for new media technology in Western Europe—some key commercial aspects," in *Medientrends,* Kongress dokumente, Inter Media Centrum Hamburg, Hamburg, West Germany, 1985, p. 86.
e: Estimate of author based on data reported in *Screen Digest,* May 1987, p. 106.
f: *Screen Digest,* June, 1987, pp. 129–133: Revenue for Europe based on projections by the author from reported data covering 6 European countries.

As Table 4 suggests, the United States has achieved a great lead in developing its pay media infrastructure. While several smaller nations in Western Europe have very high cable penetration, it is almost negligible in most of the larger nations (Müller, 1987). This difference is closely related to the far greater penetration of premium television channels in the United States, most of which offer recent theatrical movies and are distributed via cable technology.[14] VCR penetration in Western Europe and Japan has advanced much more in step with that in the United States. The still relatively great U.S. advantage in wholesale software revenues, however, reflects substantially greater expenditures on prerecorded tapes made by the average American VCR owner.[15]

By far the dominant programming on both premium television channels and prerecorded videocassettes worldwide is theatrical features. In the United States, the prevalence of American-produced films on these media is obvious.[16] By all appearances, the proportion of videocassette sales and

---

[14] By far the largest pay television service outside the United States, *Canal Plus* of France, relies on broadcast distribution.

[15] *Screen Digest* reports average expenditure by U.S. VCR owners on prerecorded videocassette software in 1986 to be $57, compared to weighted average of $24 for five European countries and $20 for Japan (converted from £) (*Screen Digest,* 1987).

[16] The major pay-cable services, HBO, Showtime and the Movie Channel, only occasionally offer foreign-made features. Numerous foreign movies appear on BRAVO, a "cultural" pay-cable network, but this service reaches only about one-half of one percent of all U.S. households.

rentals attributable to foreign-made films is probably in the same range as that of box office revenues from U.S. theaters, less than 2 or 3 percent. The U.S. video market is so large that the contribution of even these meager market slices to foreign producers would appear to be, while no doubt disappointing, at least an improvement. The contribution of U.S. pay media to American movie distributors has, on the other hand, been obviously dramatic. In 1977, before significant penetration of any pay media in the United States, about 80% of domestic distributor revenues for theatrical films came from theaters and 20% from broadcast television. An available estimate for 1986 attributes 43% of revenues to theaters and 12% from broadcast television, with 45% coming from pay television and videocassettes (*Video Marketing Newsletter,* 1986). In spite of this expansion, revenues from U.S. theaters have fallen by only 7% from 1977 to 1986 in CPI-deflated terms, resulting in nearly a doubling of the real domestic revenue base for U.S. theatrical features over this time period (Motion Picture Association of America, unpublished data deflated by the *General Consumer Price Index,* 1986). One apparent result of this market expansion has been an increase in the total number of U.S.-produced features from 226 in 1977 to 330 in 1985, with a jump to 515 reported in 1986 (*Screen Digest,* 1987). Average production costs of MPAA member-produced theatrical features have reportedly risen by 104% in CPI-deflated terms from 1978 to 1985 (MPAA, 1986).

Results of the model suggest this U.S. budget and production volume expansion would tend to increase the American competitive advantage in international motion picture and video markets. While the declining dollar has clearly been a recent factor, steadily increasing market shares of theatrical box office receipts earned by American films in the last several years (reaching all time high levels in Germany and even Italy in 1986) are consistent with this hypothesis.

The model further suggests that we should observe a substantial presence of domestic programming on the commercial pay media that have developed in foreign countries. On the major pay network in Europe, *Canal Plus,* 60% or more of the movies shown are reportedly French-language productions, but this is determined by government quota, not the free market. The proportions of EEC-produced program hours on British-originated cable TV networks, on which content is not restricted, are relatively high for advertiser-supported services, as shown in Table 5. The dominant fractions of non-EEC programs on U.K.-originated premium networks are undoubtedly accounted for by U.S.-produced theatrical features. Prevalence of American films might be expected on English-language pay networks, however, especially given the meager pickings available from the British film industry. Videocassette content data could be located only for Japan, where in the first half of 1986, Japanese-produced movies reportedly earned 22.8% and

Table 5.   Programming Content of U.K. Originated Cable
Television Channels (1986).

Channel	Means of Support	% EEC Content
Arts Channel	Advertising	84%
Bravo	Advertising	8
Children's Channel	Advertising	62
Home Video Channel	Subscription	11
Lifestyle	Advertising	55
Mirrorvision	Subscription	10
Music Box	Advertising	77
Premiere	Subscription	13
Screen Sport	Advertising	35
Sky Channel	Advertising	51

Source: Screen Digest, 1986b, p. 247, based on a 13-week sample apparently
collected in 1985 or 1986 (UK Cable Authority data).

27.2% of all retail sales and rentals, respectively. By contrast, all foreign-produced features accounted for 27.8% of sales revenues and 51.0% of rentals (Screen Digest, 1986b). If the domestic vs. foreign content proportions in Europe for prerecorded videocassettes are similar to those for movie theaters there, something less than half of all gross revenues from video software would be accounted for by non-American features.

These sparse data fail to confirm or deny that the European production is benefitting relatively more greatly from pay media development than is U.S. production, as the model predicts. It is early in the transition process, however, and it is evident that these new media are already providing at least significant sustenance to domestic producers.

CONCLUSION AND POLICY IMPLICATIONS

This analysis suggests an optimistic long-range future for the domestic motion picture and television production industries of America's trading partners. If commercial video media infrastructures in those countries do eventually prove to benefit domestic producers relatively more than they benefit importing producers, this will be reflected by comparably increasing proportions of domestically produced programs available to their television viewers.

Economic analysis offers an admittedly narrow perspective on the complex social and political issues surrounding privatization and new media development. Apart from whether domestic production industries prosper or not, for example, reliance on commercial incentives change the television product—for the worse, many would argue.[17] In such an environment, achieving the social objectives historically pursued by media policy in European and other countries becomes much more difficult. Our analysis nevertheless puts into relief the economic constraints which sovereign nations face in pursuing those objectives.

What are these constraints in practical terms? Import quotas are obvious methods to ensure that the proportions of domestic programming on broadcast and pay television media such as premium cable channels remain high. In the short term, such policies undoubtedly succeed in stimulating both the quantity of domestic programs and the viewing of them. In a competitive media environment, however, quotas tend to undermine these very objectives over the long term. In order for import quotas governing one medium to be effective, alternative delivery systems for the products which are restricted, notably American movies, must also be controlled. A profound blow to this possibility has been forever dealt by the videocassette recorder, a technology whose diffusion and usage is defiant of public control. A second undermining effect of quotas is that they constrain the development of strong commercial media infrastructures by restricting the main available supply of programming needed to support expanded system capacity in the near term. In the long term, however, these commercial infrastructures must be relied upon to support domestic production activity.

Another category of government controls common in Europe is regulations which limit the profitability of licensing theatrical feature films to video media. France, in particular, has maintained a myriad of regulations on pay media, including control of the time windows when films may be exhibited on pay TV and videocassettes, and heavy taxes on both videocassette hardware and software. Like quotas, such policies constrain the development of infrastructures capable of supporting domestic film production— and with that, the competitive positions of those countries in both their domestic and international markets.

A public policy which clearly benefits both domestic motion picture and television production industries is the subsidy or promotion of coproductions, both among American trading partner countries and with American producers. History has demonstrated that without the additional economic resources these arrangements mobilize, the potential to maintain either domestic market shares or to increase export potential will remain very limited. It is noteworthy that the reported resurgence of Italian production is heavily weighted toward co-productions with other countries (Reteitalia, 1986; Werba, 1986b). Without the benefit of its newly created commercial broadcasting infrastructure, it seems unlikely that the leadership role Italian producers have taken in European co-production activity could have been achieved.

---

[17] For an extended analysis of this point, see the Peacock Commission Report (1986).

Finally, the economic growth of production industries, and even of a shifting balance toward domestically produced programming on television screens, may seem small consolation to those committed to the historical objectives of public service broadcasting. Can public television systems survive and prosper in an open-trade, competitive media environment? In the past, government-imposed insulation of public television systems from competition with commercial television has provided them not only with largely captive audiences but with cheap production resources. Notorious increases in the prices recently commanded by top performers in the United States and Europe, however, suggest that the supply of human resources for the entertainment industries is relatively inelastic and potentially consists largely of economic rents.[18] No longer can public television systems avoid paying these higher competitive prices for program production resources and expect to attract large audiences. A very tempting alternative of course, is collusion among public and private program buyers, a subject of frequent discussion, for example, in Italy. As alternative media proliferate, the difficulties of maintaining collusion will increase.

Such financial prospects only sharpen, of course, the dilemma of how public television systems can continue to be supported. Some assistance might come from adopting the recommendation of the 1986 Peacock Commission Report that, in the future, commercial independent television licenses in Britain be auctioned off, and the proceeds be used to fund public television (Peacock, 1986). Other methods of taxation might be applied to commercial pay media enterprises. As long as these taxes are relatively painless—designed for effective revenue production rather than set at punitive levels to protect politically powerful interest groups—they might permit public broadcasting to benefit rather than only suffer, from the prosperity of the commercial media sector.

REFERENCES

Antola, L., & Rogers, E. (1984). Television flows in Latin America. *Communication Research, 11*(2), 183-202.

Cable TV Programming Newsletter. Carmel, CA: Paul Kagan Associates.

de Sola Pool, I. (1977). The changing flow of television. *Journal of Communication, 27*(1), 139-149.

Dossiers de l'Audiovisuel, No. 13. (1987, May–June). Paris: Institut National de l'Audiovisuel.

Les 15 meilleures émissions en décembre 86 en France, au Royaume-Uni, en RFA (The 15 best-scoring programs in France, in U.K. in W.G.) *Eurodience,* pp. 8, 9.

Global prices for TV film. (1985, April 17). *Variety,* p. 86.

---

[18] For a related analysis, see Rosen (1981).

Katz, E., & Wedell, G. (1977). *Broadcasting in the Third World: Promise and performance.* Cambridge, MA: Harvard University Press.

Kierzkowski, H. (Ed.). (1984). *Monopolistic competition in international trade.* Oxford, U.K.: Clarendon Press.

Mandese, J. (1987, December). The network's revenge: How high will it go? *Channels,* p. 39.

Michie, L. (1984, April 18). Program pricing stabilities in Italy after M.P.E.A. pact. *Variety,* pp. 113, 136.

Mills, P. (1985). An international audience. *Media, Culture and Society, 7,* 487–501.

Motion Picture Association of America (MPAA). (1986). *1986 U.S. Economic Review* (mimeo).

Müller, J. (1987). Cable policy in Europe: The role of transborder broadcasting and its effect on CATV. *Telecommunications Policy, 11* (3), 259–268.

Nielsen, A.C. (1987). *Television 1987 Nielsen Report.* New York.

Noll, R., Peck, M., & MacGowan, J. (1973). *Economic aspects of television regulation.* Washington, DC: Brookings Institution.

Pasquarelli, G. (1985, July). Television advertising in Italy. *EBU Review, 36* (4), 10–12.

Pay TV Newsletter, p. 4. (1987, Jule 26). Carmel, CA: Paul Kagan Associates.

Peacock, A. (1986). *Report of the Committee on Financing the BBC.* Presented to Parliament by the Secretary of State for the Home Department by Command of Her Majesty, Cmdn 9824, London, United Kingdom.

Pragnell, A. (1985). *Television in Europe: Quality and values in a time of change* (Media Monograph No. 5). European Institute for the Media.

Reteitalia manage to read 43 hours of Mipcom sales while casting eyes at Coprod. (1987, October 14). *Variety,* p. 70.

Rosen, S. (1981). The economics of superstars. *American Economic Review, 71,* 845–858.

Screen Digest, pp. 129–133. (1987, June).

Screen Digest, pp. 207–208. (1986a, October).

Screen Digest, p. 251 (1986b, December).

Shimuzu, S. (n.d.) Public Service Broadcasting in Japan: How NHK faces the future. Nippon HOSO Kyokai, Tokyo.

Tracey, M. (1985, Fall). The poisoned chalise? International television and the idea of dominance. *Daedalus,* p. 114.

Tully, S. (1987, April 13). U.S.-style TV turns on Europe. *Fortune,* pp. 96–98.

Tunstall, J. (1977). *The Media are American.* New York: Columbia University Press.

Varis, T. (1974). Global traffic in television. *Journal of Communication, 24* (1), 102–109.

Varis, T. (1984). The international flow of television programs. *Journal of Communication, 34* (1), 143–152.

Video Marketing Newsletter, (Baskerville Associates, Los Angeles), August 10, 1986, p. 3.

Waterman, D. Structural development of the motion picture industry. *The American Economist,* Spring, 1982, 17–27.

Werba, H. (1986a, April 23). 10 years of commercial television in Italy. *Variety,* pp. 143–144.

Werba, H. (1986b, October 15). Italo TV ends its Yank program spree. Native product gets bear hug. *Variety,* p. 125.

Whitten, P. (1985). The potential for new media technology in Western Europe—some key commercial aspects. In MEDIENTRENDS, Congress dokumente, Inter Media Centrum Hamburg. (Hamburg, West Germany).

Wildman, S.S., & Siwek, S.E. (1988). *International trade in film and television programs.* Cambridge, MA: Ballinger.

5

The Gray Market in Video, Consumer Welfare, and Public Policy: An Economic Analysis*

Jonathan B. Baker

INTRODUCTION

Two generations ago, the only audiences for recorded visual entertainment products patronized movie theaters. Today films are shown on airplanes, televisions are commonplace household appliances throughout the world, and a dazzling variety of technologies allows viewers to tape television programs, purchase prerecorded videocassettes, and receive direct satellite transmissions of television programming. The same technology has facilitated the unauthorized sale or use of video products: It is now possible for unauthorized sellers to copy videocassettes (or live performances) for resale,[1]

---

* The Amos Tuck School of Business Administration, Dartmouth College. The author once represented a U.S. trademark owner in gray market litigation. The present chapter consists of his personal views. The author is indebted to Michael Knoll for helpful comments on an earlier draft and to James Bierman, Gregg Dwyer, David Eames, and Sheila Gill for valuable discussions concerning the gray market.
[1] See, e.g., "On Bluebeard's Tapedeck," 1984, p. 56; "How Pirates are Plundering the Studios," 1983, p. 81; J. Melanson, 1983, p. 45; D. Groves, 1986, pp. 374, 418. The Motion Picture Association of America (MPAA) has traced some of the worldwide unauthorized videocassette sales to the unauthorized taping of movie theater prints (W. Nix, 1986). However, another spokesman for that trade association has indicated that almost all unauthorized videocassettes sold in the U.S. are copied from legitimate tapes or off cable television rather than made from stolen theater prints (Spillman, 1984).

for unauthorized viewers to intercept satellite or cable broadcasts,[2] and for unauthorized broadcasters to evade regulatory schemes by operating in international waters or territories outside governmental control (Growth in piracy, 1986; How pirates are plundering, 1987; Wentz, 1985). In addition, unauthorized distributors may import video products for resale.[3] The film and television producers term all of these unauthorized practices "video piracy."

If film and television producers' estimates are to be believed, the extent of the unauthorized prerecorded videocassette trade in many countries is astounding.[4] The market share of unauthorized videocassettes, measured in quantity units, is estimated at 100% in Turkey and Egypt[5], 40% to 50% in Japan (Valenti, 1987; Melanson, 1987), 50% in Iceland (including 80% in Reykjavik; Keller, 1986), 20% in Australia (Groves, 1986), 85% in Panama (Besas, 1986), 100% in the Phillippines (Giron, 1986),[6] 30% in Venezuela (Besas, 1986), and 70% in West Germany, France, and the Benelux countries (On Bluebeard's Tapedeck, 1984). Further, despite substantial decreases in share in the recent past, unauthorized video products account for a large fraction of the prerecorded videocassette trade in Britain (down from 65% in 1981 to 35% in 1983 and 25% in 1986; On Bluebeards Tapedeck, 1984;

---

[2] See Chad, 1987, p. C18; "Federal Injunction Bars Florida Motels From Cable-TV Theft," 1986, p. 1; Guild, 1986, pp. 1, 44. The MPAA contends that satellite signal and cable interception is the leading source of unauthorized video activity in the United States (Nix, 1986, p. 34), although new technology has increased the ability of cable companies to detect unauthorized users (Cleaver, 1984).

[3] This is said to be the major source of unauthorized video cassette sales in New Zealand (Nicolaidi, 1987, p. 130). The MPAA claims that Venezualen cassettes have been sold in other Latin American countries, Puerto Rico, and the United States, while United Kingdom cassettes "regularly appear" in Australia, Hong Kong, and New Zealand (Nix, 1986, p. 33; D. Groves, 1986, pp. 347, 418).

[4] The primary source of these estimates appears to be the Motion Picture Association of America (MPAA), a film and television producer trade association strongly opposed to the unauthorized sale of these products. The American Film Marketing Association, an organization of smaller independent film producers, also opposes the unauthorized sale of video products (Rosenfield, 1986, p. 83).

Similarly, studies commissioned by record and tape producers show that a high fraction of sound recordings sold in many countries (excluding home taping or the unauthorized recording of live performances) are duplicated without authorization and sold under a label resembling the original. The market share of these unauthorized products is estimated at 90% in Turkey, 80% in Portugal, 70% in Greece, 50% in Spain, and 25% in Italy (Ruzicka, 1986). U.S. record companies have aggressively prosecuted U.S. record chains importing and selling compact disks purchased abroad whent he same title is distributed domestically (Goldberg, 1986, p. 17).

[5] These countries have an installed base of videocassette recorders and television sets in the millions. See the testimony of Jack Valenti, President, Motion Picture Association of America, Inc., Joint Economic Subcommittee on Trade, Productivity, and Economic Growth, Hearing on International Piracy and Counterfeiting, March 31, 1986.

[6] The article reports that most of the unauthorized sales consist of feature films, principally from the U.S.

Stuart, 1986), in Brazil (down from 90% in 1984 to 50% in 1986; Besas, 1986),[7] in Spain (down from 100% in 1983 to 30% in 1986; Stuart, 1986; Besas, 1987), and in Holland (down from 90% in 1983 to 40% in 1987; Variety, 1987).[8] Yet in other countries with large markets for prerecorded videocassettes, the market share of unauthorized products is much lower, under 10%. That share is estimated at between 2% and 5% in Denmark, Sweden, and Norway (Keller, 1986) and 5% to 10% in the United States (Melanson, 1987).

The unauthorized sale or use of video products in general violates the law of most countries. However, the extent of copyright and trademark law protection for authorized sellers has been disputed, primarily because of the ambiguity of extending laws created for other products to video practices made possible by new technology.[9] Even when such conduct is unambiguously illegal, it may be difficult and costly to police. For example, most unauthorized videocassette production in West Germany is reportedly undertaken in residential areas, where it is difficult to detect, and may be sold informally through "photocopy lists...circulated discreetly among acquaintances and colleagues at work" (Kindred, 1987). Further, countries that consume but do not produce video products may enact laws barring unauthorized distribution of those goods under pressure from trading partners who produce video products, but may find it expedient in terms of domestic politics not to enforce those laws. Enforcement initiatives advocated by the film and television industry or implemented in various countries have included increasing the civil and criminal penalties for copyright law violations, raising the cost of blank video recording tape through a tax, and increasing the public and private resources devoted to detecting and convicting violators.[10]

---

[7] However, another estimate puts the market share of unauthorized sales in Brazil at 80% in 1986 (Hoineff, 1986).

[8] In each of these countries the decline in the market share of unauthorized videocassette sales has been attributed at least in part to increased governmental enforcement efforts against the practice.

[9] See, e.g., *Sony Corp. v. Universal City Studios, Inc.,* 464 U.S. 417 (1984) (*Betamax*); *Columbia Broadcasting System, Inc. v. Scorpio Music Distributors, Inc.,* 569 F. Supp. 47, 222 U.S.P.Q. 975 (E.D. Pa. 1983); *aff'd without opinion,* 738 F.2d 424 (3d. Cir. 1984).

[10] Each of these methods has been employed or considered in EEC countries, the U.S., Singapore, and Australia ("On Bluebeard's Tapedeck," 1984, p. 56 (EEC); "How Pirates are Plundering the Studios," 1983, p. 81 (US); "Taping the Pirates," 1986, p. 71; D. Groves, 1986, p. 41; J. Stuart, 1986, pp. 5, 35). In 1984 the MPAA reportedly employed six full-time and 30 part-time ex-FBI agents investigating the unauthorized sale of video products in the United States (Spillman, 1984, p. 105). Film producers are also employing sophisticated labeling technology to detect the source of theater prints copied without authorization (Nix, 1986, pp. 33, 35) and are making videocassettes more difficult to copy (Bierbaum, 1986, pp. 5, 92).

Private litigation by copyright holders also deters unauthorized use. For example, the National Football League is embroiled in disputes with bar owners over the rights to view satellite disk pickups of sports event broadcasts (Chad, 1987, p. C18; see "Federal Injunction Bars Florida Motels From Cable-TV Theft," 1986, p. 1).   (*continued*)

Those retailers who defend various forms of unauthorized videocassette distribution argue that the practice permits lower consumer prices (Allen, 1980) and greater product variety.[11] The authorized distributors, in contrast, emphasize that a reasonable markup of price over marginal cost is necessary for producers to cover the high fixed costs for film production and the risks of box office flops.[12] Without the ability to recover such costs on box office successes, the video products most likely to be the subject of unauthorized distribution, the producers of authorized products may be forced to exit from the film business entirely, reducing over time the number and variety of new film products available to consumers.

The underlying policy tradeoff suggested by the debate over unauthorized video products is between the lower consumer prices that result from allowing their distribution and the reduction in producer incentives to invest in new products or services that results from permitting unauthorized distributors to compete with authorized firms. This tradeoff appears whenever firms can make investments that increase the value of their product to consumers, including the policy debates over patent protection, vertical restraints on distributors, counterfeit sales, and "gray market" goods.

In the familiar context of inventions, the tradeoff is resolved by allowing manufacturers to patent innovations for a term of years. Governments award patent monopolies even though consumer prices would be lower were unauthorized producers allowed to sell new products created by others, in order to preserve economy-wide incentives for investment in new techniques and products.

A similar policy tradeoff arises when governments decide whether to allow manufacturers to impose nonprice vertical restraints on distributors. Since 1977, U.S. antitrust law has recognized that limitations on intrabrand competition, as through territorial restraints on distributors, can be pro-competitive if they improve interbrand competition.[13] In this way, dealers are encouraged to offer valuable point of sale services to consumers without fear that competing dealers will free ride on those actions. This antitrust

---

Some proposals for limiting the trade in unauthorized informational products seek governmentally imposed technological standards to raise the cost of evading the copyright and trademark laws. For example, record companies wish to restrict the sale or recording ability of new digital audiotape recorders (Burgess, 1987, p. H1; Mesce, (Associated Press report); B. Davis, 1987, p. 33). For an overview of the current U.S. policy debate on this topic, see generally, Burgess, 1987, p. H1.

[11] Some countries believe that the sale of both authorized and unauthorized foreign videocassettes reduces product variety, to limit the sale of foreign video products to preserve the local culture (Chilean vid distribution, 1986). See generally, C. Ogan, 1985, p. 63).

[12] See the testimony of Jack Valenti, President, Motion Picture Association of America, Inc., Before the Joint Economic Subcommittee on Trade, Productivity and Economic Growth, Hearing on International Piracy and Counterfeiting, March 31, 1987, p. 8. See also Spillman, 1984, p. 105.

[13] *Continental TV Inc. v. GTE Sylvania, Inc.* 433 U.S. 36 (1977).

policy allows manufacturers to preserve distributor investment incentives by restricting competition among dealers. This chapter analyzes the welfare consequences of the unauthorized sale of video products as a species of another question raising the policy tradeoff between preserving producer investment incentives and preserving low consumer prices: whether to allow the "gray market."[14] This term refers to the unauthorized importation of trademarked or copyrighted products. In the 1980s U.S. consumers have been able to purchase a wide variety of branded products on the gray market, including Opium perfumes, Seiko watches, Mercedes automobiles, Duracell batteries, and Nikon cameras.

Among the many practices termed "video piracy" by the film and television producers, one of the most widespread is a form of gray-market sales: the unauthorized importation of copyrighted material. Other video piracy practices fit different legal categories more closely. The unauthorized resale of copied or covertly taped videocassettes is counterfeiting in legal schemes awarding property rights in visual recordings. Satellite and cable interceptions involve the resale of stolen goods when property rights in broadcasting exist. Regardless of legal category, all of these practices raise the same policy tradeoff, and all may be analyzed with the same economic model. Thus, for expositional convenience, the model of this paper will be discussed in terms of the gray market, and the examples of video piracy will emphasize the unauthorized trade in prerecorded video-cassettes. With the appropriate redefinition of variables, the same economic model could equally well describe counterfeiting or the fencing of stolen property, and thereby accommodate all the practices labeled video piracy. Further, the economic model could be recast to evaluate patent laws, vertical restraints, and other policy questions raising the tradeoff between low consumer prices and high manufacturer or distributor incentives to invest.

Unlike most gray markets, which involve small market shares, the trade in unauthorized prerecorded videocassettes often appears to result in a market share over 50%. The model presented in this chapter accommodates this wide disparity in market shares by relating it to the marginal cost curve of the unauthorized sector. The model therefore implicitly attributes the high market share of unauthorized video products, compared to the small market share of other gray market sectors, to the low cost of copying video-cassettes and the low expected penalties facing gray market distributors resulting from difficulties enforcing laws prohibiting the practice.[15]

---

[14] In the video realm, the manufacturers are winning the semantic battle, by the widespread adoption of the connotatively unfavorable term "video piracy" to describe the sale of unauthorized video products. The gray-market question is the subject of a semantic as well as a legal debate: The term "gray market" is employed by manufacturers to describe the unauthorized importation of trademarked or copyrighted products, while importers refer to the practice as "parallel importation."

[15] So long as gray market sellers are small and numerous, they will act as a competitive fringe in a dominant firm model even in markets where they collectively hold a high share.

In discussing the gray market and video piracy, this chapter evaluates the underlying consumer welfare tradeoff. The gray market can harm consumers by removing producer incentives to invest in reputation, because it allows unauthorized distributors to free ride on the reputational investments of the authorized distributors. On the other hand, it may benefit consumers by lowering prices for the gray market product. The primary conclusion of this chapter is that, in most cases, the gray market is on balance detrimental to consumers, because the harm to consumers from deterring valuable investments will likely outweigh the consumer benefit from lower prices.

This result is shown for a world biased in favor of the gray market, because it assumes away a second likely form of consumer harm from the gray market, consumer confusion. Appendix E to this chapter extends the model to allow for the possibility that consumers of gray market products mistakenly think they are purchasing a more valuable authorized good, and shows that this possibility likely strengthens the case against the gray market. In the video piracy context, these results suggest that higher penalties and increased enforcement efforts aimed at reducing the unauthorized sale or use of video products will improve consumer welfare.

PREVIOUS ECONOMIC ANALYSES

The present analysis adds to the economic literature on the gray market by creating a formal economic model in order to derive conditions under which policies affecting the gray market improve consumer welfare. This model incorporates the primary arguments of the economists on each side of the policy debate.

Economists opposing the gray market emphasize the welfare costs of free riding by gray market sellers and dismiss the possibility that arbitrage will create welfare gains by lowering consumer prices. These authors argue that consumer prices can fall no further following the creation of a gray market because entry is already easy into most domestic markets selling the branded products that are prey to gray market competition. As entry will compete price down to long run average cost, the long run competitive equilibrium, gray market imports are said to be unnecessary for consumers to receive the benefits of competition (Knoll, 1986; Miller, 1986).

The argument against the benefits of additional competition depends crucially on its free entry assumption. Yet this assumption is not unchallengeable. Economists have applied strategic entry deterrence models to industries selling differentiated products, such as the branded goods subject to gray markets. In these models, entry is deterred by the credible threat of post-entry competition, allowing supercompetitive pricing by incumbent firms (Schmalensee, 1978; Mankiw & Whinston, 1986). Further, in order to compete away incumbent firm market power in differentiated product industries, entrants must create a new product with characteristics similar to those of the brand sold by the successful incumbent. Yet this competitive response is problematic in the prerecorded videocassette industry, for one, as it can be difficult to replicate the attributes of a successful film in a later product.[16] Because entry need not be easy, the possibility of consumer benefits from lower prices resulting from the gray market cannot be dismissed cavalierly.

The primary economic argument in favor of the gray market, in contrast, dismisses the incentive effects of gray market competition on the reputational investments of the authorized producer and emphasizes the lower prices created by international arbitrage (Hilke, 1987). If free riding were a problem, this argument contends, private contracting for exclusive distribution territories and the prevention of resale except to consumers would eliminate it.

This argument fails to recognize that if firms were able to contract to eliminate free riding, they could also contract to eliminate international arbitrage.[17] In other words, this position ignores enforcement costs; private contracting to prevent resale may well be prohibitively expensive to enforce for consumer products sold in complex distribution chains, such as the branded consumer products most affected by the gray market.[18] In consequence, a gray market may create a substantial disincentive for producer investments in reputation; importer free riding rather than arbitrage could be the primary economic force underlying the practice. To incorporate this possibility, the present model expressly allows for gray market sales to appropriate the benefit of the reputational expenditures of the authorized distributor.[19]

---

[16] A successful film will often be followed by less successful imitations.

[17] Further, this position's emphasis on the consumer benefits resulting from low gray market prices understates the social costs of the reduction in reputational investments that will occur if authorized sectors are unable to cover average costs.

[18] The most cost-effective way to enforce such contracts in the international trade context is likely at the border, through the Customs Service. This is the remedy generally advocated by anti-gray market forces. The expenses of policing the unauthorized copying of videocassettes are equally high.

[19] Gray market foes sometimes suggest that the consumer gains from international arbitrage necessarily exceed the costs of free riding on the authorized firms' reputational investment whenever the (domestic) wholesale price of the authorized product exceeds the (foreign) wholesale price of the gray market product. This position implicitly presumes that the authorized distributor makes no reputational investments valuable to domestic consumers.

When domestic distributions make reputational investments, the authorized foreign product can be thought of as a different good from the authorized domestic product. To the extent the domestic and foreign distributors invest in creating different physical or nonphysical product attributes, the two goods can be said to have "separate goodwills." For example, one distributor might provide more point of sale services, greater warranty protection, or a better reputation for quality than the other.   (continued)

A recent economic analysis of counterfeit goods by Grossman and Shapiro addresses some of the issues confronted here.[20] These authors develop a two-country model of international trade in which foreign firms choose to produce either low-quality legitimate merchandise or counterfeit products, and in which the domestic producer chooses his quality level. Grossman and Shapiro focus primarily upon two issues of secondary importance for this chapter. They address the adverse selection problems associated with the marketing of counterfeit merchandise when consumers have imperfect information, by finding a rational expectations (subgame-perfect) steady-state equilibrium for their model. Further, Grossman and Shapiro examine the welfare effects of several policies for the disposal of confiscated products, an issue that is not a concern of the present chapter.

In a very general way, Grossman and Shapiro's results corroborate the welfare tradeoff emphasized here. When the number of sellers in the domestic market is fixed so that domestic producers have market power, these authors find that marginal increases in the enforcement of counterfeiting prohibitions may or may not improve domestic welfare. Welfare may fall if increased enforcement exacerbates a preexisting market distortion. Although the distortion emphasized by Grossman and Shapiro concerns producer choice of product quality, an issue not incorporated into the present analysis, this result parallels the discussion below. The present chapter similarly finds that a marginal increase in the marginal costs facing the gray market fringe (as from greater enforcement efforts) can either improve or reduce domestic welfare. Welfare may fall if the reduction in gray market imports exacer-

---

This chapter shows that the gray market sector will be most active when its marginal cost is low, as when authorized foreign distributors do not invest heavily in (foreign) reputation, and when the domestic selling price is high, as when authorized domestic distributors invest heavily in reputation. Under these circumstances, the gray market sector is free riding substantially on the reputational investments of the domestic distributor. This result is not inconsistent with the possibility that both authorized distributors, foreign and domestic, purchased the product for the same wholesale price; indeed free riding will be profitable for the gray market sector so long as the value to domestic consumers of the authorized distributor's reputational expenses exceeds the transportation and other marginal costs of importation (see generally, Lexecon Inc., 1986).

[20] See G. Grossman and C. Shapiro, 1986. For more general, nontechnical, and stimulating discussions of the welfare effects of trademarks, see Shapiro, 1982; Craswell, 1979.

Two recent papers analyze the welfare effects of counterfeiting snob goods, but neither confronts the issues addressed in the present discussion. The first emphasizes that some consumers benefit when they are able to purchase the prestige aspect of such products at a low price without the buying the quality attributes, but that the sale of fake products degrades the status associated with a given trademark for snobbish consumers (G. Grossman & C. Shapiro, forthcoming). The other emphasizes that the value of prestige goods to snobbish consumers may fall if the amount of goods in circulation rises (R. Higgins & P. Rubin, 1986, pp. 211–230). Neither of these dynamics applies to the gray market generally, or to the unauthorized sale of video products in particular.

bates the distortion created by the monopoly pricing of the trademarked product by more than it improves the incentives of authorized producers to invest in reputation. This chapter goes beyond Grossman and Shapiro on this issue, however, by assessing the practical significance of this tradeoff.

A MODEL OF GRAY MARKET TRADE

The model of the gray market described in this section is designed to examine the policy tradeoff between free riding and arbitrage. Gray market sellers free ride on the reputational investments of the sellers of the authorized product, thereby reducing the incentive of authorized sellers to undertake such investments regardless of the value of those investments to consumers. However, the gray market may also allow the arbitrage of international price differences, lowering consumer prices.

The discussion below uses the term ''authorized'' product to describe a good placed into domestic commerce by the domestic trademark or copyright owner, and employs the term ''gray market'' product for a good with similar physical characteristics placed into domestic commerce by anyone else. In the videocassette context, the gray market product represents both unauthorized parallel imports of video products (true gray market sales), and, more generally, unauthorized copies whether or not imported.

The industry is modeled as composed of a dominant firm, namely the authorized seller, and a gray market fringe. The industry produces a differentiated product, so its demand curve is downward sloping. The model assumes that only one authorized distributor exists for each product. The gray market is treated as a competitive fringe, selling a product perceived by consumers as identical to the authorized good along its upward sloping marginal cost curve.[21]

These assumptions plausibly characterize the video industry. For most video products, the authorized distributor makes reputational investments, while gray-market importers (or video cassette copiers) are small and numerous, and do not make such investments. The model implicitly treats possible

---

[21] The gray market is implicitly characterized as a large number of independent distributors who act competitively, not as a small number of sellers involved in a more complex noncooperative interaction with the authorized domestic producer. This interpretation is consistent with the characteristics of many gray markets in the United States. This view may be less plausible when gray market sales equal half or more of total product sales, to the extent the larger share is serviced by a large importer able to take advantage of the downward-sloping industry demand curve. However, the model continues to apply in those situations if there are many importers, each of whom prices at marginal cost. If the gray market sector did not act competitively, the consumer welfare loss from allowing a gray market to exist would likely increase over the levels observed in the present model, even if the gray market sector also undertook its own reputational investments.

sanctions against the illegal acts of video pirates as a marginal cost, and ignores the possibility that the authorized producer might obtain damages in a private action against unauthorized firms.

The model presumes that the authorized and gray market products are identical. By assuming away the possibility of consumer confusion between the authorized and gray market products, the model highlights the policy tradeoff between encouraging new products by preserving the authorized firm's incentives to invest in reputation, and lowering consumer prices by allowing gray market sellers to compete with authorized distributors. However, courts have often, but not always, found consumer confusion in gray market litigation in the United States. When consumer confusion is important, the analysis below will likely underestimate the costs of gray market activities, perhaps substantially so. The significance of consumer confusion is treated in detail in Appendix E of this chapter.

The dominant firm, selling the authorized product, distributes Q units of the authorized product at marginal cost C and sells them for price P.[22] Aside from the expenses included in the marginal cost function, distribution of the authorized product may require an investment A in reputation-creating activities. As the model has only one period,[23] A should be viewed as the discounted present value of all reputational investments.

The variable A may be thought of as advertising, although it may also represent a variety of other firm investments depending on the product, including other forms of promotion, warranty service, point of sale services, and expenses on preserving quality. The model presumes that all reputational investments benefit consumers (Telser, 1968). This assumes away the possibility that advertising by branded good distributors is a device for strategic entry deterrence,[24] and it presumes that all reputational investments are valued identically by marginal and inframarginal customers. If

---

[22] The assumption that price is well defined for sellers of prerecorded videocassettes abstracts from several complications. Most importantly, video distributors must decide whether to rent or sell their products, or whether to do both simultaneously at different prices ("A No-Win War in Videocassettes," 1987, p. 152). Other pricing complexities arise from the ability of film and television producers to shift distribution from theater or television to cassette sales, and from the presence of alternative standard formats, Beta and VHS. In order to isolate the gray market issue, the price of a videocassette as used in the present model will be thought of as the discounted present value of the revenue stream resulting from the best set of marketing decisions available to the firm, divided by the number of cassettes placed in distribution. In other industries where gray market sales are prevalent (such as watches, perfume, and cameras), the good and its price are better defined.

[23] Profits in the model can be thought of as the discounted present value of an expected profit stream. Even if lower consumer prices from gray market competition occur before the dominant firm's foregone reputational investments would have been made, the model will fairly represent the consumer welfare tradeoff between lower consumer prices and reduced innovation because the value of future reputational investments is also discounted to the present.

[24] This assumption does not assume away all entry barriers, only the use of advertising to deter entry (Salop, 1979).

these assumptions are inaccurate, an observed advertising/sales ratio may overstate the level of the reputational investment relevant to the consumer welfare calculation.

In the model, the dominant firm's profits take the form:

$$\pi = (P - C)Q - A \tag{1}$$

Marginal cost C is assumed constant. For analytic simplicity, equation (1) assumes that there are no fixed costs of production (other than the investment in reputation). This assumption does not affect the welfare analysis of the model because that analysis is local rather than global. Thus, the role of dominant firm fixed costs in creating scale economies and the role of dominant firm sunk costs in creating entry barriers against the fringe are ignored, and a profit constraint is assumed satisfied.

The brand (inverse) demand function (2) depends upon the total of both authorized firm output Q and gray market output G, because consumers do not differentiate between the two goods. The notation X represents the total quantity of brand sales: $X = Q + G$. Brand demand also depends on the reputation created by advertising or other reputational expenditures A.

$$P = F(X,A) \tag{2}$$

The inverse demand curve is downward sloping in quantity $(F_X < 0)$. Its slope will be steepest when competing brands are poor substitutes for the brand at issue.[25] Increasing expenditures on goodwill are assumed to increase the value of the product to consumers $(F_a > 0)$.[26]

The gray-market fringe sells at its marginal cost, so its output is determined by the fringe supply function (3).

$$P = T + K(G) \tag{3}$$

The fringe supply curve shifts vertically through changes in the intercept T. Exchange rate fluctuations are likely the most important source of shifts in T. This parameter permits investigation of the welfare consequences of policies encouraging or discouraging gray market imports. The model ignores the role of fixed costs in determining the number of fringe producers and in creating the possibility of scale economies in fringe production.

The fringe marginal cost curve is an increasing function of fringe output $(K_g > 0)$. This slope reflects both the difficulties gray market importers have

---

[25] The greater the extent of product differentiation, the less important oligopoly behavior is in affecting the demand for any one brand. This chapter ignores rival brand reactions on the assumption that differentiation is extensive for brands subject to gray market competition. Thus, the output of competing brands is neglected in specifying equation (2).

[26] The second-order conditions will require that $F_{aa} > 0$.

in obtaining assured foreign supplies and domestic distribution as their sales increase, and gray market importers bidding up the foreign price of imports as their purchases increase.

Equations (2) and (3) imply equation (4), a residual demand curve facing the dominant (authorized) seller.

$$P = R(Q,A) \tag{4}$$

As is demonstrated in Appendix B, the residual demand curve facing the dominant firm is downward sloping in output ($R_q < 0$).

The dominant firm is the only nontrivial decision maker in the model. It chooses Q and A to maximize profits (1), thereby solving the optimization problem (5).

$$\max_{Q,A} \pi = (R(Q,A) - C)Q - A \tag{5}$$

The first-order conditions for an interior maximum are stated as equations (6) and (7).[27]

$$QR_q + R - C = 0 \tag{6}$$

$$QR_a = 1 \tag{7}$$

Through algebraic manipulation, these first-order conditions take on familiar forms:

$$L \equiv (P - C)/P = - E_{rq} \tag{8}$$

$$\Psi \equiv A/(PQ) = E_{ra} \tag{9}$$

According to equation (8), a firm with market power chooses a price such that the Lerner Index (L) of markup of price over marginal cost equals the absolute value of the elasticity of inverse residual demand with respect to output. Equation (9) is the Dorfman-Steiner condition that a firm with monopoly power advertises until the advertising to sales ratio (Ψ) equals the advertising elasticity of inverse residual demand.[28] These first-order conditions, along with definitions (2) and (3), are sufficient to determine P, Q, G, and A; they define the equilibrium.

---

[27] The two second-order conditions are: $R_{qq} + 2R_q < 0$ and $R_{aa} < 0$. The former condition is guaranteed by the assumption that $R_q < 0$, unless R_{qq} is large and positive. In the "linear" model that generates the primary results of this chapter, $R_{qq} = 0$, so this condition will necessarily be satisfied. Further, the proof of Corollary A.1 of Appendix A implies that R_{aa} has the same sign as F_{aa}, previously assumed negative. This guarantees that the condition $R_{aa} < 0$ holds.

[28] Note that both Ψ and L must be found in the interval [0,1].

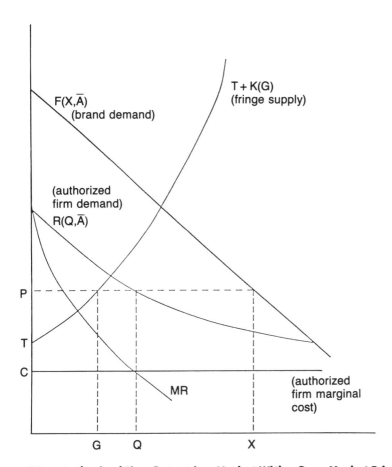

Figure 5.1.   Authorized Firm Output in a Market With a Gray-Market Fringe

The equilibrium derived above is depicted in Figure 1. This diagram is similar to the familiar diagram of the equilibrium in a market with a dominant firm and competitive fringe. Unlike the familiar case, however, the curves drawn in Figure 1 hold constant the level of advertising. Thus, only first-order condition (6) is shown.

The comparative statics of this equilibrium, derived and signed in Appendix B, are summarized here. The derivatives of inverse residual demand (price) with respect to the dominant firm's two decision variables (Q and A) and the policy parameter (T) are:

$$R_q = -K_g F_x / (F_x - K_g) < 0,\tag{10}$$

$$R_a = -K_g F_a / (F_x - K_g) > 0, \text{ and}\tag{11}$$

$$R_t = F_x / (F_x - K_g) > 0.\tag{12}$$

Equation (10) shows that an increase in the dominant firm's output reduces price, because the dominant firm faces a downward sloping residual demand curve. When the dominant firm increases its investment in reputation, equation (11) shows that it raises consumer willingness to pay and raises the equilibrium price. Finally, if the marginal cost of gray market sales increase, equation (12) shows that the equilibrium price rises because the fringe provides less competitive discipline for the dominant firm. Intuitively, the higher cost to the fringe allows the dominant firm to internalize more of the benefits of the reduction in total brand sales, so the dominant firm increases output by less than the fringe reduces output. As total output declines, equilibrium price rises.

The derivatives of fringe output with respect to the same three variables are:

$$G_q = -F_x/(F_x - K_g) < 0, \tag{13}$$

$$G_a = -F_a/(F_x - K_g) > 0, \text{ and} \tag{14}$$

$$G_t = 1/(F_x - K_g) < 0. \tag{15}$$

Equation (13) shows that an increase in dominant firm output takes sales away from the fringe.[29] The remaining equations show that an increase in the dominant firm's reputational investment allows fringe producers to increase sales by free-riding on that investment (equation (14)), and that an increase in the marginal cost of gray-market products reduces fringe output (equation (15)).

The effects of changes in T, vertical shifts in fringe marginal cost, on the dominant firm's decision variables are derived and signed in Appendix B under the assumptions of the "linear" model defined in Appendix A. The "linear" model sets all second derivatives to zero except F_{aa} and R_{aa}, which must be negative in order for the second order conditions for an interior profit maximum to hold.

$$A_t = R_a R_t/[4R_q Q R_{aa} - (R_a)^2] > 0 \tag{16}$$

$$Q_t = -(2R_{aa}Q R_t/(4R_q Q R_{aa} - R_a^2)) > 0 \tag{17}$$

The conclusion that both Q_t and A_t are positive in the "linear" model is a sensible one. First, an upward shift in fringe marginal cost will make the dominant firm's reputational investments more valuable on the margin by reducing fringe free riding, and thus will cause the dominant firm to increase

---

[29] In this case, fringe sales may decline less than dominant firm sales rise.

those investments. Second, a higher fringe supply curve will raise dominant firm output because the dominant firm will take sales away from the fringe. As is evident from the comparative statics of G, the fringe's market share will be large whenever total brand demand is elastic, fringe marginal cost is flat, and fringe marginal costs are low. The model is not inconsistent with a high market share for the fringe, as has been observed for videocassettes in many countries. The most likely explanation for this observation in terms of the model is that T, the parameter generating vertical shifts in fringe supply, is low. Indeed, in comparison with the costs facing sellers of most gray market products, the marginal cost curve for fringe sellers of unauthorized videocassettes is probably very low, because unauthorized videocassettes can be obtained by copying without need for importation or the payment of royalties to trademark owners.

In terms of the model, the variation in market share of the unauthorized video product sector across countries may also be explained by variation in T, in this case by differences in the enforcement of intellectual property protections. It is unlikely that the slope of brand demand or fringe marginal cost differs substantially from one country to the next for the videocassette industry. Hence the large cross-sectional variation in the market share of unauthorized videocassettes is most likely explained by disparities in the level of gray market marginal costs. In particular, the U.S. and various Scandinavian countries most likely have a much lower incidence of video piracy than other market economies because more governmental resources are devoted to enforcement actions to prohibit this trade in those countries. This inference is consistent with the behavior of the film and television producers and their authorized distributors, who have emphasized private enforcement and lobbying for public enforcement in their efforts to stem the unauthorized trade. Intertemporal variation in gray market significance also is explained by variation in marginal cost. The size of the gray market sector in the U.S. has altered over the past decade along with the strength of the dollar. The stronger the dollar, the cheaper are imports in dollar terms, and the larger the gray market.[30]

DETERMINANTS OF CONSUMER WELFARE

The welfare analysis of this chapter focuses on the surplus accruing to domestic consumers. This emphasis excludes the domestic benefit of the

---

[30] Thus, in a case involving gray market Duracell batteries, the U.S. International Trade Commisson found that gray market transactions were "profitable to the importer due to the strong position of the U.S. dollar as against European currencies." *In re Certain Alkaline Batteries,* 225 U.S.P.Q. 823, 825 (U.S.I.T.C. 1984); *remedy disapproved,* 225 US12 862; *aff'd sub nom., Duracell Inc. v. U.S.I.T.C.,* 778 F.2d 1578 (Fed. Cir. 1985).

producers' surplus accruing to the authorized and gray market sectors, and it excludes all benefits to foreign consumers.[31] The domestic benefit of the producers' surplus is analyzed in Appendix D of this chapter.

The focus on consumer welfare is consistent with the consumer welfare emphasis of the gray market policy debate.[32] Further, under one set of assumptions, described in Appendix D, producers' surplus will be zero, so that total surplus will consist solely of consumers' surplus. Although gray markets involve international trade, the welfare of foreign consumers is excluded on the view that sovereign policy makers are primarily concerned with their domestic consumers.

Consumer welfare is defined in this chapter as equal to the domestic consumer's surplus associated with purchases of Q and G, as indicated in equation (18).[33]

$$CS = S(X,A) - R(Q,A)X, \text{ where } S(X,A) = \int_0^X F(X,A)dX \qquad (18)$$

In equation (18), the expression $S(X,A)$ represents the aggregate consumer benefit of domestic consumers' purchases of both the authorized and gray market products, measured as the area under the demand curve. The expression $R(Q,A)X$ equals total consumer payments for those products.

The policy question addressed by this chapter—whether promoting or hindering the gray market aids consumer welfare—will be analyzed by computing dCS/dT, the change in consumer's surplus resulting from a small vertical shift in gray market marginal cost.[34] If this expression is positive,

---

[31] The welfare analysis also excludes the social resources devoted to the enforcement of intellectual property laws limiting or prohibiting the gray market. In consequence, if enforcement costs are large relative to changes in consumers' surplus, as seems unlikely, the analysis in this chapter will overstate the case against the gray market.

[32] The authorized and gray market production and distribution sectors will likely be vocal advocates of their position on the gray market, as the producer benefits and costs of gray market policy are typically concentrated in a few firms or trade associations with a direct economic stake in governmental policy. In U.S. debates over the gray market, the policy arguments of the producers and distributors are often framed around the impact of such policies on domestic consumers, for whom the benefits and costs of policies are typically diffuse.

[33] The analysis below assumes that consumers' surplus is an exact welfare measure, ignoring income effects. It further assumes that consumers have full information about the value of all products in the economy, including the authorized product (other than the possibility of confusion from the gray market good in the discussion of Appendix E). Thus, the downward sloping demand curve for the authorized product results from spatial location, not from imperfect buyer information. Under this assumption, the market demand curve reflects underlying preferences under full information, and is appropriately considered a welfare measure.

[34] This welfare analysis assumes that the dominant firm's foreign affiliate does not alter the foreign wholesale price in response to variation in domestic government policy affecting T. The foreign affiliate (foreign distributor) is taken to be an independent decision maker maximizing its own profits without regard to the impact of its decisions on affiliated entities. This assumption is most plausible when the gray market exports account for only a small fraction of foreign source sales. It is particularly plausible with respect to video piracy, to the extent this problem involves unauthorized cassette copying.

then policies which raise the marginal cost of gray market imports move the equilibrium locally in the direction of higher consumer welfare.[35] If the expression is negative, then policies reducing the cost of those imports on the margin will improve consumer welfare. The test statistic dCS/dT is derived in equation (19).[36]

$$dCS/dT = S(X,A)_x X_t + S(X,A)_a A_t - PX_t - XR_t = S(X,A)_a A_t - XR_t \qquad (19)$$

The first expression in equation (19), $S(X,A)_a A_t$, represents the influence of a change in gray market policy on the consumer welfare costs resulting from unauthorized distributors free riding on the authorized firm's reputational investment A. This expression has a positive sign. As indicated in equation (11), increased reputational expenditures by the dominant firm increase the market price ($R_a > 0$). This guarantees that $S_a > 0$ under the "linear" model.[37] Further, as indicated in equation (16), a policy raising fringe marginal cost increases dominant firm reputational investments by raising their marginal value ($A_t > 0$). Intuitively, higher gray market marginal costs lead the authorized firm to increase its investment in goodwill, and those investments increase the consumer benefit from the consumption of both goods. Hence, policies raising gray market marginal costs improve social welfare by reducing the inhibitions on authorized producer reputational investments created by fringe free riding.

In contrast, the second expression, $-XR_t$, representing the beneficial effect of arbitrage on domestic prices, is negative. As indicated in equation (12), an increase in gray market marginal costs leads to a higher market price for sales of both the authorized and gray market goods ($R_t > 0$). Thus, policies harming the gray market reduce consumer welfare insofar as they raise consumer prices.

Proposition 1 summarizes the analysis of equation (19), identifying the mechanisms by which policies regarding the gray market affect consumer welfare in the absence of consumer confusion. Appendix E examines the significance of consumer confusion, and demonstrates that omitting this

---

[35] Although the welfare analysis of this chapter is local, it is possible under some circumstances to make inferences from dCS/dT about the welfare effects of substantial changes in T. Substantial shifts in T are proposed by the advocates of complete prohibition or unimpeded sale of gray market products. Inferences about the welfare effects of these policies require the additional (and potentially controversial) assumption that the magnitudes of the various derivatives comprising equation (19) do not change following substantial fluctuations in the values of Q and G implied by large changes in T. In general, local analysis will show the likely direction of policy improvements resulting from an increase or decrease in T, although policies involving large changes in T may overshoot the welfare optimum.

[36] The equation simplified by recognizing that $S(X,A)_x = F(X,A) = P$.

[37] Under the "linear" model, S_a is related to R_a by the following equation: $S_a = \int F_a(X,A)\, dx = \int R_a F_{aa}/R_{aa}\, dx$. Both second derivatives are always negative by virtue of Assumption A of the "linear" model. As R_a is positive (see equation (A.8) of Appendix B), S_a must be positive as well.

effect likely biases the consumer welfare tradeoff described in Proposition 1 in favor of the gray market.

Proposition 1: In the absence of consumer confusion, a policy making the gray market more expensive affects consumer welfare by:

- increasing reputational investments by the authorized producer through limiting the effects of free riding by gray market sellers, thereby improving consumer welfare; and
- raising consumer prices on both authorized and gray market products, thereby reducing consumer welfare.

In the event the authorized and the gray market products are differentiated from each other, contrary to the assumption made for analytic convenience in the present model, some of the welfare loss attributed here to higher consumer prices will instead take the form of reduced product variety. Although the analytic details of the model will alter if differentiation is allowed, the main conclusions of the analysis will likely remain unaffected.[38]

---

[38] The present model will continue to apply when consumers can distinguish authorized from gray market products, and when they prefer the authorized goods, so long as: (a) the two products are sufficiently close substitutes so that the reputational investments of the authorized producer raise consumer willingness to pay for both products in a similar way; and (b) the units of the gray market product are altered so that, in adjusted units, the two goods sell for the same price. Under these assumptions, for the purpose of applying the model the two products may be treated as identical.

Alternatively, the gray market product may provide more competitive discipline for other brands, such as low-quality fringe brands, than for the authorized branded product. The welfare consequences of this situation depend on entry conditions in the industry. In a zero-profit free-entry equilibrium with price discrimination, the gray market may harm consumers because authorized firms may well create optimal product variety, which the gray market disturbs. (Incumbent manufacturers can capture the social benefit of product variety while preserving production economies by creating private labels. The gray market sector has less control over the attributes of its good than a manufacturer selling a private label, so optimal variety is likely sacrificed in an equilibrium including a nontrivial gray market sector.)

If instead incumbent firms earn economic profits, as may occur if product differentiation deters entry, gray market competition will benefit consumers by increasing product variety, although it will also harm consumers by reducing the reputational investments of the authorized distributor whose product's attributes are closest to those of the gray market good. This observation generalizes to the differentiated product case the policy tradeoff between lower prices and free riding characteristic of the homogeneous product case described in the present model.

Retailers of gray market products on occasion make reputational investments, as by providing warranties different from the manufacturer's warranty. These investments may differentiate the gray market goods from the authorized product. The effect of such investments is ignored in this model.

FREE RIDING VERSUS ARBITRAGE IN THE "LINEAR" MODEL

The primary results in this chapter are derived for the special case termed the "linear" model. This model presumes that all second derivatives are zero, except the second derivatives of brand and dominant firm inverse demand, which must be negative in order for the second order conditions to be satisfied. The assumptions of the "linear" model are stated in Appendix A.

Propositions 2 and 3, stated below and proved in Appendix C, identify conditions under which consumers benefit from policies tending to raise gray market costs. These propositions assess the policy tradeoff presented by the gray market, between lower consumer prices and free riding on authorized producer investments in reputation.

One new variable is introduced in order to simplify notation: $\lambda = [E_{fx}Q/E_{rq} X - 1] = [-E_{fx}Q/LX - 1]$. The variable λ depends upon the ratio of the elasticity of the inverse structural demand curve with respect to output (E_{fx}), to the elasticity of the inverse residual demand curve with respect to output (E_{rq}). This ratio will always exceed unity, but will be close to one if the fringe supply curve is very inelastic. Equation (8) allows the substitution of the Lerner Index (L) for $-E_{rq}$ in the definition of λ. The variable λ also depends on the quantity share of the authorized product (Q/X), a number between zero and one. As the product of these quantities must be greater than one,[39] the variable λ cannot be negative ($\lambda > 0$).

Proposition 2: In the "linear" model, without consumer confusion, a policy marginally hindering the gray market improves consumer welfare if $[\Psi(2+\lambda)/4(1-\Psi)] > L$, but reduces consumer welfare if $[\Psi(2+\lambda)/4(1-\Psi)] < L$.

Proposition 2 is important because it shows that the resolution of the fundamental gray market policy tradeoff—stopping free riding versus allowing lower consumer prices—turns on the size of the Lerner Index (L) of the authorized producer's markup of price over marginal cost.[40] If the

---

[39] In the proof of Theorem 2, it is demonstrated that $(1+\lambda) = F_x/R_q$. Equation (A.7) of Appendix B requires that the market demand curve be steeper than the dominant firm's residual demand curve. Hence, λ cannot be negative. In the limiting case in which the gray market disappears, Q/X goes to one. Further, as the residual demand curve approaches the market demand curve, $-E_{rq}$ rises to $-E_{fx}$. In this polar case, λ shrinks to zero.

[40] At least two approaches to inferring the Lerner Index of markup are available. The accounting approach to estimating the markup from annual report data employs the dominant firm's short run average variable cost as a proxy for its marginal cost, and employs average revenue as a proxy for price. This approach presumes that marginal cost is constant for large changes in output. For example, if marginal cost is rising, average variable cost will understate marginal cost, so this accounting approach will overstate the markup L.

(continued)

dominant firm's markup is high relative to the dominant firm's reputational expenses, measured in terms of the advertising/sales ratio (Ψ), then consumer welfare is improved by policies benefitting the gray market. In that case, the consumer gains from lower prices exceed the consumer harm created by the reduction in incentives of the authorized producer to invest in improving the value of his product to the consumer. In contrast, when prices are low relative to reputational expenses, a policy hindering the gray market benefits consumers on the margin.

The size of the observed markup depends in part upon the level of reputational expenses. (The markup also varies with the height of entry barriers, dominant firm market share, the slope of the fringe supply curve, and the demand substitutability of competing brands.[41]) Because the parameter λ does not remain constant as L changes, the condition in Theorem 2 cannot be used to compare observed values of L and Ψ. This comparison is instead the subject of Proposition 3.

> *Proposition 3:* In the "linear" model, without consumer confusion, $dCS/dT > 0$ if and only if $L < L^*$, where $L^* = \Psi/8(1 - \Psi) + [\Psi^2 - 16(1 - \Psi)E_{fx}Q/X]^{1/2}/8(1 - \Psi)$.

Proposition 3 identifies the critical markup value L^*. If, for a particular product, L is greater than the indicated value of L^*, the gray market improves consumer welfare on the margin. If L is less than the appropriate critical value, a policy raising gray market costs improves consumer welfare on the margin. Proposition 3 shows that the critical value of the markup, that is, the markup level at which the gray market does not affect consumer welfare on the margin, depends on the level of reputational expenses (Ψ), and on the elasticity of industry demand ($-E_{fx}$) weighted by dominant firm market share (Q/X).

In making these computations, the price P, the marginal cost C, and promotional expenditures A must be consistently defined. If these variables are defined with respect to an upstream distributor who sells at wholesale to retailers, P would be the wholesale price, C would be the distributor's marginal cost, and A would be the promotional investments made by the distributor. Alternatively, the distributor and retailers could be viewed as an integrated distribution sector. The P would be the retail price, C the sum of the distributor and the retailer's marginal costs, and A the total promotional expenses made at both levels. Further, the variables in the model are discounted present values of expense and revenue streams. If L and Ψ are inferred from one year's accounting data, that inference would implicitly presume that these variables are stable over time.

However, accounting estimates of markup are often unreliable indicators of true economic profits (Fisher & McGowan, 1983, pp. 82–97). An alternative econometric approach, available for differentiated product industries such as those susceptible to gray markets, would infer L directly from the slope of the residual demand curve (Baker & Bresnahan, 1985, pp. 427–44).

[41] See, generally, W. Landes & R. Posner, 1981, pp. 937–96.

Table 1.   Critical Values of L.

			$-E_{fx}Q/X$			
	0.25	**0.50**	**0.75**	**1.00**	**1.25**	**1.50**
Ψ						
.05	0.26	0.37	0.45	0.52	0.58	0.63
0.10	0.28	0.39	0.47	0.54	0.60	0.66
0.15	0.29	0.41	0.49	0.56	0.63	0.69
0.20	0.31	0.43	0.52	0.59	0.66	0.72
0.25	0.33	0.45	0.54	0.62	0.69	0.75
0.30	0.36	0.48	0.57	0.65	0.72	0.79
0.35	0.38	0.51	0.61	0.69	0.76	0.83
0.40	0.42	0.55	0.65	0.73	0.81	0.88
0.45	0.45	0.59	0.70	0.78	0.86	0.93
0.50	0.50	0.64	0.75	0.84	0.93	1.00

To interpret Proposition 3, it is necessary to assess the likely magnitudes of three terms: L, Ψ, and $-E_{fx}Q/X$. Table 1 reports the critical values L* for various combinations of Ψ and $-$ EfxQ/X. The values of $-E_{fx}Q/X$ in Table 1 range from 0.25 to 1.50. In the absence of econometric estimates of the demand curve for products with gray markets, this range seems plausible for three reasons. First, in the present model, the elasticity of the inverse market demand curve deflated by the market share of the dominated firm $(-E_{fx}Q/X)$ must exceed the markup chosen by the dominant firm (L).[42] If the market demand curve has a roughly constant elasticity, then $-E_{fx}$ can be thought of as the likely markup that the dominant firm would choose were there no gray market;[43] this observation suggests $-E_{fx}$ less than but perhaps close to one,[44] and $(E_{fx}Q/X)$ roughly equal to the authorized firm's market share.

Second, the markup for a branded product (L) may substantially exceed zero, even if the firm earns zero economic profits, when promotional expenditures in support of the brand are substantial. As $-$ EfxQ/X must be greater than L, this implies that $-E_{fx}Q/X$ can also substantially exceed zero. Finally, the requirement that $-$ EfxQ/X must exceed L suggests that $-E_{fx}$ will be a large multiple of L when gray market goods have a high market share (e.g., more than 50%), because a large gray market sector will limit the ability of the authorized producer to take advantage of an inelastic

---

[42] Equation (A.7) of Appendix B implies that $L = [K_g/(K_g - F_x)](-E_{fx})(Q/X)$. As $K_g > 0$ and $F_x > 0$, the expression $[K_g/(K_g^1 F_x)]$ lies in the interval from zero to one.

[43] This interpretation of $-E_{fx}$ is the most reasonable when gray market goods have a small market share (e.g., no more than 10%), as then the constant market demand elasticity assumption will be the most plausible.

[44] Because a brand monopolist would not operate on an elastic portion of its demand curve, in equilibrium it would choose an output level such that L is no larger than one.

brand demand curve. In such a case, $-E_{fx}$ could be substantially larger than one, although there is no reason to believe that the product $-E_{fx}Q/X$ will be much larger than one.[45] To the extent a typical value for $-E_{fx}Q/X$ can be assigned based on the above considerations, perhaps 0.75 is a fair estimate. The values of the advertising/sales ratio (Ψ) in Table 1 range from 0.05 to 0.50. There is some evidence that the advertising/sales ratio of typical products subjects to a gray market is high, on the order of 20% to 30%.[46] As these estimates may not take into account all forms of promotion, the highest value for Ψ in the table is above 30%.

The line separating the lower left hand quadrant of Table 1 from the rest indicates that the critical values of L in that quadrant must be higher than the actual value of L, by virtue of the condition that $L < -E_{fx}Q/X$. Hence whenever Ψ and $-E_{fx}Q/X$ map to positions to the left and below this line, a marginal increase in the costs of the gray market sector necessarily increases consumer welfare. This quadrant includes the lowest critical values in the table.

Table 1 shows that a product's markup L must be very high before a policy encouraging the gray market on the margin will benefit consumers.[47] Outside of the lower-left quadrant, where L necessarily exceeds its critical value L*, the critical markup values are in general closer to one than zero. Further, these values are in every case greater than the advertising/sales ratio for the authorized producer. Thus policies deterring the gray market on the margin will likely benefit consumers in most cases, no matter where on Table 1 the market in question is found.

Although Table 1 reflects a marginal analysis, this property permits a global policy conclusion: a complete prohibition of the gray market will, in most cases, improve consumer welfare. Even in the absence of consumer confusion, the policy tradeoff between preserving reputational incentives and lowering consumer prices is readily resolved in favor of prohibiting free riding. Hence, as discussed further in Appendix E, when gray market products are less desirable to consumers than authorized goods, and when consumers are confused at time of purchase between the two, a policy raising the costs of gray market imports almost surely benefits consumers.

This conclusion describes a general tendency; in any particular case, the balance between arbitrage and free riding may tilt the other way, to favor a

---

[45] Note that E_{fx}, X and L determine E_{fa}. This is evident from the two first order conditions and the formula for R_a of Appendix B: (L) $(E_{fa}) = (-E_{fx})(Q/X)\Psi = -E_{fx}(A/PX)$. Thus, if $(-E_{fx})(Q/X) = 0.75$, if Ψ equals 0.25, and if L equals the critical value indicated in Table 2 of 0.54, then E_{fa} will equal 0.35, a reasonable number.

[46] See Hilke, 1987, p. 17 n. 41; Miller, 1986, p. 373.

[47] Assumption C of Appendix A requires that $L > \Psi/4(1-\Psi)$. This technical condition also relating L and Ψ will readily be satisfied. If it does not hold, then the "linear" model is not an appropriate approximation for the industry at issue.

gray market. A gray market is most likely to improve consumer welfare in industries where the authorized distributor would face a steep brand demand curve ($-E_{fx}$ large) even absent substantial advertising expenses.[48] However, Table 1 suggests such a situation will be the exception rather than the rule.

CONCLUSION AND APPLICATION

The dominant firm/gray market fringe model of this paper plausibly characterizes gray markets generally, and video piracy in particular. In terms of the model, the variation in gray market share across products, across countries, and over time is explained by differences in the height of the fringe marginal cost curve, which in turn shifts primarily in response to exchange rate fluctuations and variation in governmental enforcement efforts.

The main conclusion of this chapter is that the typical gray market most likely hurts consumers more than it helps them, although it is possible for the reverse to occur in particular cases. However, the formula of Proposition 3, relating the policy tradeoff between arbitrage and free riding to the dominant firm's markup and its level of advertising, allows in principle for a case-by-case analysis.

The formula is particularly difficult to apply to the prerecorded videocassette industry because neither the advertising sales ratio (Ψ) nor the authorized distributor's markup (L) can readily be measured. Most importantly, it is difficult to measure the advertising and promotional expenses benefiting the consumers in any particular country.

The first problem in measuring the reputational investments of cassette distributors is accounting for the spillover from prior theater advertising. If a film has been released in theaters prior to its cassette release, promotional expenditures undertaken in support of the theater showings may influence later consumer decisions to purchase videocassettes. To the extent these expenditures are undertaken by an affiliate of the videocassette distributor or the party who sold distribution rights to the distributor, so that the distributor expects to internalize this spillover, some fraction should be included in A and thus recognized in Ψ.

---

[48] This exceptional case is perhaps plausible with respect to U.S. gray markets for expensive automobile brands, such as Mercedes. Consumers of gray market luxury automobiles are generally aware that they are purchasing a gray market product which will require the addition of pollution control equipment to meet U.S. standards. Thus, consumer confusion is probably not an issue for consumers of this product. If, as has been contended, the U.S. authorized distributors price these automobiles at a substantial markup over marginal cost, exceeding the critical values of L in Table 1 given the promotional investment of authorized distributors, policies encouraging the gray market in these products may benefit consumers.

A second problem for measuring reputational investments in the video-cassette industry comes from the need to account for other spillovers: Promotional expenses on related products and expenditures in other countries will affect consumer willingness to pay for videocassettes. To the extent one country's film reviews, film-related products such as toys or movie soundtracks, and film related topical illusions in the popular culture have audiences in other countries, the advertising and promotional expenditures in any one market will be difficult to determine.[49] Further, these spillovers imply that reputational expenditures affecting the value of videocassettes are unlikely to be stable from year to year, complicating the estimate of the typical value of Ψ required to apply the model.

The second difficulty applying the formula of Proposition 3 to the prerecorded videocassette industry is in measuring the markup L. Revenue and cost data on individual films will be misleading because of the high failure rate for new products in the industry. Even aggregate revenue and cost data will require smoothing over time to account properly for the occasional blockbuster.

Because of these difficulties, the accounting records of videocassette distributors are unlikely to generate the appropriate measures of Ψ and L needed to apply Table 1 to the videocassette industry. Further, this accounting data is not in general publicly available. Policy makers addressing the issue of video piracy may, by default, find it necessary to apply the above generalization concerning the gray market, as it is unlikely, even in the absence of consumer confusion,[50] that the practices termed "video piracy" will benefit consumers.

Alternatively, one might speculate that blockbuster movie successes are the subject of the most substantial fraction of unauthorized videocassette distribution. Because sales are so large for these products, the worldwide average advertising/sales ratio may be low, even if promotional expenses in film related products are higher than average. The market demand for videocassettes of blockbuster film successes is likely to be relatively inelastic ($-E_{fx}$ close to one), so that the $-E_{fx} Q/X$ term can be approximated by the authorized firm's worldwide average market share. If that share is in the broad range of 50% to 100%, Table 1 suggests that the critical value of L is likely in the 40% to 50% range. Under these assumptions, the sales price must exceed 1.6 to 2.0 times marginal cost before incremental policy shifts *in favor of the gray market benefit consumers.* However, marginal cost,

---

[49] Such spillovers may be large. They undoubtedly contribute to the success of video pirates in distributing unauthorized videocassettes in some countries before the authorized product is released there either in theaters or as cassettes.

[50] As the MPAA does not emphasize consumer confusion in its extensive publicity effort concerning video piracy, it is likely that this is no more than a second order concern in the video industry, so is not emphasized here.

measured correctly, includes the risk that new films are box office failures. If one in ten films is a blockbuster success, the sales price for an authorized videocassette must exceed 16 to 20 times the incremental costs directly related to that film before it is sufficiently high as to make a gray market benefit consumers on the margin. As it is unlikely that actual markups are this high, this back-of-the-envelope calculation suggests that video piracy is unlikely to benefit consumers.

In sum, an identical conclusion results from both the general presumption and the speculative application of the model to the videocassette industry: Video piracy likely harms consumers. Three approaches to solving the video piracy problem have been proposed by the film and television industry: raising penalties, devoting more resources to enforcement, and taxing blank videotape (to raise the cost of unauthorized taping).[51] If the demand for blank tape for uses other than the unauthorized taping of copyrighted videocassettes is large and elastic, taxing that product should be the last policy resort rather than the first, because such legislation could impose a substantial welfare loss on legitimate purchasers of the product. The first two proposals both work by increasing the expected penalty to unauthorized video product sellers; one raises the absolute penalty for those who are convicted, while the other raises the likelihood that a violator will be detected and convicted. Because of the difficulties identifying the source of unauthorized video products, and because it is easy for new individuals to enter the business of copying cassettes without permission, it is likely that public enforcement is more cost effective than private enforcement.[52]

---

[51] A higher price for videotape would create the same disincentive to unauthorized taping whether it is created by a tax, with revenues going to the government, or by awarding "royalties" to the film industry paid by blank tape purchasers. This difference in approach matters little to those who are concerned with consumer welfare, although it may have a substantial distributional effect on the film industry.

[52] This observation does not resolve whether the public or the film producers should pay for increased public enforcement, however.

The discussion in the text treats two alternative public policies toward the gray market: complete prohibition or free gray market trade. These alternatives exclude two intermediate public policies to differentiate gray market goods from authorized products—demarking and labeling—because these intermediate policies are not readily applicable to film products. As it is impossible to separate the physical film product from the identity of the authorized producer, neither demarking nor labeling will reduce free riding by unauthorized videocassette distributors.

These intermediate public policies likely have greater applicability to other gray market goods. Both demarking and labeling reduce consumer confusion and increase product variety (generating similar consumer welfare benefits as obtained from a price reduction). Further demarking, and to some extent labeling, reduces unauthorized distributor free riding. These intermediate remedies may be understood as resembling a requirement that authorized producers create private label versions of their brand name products.

(*continued*)

APPENDIX A. THE "LINEAR" MODEL

This Appendix defines the "linear" model, a set of largely linear approximations. These approximations allow various derivatives to be signed in the comparative statics exercise of Appendix B. The assumptions of the "linear" model should be thought of as plausible local approximations to the behavior of the functions at issue. The term "linear" is placed in quotes because some functions cannot be linearized without violating the second order conditions for an interior solution to the dominant firm's optimization problem.

The "linear" model makes three sets of assumptions.

Assumption A: All the second derivatives of the functions $F(X,A)$, $K(G)$, and $R(Q,A)$ equal zero, except that the two partial derivatives R_{aa} and F_{aa} are assumed negative.

Assumption A linearizes the model to the maximum extent consistent with the second order conditions. It has the following corollary:

Corollary A.1: $F_{aa}/F_a = R_{aa}/R_a$

Proof: Under the conditions of Assumption A, $R_a = -K_g F_a/(F_x - K_g)$. This is demonstrated as equation (A.8) of Appendix B. As K_g and F_x can be treated as constants under the conditions of Assumption A, equation (A.8) implies $R_{aa} = -K_g F_{aa}/(F_x - K_g)$. The corollary follows immediately.

Assumption B imposes a constant elasticity approximation on a parameter which cannot be approximated linearly.

Assumption B: The "elasticity" $R_{aa}A/R_a$ is a constant, denoted μ.

A corollary of Assumption B is employed in the later analysis.

Corollary B.1: $\mu = \Psi - 1$

Because the model of this chapter demonstrates that the consumer welfare losses from free riding generally dominate the consumer benefits of arbitrage, the demarking remedy, which most likely reduces free riding more than the labeling remedy, is probably the better of these two intermediate policies for across the board application. Further, it is possible that an intermediate policy would be superior to either of the extreme policies of gray market prohibition or free gray market trade. The United States Customs Service has been studying this question (Customs Service, Importations Bearing Recorded U.S. Trademarks; Solicitation of Public Comment on Gray Market Policy Options, 51 Fed. Reg. 22,005, 1986).

Proof: Assumption B implies that $R(Q,A)$ can be written in the form $R = \alpha(Q)A^{\mu+1}/(\mu+1)$. This equation implies that $R_a = (\mu+1)R/A$, and thus that $E_{ra} = \mu+1$. Yet first-order condition (9) requires that $E_{ra} = \Psi$.

Assumption C: $2R_qQR_{aa} - R_a^2 - 2R_qQK_gF_{aa}/(F_x - K_g) > 0$, or equivalently, $L > \Psi/4(1-\Psi)$

Comment: The equivalence depends upon Assumption A.

$2R_qQR_{aa} - R_a^2 - 2R_qQK_gF_{aa}/(F_x - K_g) > 0$
$<=> 2R_qQR_{aa} - R_a^2 + 2R_qQR_{aa} > 0$
    (applying the definition of R_{aa} in the proof of Corollary A.1 above)
$<=> R_qQ < R_a^2/4R_{aa}$
    (the inequality changes sign because $R_{aa} < 0$)
$<=> -L = R_qQ/R < (R_{aa}A/R)/4(R_{aa}A/R_a) = \Psi/4\mu = \Psi/4(\Psi - 1)$
$<=> L > \Psi/4(1-\Psi)$

Assumption C requires that the markup not be close to zero. For example, if $\Psi = .08$, a plausible number for a variety of consumer product industries, then the condition requires no more than that $L > .02$. If $\Psi = .25$, a large value sometimes found for branded products subject to gray markets, then $L > .08$. As is evident, this technical condition will be readily satisfied in the differentiated product industries, such as the sale of trademarked or copyrighted products, where gray markets can be found.

Corollary C.1: $2R_qQR_{aa} - (R_a)^2 > 0$

Comment: By an analysis similar to that in the Comment to Assumption C, this condition is equivalent to $L > \Psi/2(1-\Psi)$. This inequality is implied by Assumption C.

APPENDIX B. COMPARATIVE STATICS

This Appendix performs comparative statics on the first-order conditions to assess the likely signs of the model's derivatives. The model's four equations in four unknowns are totally differentiated. The block recursive structure of the model—the two first order conditions (6) and (7) determine Q and A, which then determine P (or equivalently R) and G using equations (2) and (3)—permits the differentiation of each subsystem of equations separately.

First, first order conditions (6) and (7) are differentiated with respect to the two variables they determine, Q and A, and with respect to the exogenous variable T creating the comparative static exercise. This procedure implicitly determines Q_t and A_t. The following equations are derived:

$$(2R_q + QR_{qq})dQ + (QR_{qa} + R_a)dA = - (QR_{Rqt} + R_t)dT \qquad (A.1)$$

$$(QR_{aq} + R_a) dQ + (QR_{aa}) \qquad dA = - (QR_{at})dT \qquad (A.2)$$

Next, the two equations (2) and (3) are differentiated with respect to the two variables they determine, R and G, and with respect to three variables predetermined from the point of view of this subsystem of equations: Q, A, and T. This determines R_t and G_t as functions of the previously derived Q_t and A_t. The following equations are generated:

$$dR + (- F_x)dG = (F_x dQ + F_a dA) \qquad (A.3)$$

$$dR + (- K_g)dG = dT \qquad (A.4)$$

The simultaneous equation system (A.3) and (A.4) implies the following expressions for dR and dG:

$$dR = [- K_g F_x dQ - K_g F_a dA + F_x dT]/(F_x - K_g) \qquad (A.5)$$

$$dG = [- F_x dQ - F_a dA + dT]/(F_x - K_g) \qquad (A.6)$$

Comparative Statics Independent of the "Linear" Model

The signs of the derivatives of R have particular interest. They can be determined for the general model, without imposing the linearity restrictions. Under the assumptions made in the text ($F_x < 0$, $F_a > 0$, and $K_g > 0$), equation (A.5) implies:

$$R_q = - K_g F_x/(F_x - K_g) < 0, \qquad (A.7)$$

$$R_a = - K_g F_a/(F_x - K_g) > 0, \text{ and} \qquad (A.8)$$

$$R_t = F_x/(F_x - K_g) > 0. \qquad (A.9)$$

Equation (A.7) implies that the sign of R_{qq} is identical to the sign of F_{xx}. This is evident from Lemma 1:

Lemma 1: $R_{qq} = [- K_g F_{xx}(F_x - K_g) + K_g F_x F_{xx}]/(F_x - K_g)^2$
$= (K_g)^2 F_{xx}/(F_x - K_g)^2$

Similarly, equation (A.6) implies:

$$G_q = -F_x/(F_x - K_g) < 0, \tag{A.10}$$

$$G_a = -F_a/(F_x - K_g) > 0, \text{ and} \tag{A.11}$$

$$G_t = 1/(F_x - K_g) < 0. \tag{A.12}$$

Comparative Statics For the "Linear" Model

Equations (A.1) and (A.2) are simplified further under the assumptions of the "linear" model of Appendix A, so that comparative statics can be performed. One additional lemma is required.

Lemma 2: Under the "linear" model,
$R_{qt} = 0$ and $R_{at} = -K_g F_{aa} A_t/(F_x - K_g)$.

Sketch of Proof: Differentiating R_a (equation A.8) with respect to T (recognizing that G, A and Q are functions of T), and applying the assumptions of the "linear" model yields this expression for R_{at}.

With the simplifications implied by the "linear" model and the above lemma, equations (A.1) and (A.2) can be written as:

$$(2R_q)dQ + (R_a) dA = -(R_t) dT \tag{A.1'}$$

$$(R_a) dQ + (QR_{aa})dA = (QK_g F_{aa} A_t/(F_x - K_g))dT \tag{A.2'}$$

This system of equations implies the following expressions for Q_t and A_t:

$$dA/dT = A_t = [2R_q QK_g F_{aa} A_t/(F_x - K_g) + R_a R_t]/D \tag{A.13}$$

$$dQ/dT = Q_t = -[QR_{aa} R_t + R_a QK_g F_{aa} A_t/(F_x - K_g)]/D \tag{A.14}$$

$$\text{where } D = 2R_q QR_{aa} - (R_a)^2$$

Rearranging equation (A.13) to group together the A_t terms leads to equation (A.13').

$$A_t = R_a R_t/[D - 2R_q QK_g F_{aa}/(F_x - K_g)] \tag{A.13'}$$

$$= R_a R_t/[D + 2R_q QR_{aa}]$$

$$= R_a R_t/[4R_q QR_{aa} - (R_a)^2]$$

The second line of this equation results from employing the definition $R_{aa} = -K_g F_{aa}/(F_x - K_g)$ in the proof of Corollary A.1. Because $R_a > 0$, $R_t > 0$, $R_q < 0$, $R_{aa} < 0$, and, by Assumption C, the denominator in (A.13') is positive, $A_t > 0$.

The expression Q_t in equation (A.14) may be simplified further by employing the formula for A_t from equation (A.13').

$$Q_t = [-QR_{aa}R_t + R_aQR_{aa}A_t]/D = R_{aa}Q[R_aA_t - R_t]/D \qquad (A.14')$$

$$= (R_{aa}Q/2R_qQR_{aa} - R_a^2)[(R_a^2R_t/(4R_qQR_{aa} - R_a^2)) - R_t]$$

$$= -(2R_{aa}QR_t/(4R_qQR_{aa} - R_a^2)) > 0$$

This expression is positive because the denominator is positive by Assumption C.

Equations (A.13') and (A.14') are identical to equations (16) and (17) of the text.

Comparative Statics Summary for the "Linear" Model

This comparative statics discussion for the "linear" model may be summarized in the following way:

positive signs: R_a, R_t, G_a, Q_t, and A_t

negative signs: R_q, G_q, and G_t.

APPENDIX C.
CONSUMER WELFARE IN THE "LINEAR" MODEL

This Appendix proves Proposition 2 and Proposition 3.

Proposition 2: In the "linear" model, without consumer confusion, a policy hindering the gray market on the margin improves consumer welfare if $[\Psi(2+\lambda)/4(1-\Psi)] > L$, and reduces consumer welfare if $[\Psi[2+\lambda)/4(1-\Psi)] < L$.

Proof: The proof of this proposition proceeds by signing dCS/dT. As indicated in equation (19), dCS/dT has the following form:

$$dCS/dT = S(X,A)_aA_t - XR_t$$

This equation is simplified through several steps.

1. Simplification of S_a

$S(Z,A) = S(X,A) = \int F(X,A)dX$. Hence $S_a = \int F_adX$. In the "linear" model, $F_{ax} = 0$, so F_a does not vary with X. Thus $S(X,A)_a = F(X,A)_aX$.

From equation (A.8), $F_a = -R_a(F_x - K_g)/K_g = R_a(1 + \lambda)$, where $\lambda = -F_x/K_g > 0$. Note that equations (A.7) and (A.8) imply alternative representations for $(1 + \lambda)$ consistent with the definition of λ in the text: $(1 + \lambda) = E_{fa}/E_{ra} = F_x/R_q = -E_{fx}Q/LX > 1$.

2. Simplification of A_t

Equation (A.14$'$) shows that $A_t = R_a R_t/[4R_q QR_{aa} - (R_a)^2]$

3. Revised Expression for dCS/dT

Substituting these expressions in dCS/dT implies:

$$dCS/dT = R_a^2 R_t X(1 + \lambda)/[4R_q QR_{aa} - (R_a)^2] - XR_t$$
$$= [R_a^2(1 + \lambda)/[4R_q QR_{aa} - (R_a)^2] - 1]XR_t$$

4. Sign of dCS/dT

The expression for dCS/dT has the same sign as $[R_a^2(1 + \lambda)/[4R_q QR_{aa} - (R_a)^2] - 1]$, because $R_t > 0$. Note that $[4R_q QR_{aa} - (R_a)^2] > 0$ by virtue of Assumption C of the "linear" model.

Hence, $dCS/dT > 0 <=>$

$R_a^2(1 + \lambda)/[4R_q QR_{aa} - (R_a)^2] > 1$

$<=> R_a^2(1 + \lambda) > [4R_q QR_{aa} - (R_a)^2]$

$<=> R_a^2(2 + \lambda) > 4R_q QR_{aa}$.

$<=> (R_a A/R)(2 + \lambda) > 4(R_q Q/R)(R_{aa} A/R_a)$

$<=> y(2 + \lambda) > 4(-L)(\Psi - 1) = 4L(1 - \Psi)$

$<=> L < \Psi(2 + \lambda)/4(1 - \Psi)$

These simplifications rely upon equations (8) and (9) and Assumption B of the "linear" model.

Similarly, $dCS/dT < 0 <=> L > \Psi(2 + \lambda)/4(1 - \Psi)$.

Corollary: The following condition is sufficient for $dCS/dT > 0$:

$L < \Psi/2(1 - \Psi)$.

The Corollary follows from $\lambda > 0$.

* * * * * * * * * * *

Proposition 3: In the "linear" model, without consumer confusion, $dCS/dT > 0$ if and only if $L < L^*$, where $L^* = \Psi/8(1 - \Psi) + [\Psi^2 - 16(1 - \Psi)E_{fx}Q/X]^{1/2}/8(1 - \Psi)$.

Proof: From the proof of Proposition 2, $dCS/dT > 0$ if and only if:

$L < \Psi(2+\lambda)/4(1-\Psi)$, where $(1+\lambda) = -E_{fx}Q/LX$

Hence, $dCS/dT > 0 <=>$

$L4(1-\Psi) < \Psi(1 + [-E_{fx}\ Q/LX])$

$<=> L^2 4(1-\Psi) < \Psi(L - E_{fx}Q/X)$

$<=> L^2 4(1-\Psi) - \Psi L + \Psi E_{fx}Q/X < 0$

The critical L^* such that $L^2 4(1-\Psi) - \Psi L - \Psi E_{fx}Q/X = 0$ can be derived (for $\Psi > 0$) by solving this quadratic equation:

$L^* = \Psi/8(1-\Psi) + [\Psi^2 - 16(1-\Psi)E_{fx}Q/X]^{1/2}/8(1-\Psi)$

The negative root is rejected because it would make the critical L negative.

The function $g(L) = [L^2 4(1-\Psi) - \Psi L + \Psi E_{fx}Q/X]$ is upward sloping in L for $L > \Psi/8(1-\Psi)$, because $g'(L) - 8(1-\Psi)L - \Psi > 0$. Hence $g(L) > 0$ (and thus $dCS/dT > 0$) if and only if $L < L^*$.

*   *   *   *   *   *   *   *   *   *   *

APPENDIX D. PRODUCER WELFARE

If producers' surplus is zero, the total social surplus is captured completely by the consumers' surplus. This can occur if the three following conditions are simultaneously satisfied. First, a zero-profits free-entry equilibrium must characterize the branded product of interest. Then the typical authorized distributor will earn no economic profit. Second, authorized firms must have roughly constant marginal costs, as is assumed by the present model. Third, the fringe's marginal cost curve must rise because the gray market sector finds it necessary to bid up the foreign wholesale price of imports in order to increase sales. Then each gray market distributor will have constant marginal costs in the equilibrium. Under these conditions, no firm earns any rents to fixed factors of production, so producer welfare can be ignored in the social welfare calculation.

This Appendix analyzes the effect of policies changing gray market costs on producers' surplus under two alternative plausible assumptions that make producers' surplus non-zero. First, the analysis below allows the authorized distributor to earn economic profits. This assumption takes seriously the possibility of entry barriers into branded product industries. Second, the analysis presumes that fringe marginal cost rises because gray market importers find it increasingly costly to locate product overseas as the quantity they wish to import rises. Then marginal cost rises for each gray market distributor whenever it rises for the gray market sector.

This Appendix shows that, under these assumptions, the effect of policies concerning the gray market on domestic producer welfare is crucially dependent on the slope of the fringe supply curve (K_g). In particular, when fringe marginal cost is steeply sloping and the gray market sector is large, policies harming the gray market in the margin will reduce producers' surplus because that surplus will accrue largely to the gray market sector. Conversely, if fringe marginal cost is flat, the effect of the gray market on aggregate producers' surplus is dominated by its effect on the authorized production sector, so a policy hindering the gray market improves aggregate producer welfare.

Aggregate domestic producers' surplus (PS) can be written in the following form:

$$PS = \Gamma_1[(R(Q,A) - C)Q - A] + \Gamma_2 \int_0^G [R(Q,A) - (T + K(G))]dG + \Gamma_3 MG \quad (A.15)$$

where $\Gamma_i \in [0,1]$

The first component of aggregate domestic producers' surplus is the profits of the authorized domestic seller. Because marginal cost is assumed constant, firm profits are identical to the total surplus accruing to this firm. These profits are weighted by Γ_1, representing the fraction of the authorized firm owned by domestic entities. This adjustment is required in order to exclude the surplus accruing to foreign countries.[53]

The second component of aggregate domestic producers' surplus is the producers' surplus accruing to the domestic gray market sector, weighted by Γ_2, the share of that sector owned by domestic entities. The final component of the aggregate surplus is the producers' surplus accruing to the foreign source of the gray market imports. This surplus is assumed to equal the profits of that sector, defined by a fixed markup M of price over (constant) foreign marginal cost times the number of imports G. These profits are weighted by Γ_3, representing the domestic fraction of the ownership of the source of the gray market imports.[54]

In the model, the authorized sellers' marginal costs are constant and no costs are fixed. This assumes away another possible effect of the gray market on producer welfare. If the gray market sector is large, the authorized seller may be forced to operate at an inefficiently small scale, raising the social costs of production. However, this social cost may to some extent be offset if gray market distributors are able to achieve scale economies of their own.

---

[53] It may not be easy to determine the location of the firm's shareholders. For example, if a company has substantial institutional ownership, as by pension funds and mutual funds, one could take the view that those entities have legal personality in their country of incorporation. Alternatively one could identify the locations of an institution's ownership with the domiciles of its shareholders.

[54] To the extent that authorized film and television distributors are owned by U.S. citizens, whatever producers' surplus exists in this industry may be greatest in the United States.

The effect of a marginal change in policy on aggregate domestic producers' surplus can be derived from differentiating equation (A.15), assuming the restrictions on second derivatives of the "linear" model.

$$dPS/dT = \Gamma_1[(R(Q,A) - C)Q_t + R_tQ - A_t] \qquad (A.16)$$
$$+ \Gamma_2[(R_t - 1)G + (R(Q,A) - T - K(G))G_t] + \Gamma_3MG_t$$
$$= \Gamma_1[(R(Q,A) - C)Q_t + R_tQ - A] + \Gamma_2(R_t - 1)G + \Gamma_3MG_t$$

Equation (A.16) was simplified by applying equation (3), which presumes that the gray market fringe acts competitively to equate price with marginal cost.

The first term in this expression represents the change in the authorized firm's producers' surplus resulting from an exogenous increase in fringe costs. This term is likely to be positive. If A_t is a large negative number, however, a policy raising gray market marginal costs may reduce authorized firm profits by placing the authorized firm in a new environment in which its optimal decision involves a substantial increase in advertising. The second term reflects the reduction in producers' surplus of the gray market distributors resulting from an exogenous increase in their costs.[55] The final term indicates the reduction in profits of the foreign supplier of gray market profits resulting from an increase in domestic gray market distribution costs.

The further analysis of producers' surplus specializes to what will be termed the "benchmark" ownership case. This case presumes that gray market goods are purchased by the gray market distribution sector from a firm wholly owned by foreigners, while both the authorized and gray market distributors are completely owned by domestic citizens. These assumptions will represent the gray market in video products well in at least two cases. First, the gray market sellers may import their product from abroad. Second, the gray market sellers may undertake most of their own "production" in the form of cassette copying, so there is in effect no source for the product.

By the assumptions of the benchmark case, $\Gamma_1 = \Gamma_2 = 1$, and $\Gamma_3 = 0$. Hence, equation (A.16) becomes:

$$dPS/dT = [(R(Q,A) - C)Q_t + R_tQ - A_t] + (P_t - 1)G \qquad (A.17)$$
$$= R_tX + (R(Q,A) - C)Q_t - G - A_t$$

In addition to the benchmark ownership assumptions, the welfare calculation of Proposition 4 assumes that $L = L^*$, that is, that the markup is such that a policy maker concerned solely with consumers' surplus will be indifferent between a marginal increase in gray market costs and a marginal decrease. This assumption guarantees that the change in producers' surplus

---

[55] The expression $R_t - 1$ will be negative so long as $K_g > 0$.

will dominate the change in consumers' surplus, and thus creates a situation where welfare analysis properly focuses on the effect of the gray market on producers' surplus.

Proposition 4: For the "benchmark" ownership case, and the "linear" model, assume that a marginal change in the policy parameter T has no effect on consumer welfare ($dCS/dT = 0$). Then $dPS/dT > 0$ if and only if $F_x/(F_x - K_g) > G/X - A_t\lambda/X$, and $dPS/dT < 0$ if $F_x/(F_x - K_g) < G/X$.

Note that the terms $F_x/(F_x - K_g)$ and G/X both fall in the open interval between zero and one.

Proof:
$$dPS/dT = R_tX + (R(Q,A) - C)Q_t - G - A_t$$
$$= R_tX - G + [-2(R - C)R_{aa}QR_t - R_aR_t]/(4R_qQR_{aa} - R_a^2)$$
(for the "linear" model)
$$= R_tX - G + R_tR_a[2L(1 - \Psi)/\Psi - 1]/(4R_qQR_{aa} - R_a^2)$$

By assumption $dCS/dT = 0$, so, for the "linear" model, when $\lambda = 0$, $L = \Psi(2 + \lambda)/4(1 - \Psi)$. Thus,

$$dPS/dT = R_tX - G + R_tR_a(\lambda/2)/(4R_qQR_{aa} - R_a^2)$$
$$= F_xX/(F_x - K_g) - G + A_t(\lambda/2)$$
(by equation (A.9))

Thus, $dPS/dT > 0 <=> F_x/(F_x - K_g) > G/X + A_t\lambda/2X$

Because $A_t\lambda/2X > 0$, $dPS/dT < 0$ if $F_x/(F_x - K_g) < G/X$.

*   *   *   *   *   *   *   *   *   *   *

The significance of Proposition 4 is suggested by its corollary.

Corollary: If fringe marginal cost is steeply sloping (K_g large) and gray market sellers' market share is large (G/X near one) then, under the conditions of Proposition 4, $dPS/dT < 0$. Conversely, if fringe marginal cost is nearly flat (K_g large) then, under the conditions of Proposition 4, $dPS/dT > 0$ unless gray market sellers' market share is large (G/X near one).

The intuition behind this corollary is that a small increase in the marginal costs of gray market distribution will lead to a large decrease in net producers' surplus if it lowers substantially the surplus accruing to the gray market sector. This will occur when the fringe supply curve is steeply sloping, so that earlier gray market sales were lower costs than later sales, and when there are many such earlier sales.[56] On the other hand, if fringe marginal cost is flat, the gray market sector earns little surplus, because marginal cost pricing generates little rent for the early gray market imports. Hence a policy harming the gray market on the margin does not affect the surplus of the unauthorized production sector, although it reduces the surplus of the authorized production sector. As the authorized distribution sector loses profits, on balance, total producers' surplus declines.

APPENDIX E. CONSUMER CONFUSION

Consumers are "confused" by the gray market if they are unable to distinguish between authorized and unauthorized products at point of sale, yet would be willing to pay more for authorized goods.[57] In the videocassette context, consumer confusion could arise if consumers think that unauthorized cassettes are on average less likely to have high technical quality than the authorized goods, but cannot tell whether a cassette is authorized at point of sale.[58] Consumer confusion does not require physical quality differences; consumers may prefer the authorized product because it is sponsored by the manufacturer or because of other nonphysical attributes of the product image. The confusion question is often raised in discussions of gray market goods (see Hilke, 1987; Knoll, 1986; Miller, 1986). This Appendix shows how the model of this paper extends to the case of consumer confusion, and demonstrates the plausibility of the generally accepted view that consumers are harmed by confusion.

Consumer confusion creates an adverse selection problem (see generally, Akerlof, 1970; Wilson, 1978). This Appendix presumes a pooling equilibrium, where the authorized and gray market products sell for the same price. Con-

---

[56] In the "linear" model, $A_t = \Psi PL/K_g[4L(l - \Psi) - \Psi]$. With estimates of K_g and λ, further analysis of the sign of dPS/dT would be possible because the magnitude of the expression $A_t\lambda$ could then be assessed.

[57] Consumer confusion between gray market and authorized products, in the sense that two products valued differently sell at the same price, is not uncommon. For example, one reporter discovered gray market film, which may be substantially more likely to have been damaged in distribution than the authorized product, selling at the same price, side by side with the authorized good (Grundberg, 1987, p. 63). Similarly, although U.S. consumers preferred authorized Duracell batteries to the gray market product, the two goods sold at the same price because consumers were confused. *In re Certain Alkaline Batteries,* 225 U.S.P.Q. 823, 835 (1984); *remedy disapproved,* 225 U.S.P.Q. 862; *aff'd sub nom., Duracell Inc. v. U.S.I.T.C.,* 778 F.2d 1578 (Fed. Cir 1985).

[58] In Brazil, unauthorized videocassettes sell at a price 2/3 of authorized cassettes (Hoineff, 1986, p. 41). This anecdote suggests both that consumers are willing to pay more for authorized products and that consumer confusion may not arise in the sale of videocassettes, although it is far from conclusive evidence on either question.

sumers may know that the goods differ, but remain unable to distinguish them at time of purchase (although they may discover the truth at time of consumption).

If consumers prefer the authorized product, but cannot tell at point of sale which goods are gray market products, consumers will obtain the fraction Θ of the benefits of the authorized product from the gray market product, where $\Theta \in [0,1]$ (and small Θ reflects very costly confusion). In the limiting case where consumers are not confused, so buyers obtain equal value from a purchase of the gray market good as of the authorized good, Θ equals one. The model assumes that Θ is the same for all consumers, implicitly presuming that any buyer who values a unit of the authorized good highly also values a unit of the gray market product fairly highly.

This Appendix assumes that consumers treat the authorized and gray market products as identical at time of purchase. This assumption is most appropriate in two situations. First, it is appropriate when the authorized and gray market products are in fact identical. In this case Θ is near one. In addition, the assumption is appropriate when the authorized and gray market products are different, but when consumers are unaware at time of purchase that they are buying the gray market product (although they discover the truth at time of consumption). In the latter case, confusion is substantial, so Θ is low; the gray market seller free rides extensively on the reputation of the authorized seller. In either case the two goods will sell for the same price.

Under these assumptions, consumer welfare depends upon the benefits of purchases of "authorized good equivalents," where one unit of the gray market product equals the fraction Θ of a unit of the authorized product. These authorized good equivalents are denoted Z, where $Z = Q + \Theta G$. Consumer welfare CS is then written as equation (A.18).

$$CS = S(Z,A) - R(Q,A)X, \text{ where } S(Z,A) = \int_0^Z F(Z,A)dz \qquad (A.18)$$

In equation (A.18), the expression F(Z,A) represents the aggregate consumer benefit of domestic consumers' authorized good equivalents, measured as the area under the demand curve. CS is the consumers' surplus associated with buyer purchases of both products. When confusion disappears, so $Q = 1$ and $Z = X$, equation (A.18) reduces to equation (18), the definition of consumers' surplus in the text.

This Appendix section analyzes dCS/dT when consumer confusion is present, generalizing Proposition 3 to this case. From equation (A.18), the relation $S(Z,A)_z = F(Z,A)$ and the definitions of X and Z:

$$dCS/dT = [F(Z,A)(Q_t + \Theta G_t) - P(Q_t + G_t)] + S(Z,A)_a A_t - X R_t.$$

This expression is simplified using the definition (2), the implication of the "linear" model that $S(Z,A)_a = F(Z,A)_a Z$, and the relation $P_t = R(Q,A)_t$.

$$dCS/dT = Q_t[F(Z,A) - F(X,A)] + G_t[\Theta F(Z,A) - F(X,A)] \qquad (A.19)$$
$$+ F(Z,A)_a ZA_t - XR_t$$

Equation (A.19) adds consumer confusion to the free riding/arbitrage tradeoff raised in the gray market policy debate. The first two expressions, $Q_t[F(Z,A) - F(X,A)]$ and $G_t[\Theta F(Z,A) - F(X,A)]$, represent the effect of a policy changing gray market costs on the welfare losses from consumer confusion. When consumers increase their purchases of the authorized and gray market products, the consumer benefit from authorized and gray market purchases rises by $Q_t F(Z,A)$ and $G_t \Theta F(Z,A)$ respectively, while the costs of those purchases rise by $Q_t F(X,A)$ and $G_t F(X,A)$ respectively. These expressions differ only when $\Theta < 1$ (and thus when $Z < X$), namely when consumer confusion is present. Thus, these two terms measure the marginal change in the consumer welfare costs of consumer confusion.

The third and fourth expressions are similar to those analyzed previously in Proposition 1. The expression $F(Z,A)_a ZA_t$ represents the influence of a change in gray market policy on the welfare costs of gray market free riding on the authorized firm's reputational investment. The last expression, $-XP_t$, represents the beneficial effect of arbitrage on domestic prices.

Equation (A.19) is subject to further analysis under the consumptions of the "linear" model. Here the notation F refers to the function $F(X,A)$, with X as an argument; $\alpha = G/X$ is the market share of the gray market sector; and $(1 - \alpha) = Q/X$ is the market share of the authorized producer.

Proposition 5: For the "linear" model, when consumers may be confused, $dCS/dT > 0$ if and only if

$$\{2L(1 - \Theta)\alpha(1 - \Psi)(1 + \lambda) + (1 + \lambda)\Psi[(1 - \alpha) + \alpha\Theta]\}/[4L(1 - \Psi) - \Psi]$$
$$+ (1 - \Theta)(1 - \alpha)/[(1 + \lambda)L] > 1 + \Theta(1 - \Theta)$$

Proof: The following approximations are implied by the assumptions of the "linear" model:

$$F(Z,A) = F(X,A) + F(X,A)_x(Z - X) = F(X,A) - F(X,A)_x(1 - \Theta)G$$
$$F(Z,A)_a = F(X,A)_a$$

With these approximations, equation (A.19) becomes:

$$dCS/dT = -Q_t F_x(1 - \Theta)G + G_t[-(1 - \Theta)P - F_x(1 - \Theta)G] + F_a AZ_t - XR_t$$

Substituting in the expressions (A.13 ') and (A.14 '), the relationship $G_t = R_t/F_x$ from the "linear" model, the definition of Z, the relationship $F_a = R_a(1 + \lambda)$ derived from equations (A.7) and (A.8) and the definition of λ, and rearranging terms, implies:

$$[dCS/dT][1/R_t] =$$
$$\{2F_x(1 - \Theta)GR_{aa}Q + (1 + \lambda)[Q + \Theta G]R_a^2\}/(4R_q QR_{aa} - R_a^2)$$
$$- (1 - \Theta)[P + \Theta F_x G]/F_x - X$$

Further simplification comes from recognizing that $-E_{fx} = (1 + \lambda)$ XL/Q, and from applying equations (8) and (9) and Assumption B of the "linear" model. Thus:

$$[dCS/dT][1/XR_t] = \{2L(1 - \Theta)\alpha(1 - \Psi)(1 + \lambda) + (1 + \lambda)\Psi[(1 - \alpha) + \alpha\Theta]\}/[4L(1 - \Psi) - \Psi] + (1 - \Theta)(1 - \alpha)/[(1 + \lambda)L] - 1 - \Theta(1 - \Theta)$$

The condition in Proposition 5 now follows, as X and R are positive.

* * * * * * * * * * *

To analyze the condition in Proposition 5, note first that when $\Theta = 1$ so confusion disappears, the condition reduces to the following condition found in Proposition 2: $(1 + \lambda)\Psi/[4L(1 - \Psi) - \Psi] > 1$. Further analysis of the consumer confusion case is the subject of Proposition 6.

Proposition 6: For the "linear" model, consumer confusion makes the gray market more likely to harm consumers on the margin if and only if:

$$0 > \alpha(1 + \lambda)[\Psi - 2L(1 - \Psi)] + [\Psi L(1 - \Psi) - \Psi][\Theta\alpha - (1 - \alpha)/(1 + \lambda)L]$$

Proof:

When consumer confusion is assumed away, Proposition 2 implies that $dCS/dT < 0$ if and only if $\Psi(1 + \lambda) - [4L(1 - \Psi) - \Psi] > 0$.

When consumer confusion is present, Proposition 5 implies that $dCS/dT > 0$ if and only if $(1 + \lambda)\Psi - [4L(1 - \Psi) - \Psi] > (1 + \lambda)(1 - \Theta)\alpha[\Psi - 2L(1 - \Psi)] + [4L(1 - \Psi) - \Psi](1 - \Theta)[\Theta\alpha - (1 - \alpha)/(1 + \lambda)L]$

Proposition 6 follows directly.

* * * * * * * * * * *

To interpret the condition in Proposition 6, note that $(\Psi L(1 - \Psi) - \Psi) > 0$ by Assumption C of the "linear" model, and that $[\Psi - 2L(1 - \Psi)] < 0$ by Corollary C.1. When confusion is extensive, so that Θ is small, the primary determinant of whether the condition in Proposition 6 is satisfied will therefore be the gray market sector's market share, α. If this share is small, the condition in Proposition 6 will readily be met. In this case, consumer welfare will be improved by a policy harming the gray market, because that policy will reduce consumer confusion. If instead the gray market share is very large, a policy harming the gray market can increase consumer confusion and, in this limited respect, harm consumer welfare.

As a general rule, the condition in Proposition 6 will be satisfied for plausible parameter values. For example, suppose L equals 0.5, Ψ equals 0.3, and $\lambda = 1.0$. Further, assume that confusion is significant and fairly costly so Θ equals 0.5. Then the test condition is satisfied so long as $1.1 > 0.85$ α, which will always hold as α lies in the interval $[0,1]$.

REFERENCES

Akerlof, G. (1970). The market for lemons: Qualitative uncertainty and the market mechanism. *Quarterly Journal of Economics, 84,* 488–500.

Allen, J. (1980, December). Piracy, still a thriving business, costing millions in lost sales. *Merchandising.*

Baker, J., & Bresnahan, T. (1985, June). The gains from merger or collision in product differentiated industries. *Journal of Industrial Economics, 33,* 427–444.

Besas, P. (1986, March 19). MPEA tackles Latin pirates. *Variety,* p. 72.

Besas, P. (1987, February 18). Spanish homevidders claim piracy battle is ineffective; community vid draws fire. *Variety,* pp. 2, 151.

Bierbaum, T. (1986, March 19). MPAA claims progress in piracy fight. *Variety,* pp. 5, 92.

Burgess, J. (1987, March 29). DAT recorder sounds alarm for industry. *Washington Post,* p. H1.

Chad, N. (1987, March 1). NFL may have to scramble to stop end-around by satellite-dish entrepreneurs. *Washington Post,* p. C18.

Chilean vid distribution grow, but legit tapes too few to kill piracy. (1986, December 10). *Variety,* p. 43.

Cleaver, J. (1984, May 31). Technology, laws sinking plundering pirates. *Advertising Age,* p. 39.

Crasswell, R. (1979, January). *Trademarks, consumer information, and barriers to competition* (Policy Planning Issues Paper). Washington, DC: Federal Trade Commission.

Davis, B. (1987, April 16). Debate heats up over digital recorders as Congress weighs anti-taping measure. *Wall Street Journal,* p. 33.

Federal injunction bars Florida motels from cable-TV theft. (1986, February 26). *Variety,* p. 1.

Fisher, F., & McGowan, J. (1983, March). On the misuse of accounting rates of return to infer monopoly profits. *American Economic Review, 73,* 82–97.

Giron, M. (1986, October 22). Filipino video piracy virtually 100%. *Variety,* pp. 443, 446.

Goldberg, M. (1986, Summer). Imports under fire. *Rolling Stone,* p. 17.

Grossman, G., & Shapiro, C. (1986, August). *Counterfeit-product trade.* Princeton, NJ: Princeton University.

Grossman, G., & Shapiro, C. (forthcoming). Foreign counterfeiting of status goods. *Quarterly Journal of Economics.*

Groves, D. (1986a, March 5). Oz film, TV & homevid factions pushing for higher pirate fines. *Variety,* p. 41.

Groves, D. (1986b, May 7). OZ up for tougher antipiracy laws. *Variety*, pp. 374, 418.

Growth of piracy in Mideast has MPEA, prds. seeing red; new laws on local books help. (1986, May 7). *Variety*, pp. 487, 494.

Grundberg, A. (1987, February 1). Beware of aging gray-market film. *New York Times*, p. 63.

Guild, H. (1986, September 3). Cable systems lift AFN shows in German mkt. *Variety*, pp. 1, 44.

Higgins, R., & Rubin, P. (1986, October). Counterfeit goods. *Journal of Law and Economics*, pp. 211–230.

Hilke, J. (1987, February). *Free trading or free riding: An examination of the theories and available empirical evidence on gray market imports* (Working Paper No. 150). Washington, DC: Bureau of Economics, Federal Trade Commission.

Hoineff, N. (1986, November 26). Homevid pirates still holding 80% in 1986. *Variety*, p. 41.

How pirates are plundering the studios. (1983, February 21). *Business Week*, p. 81.

Keller, J.R.K. (1986, December 3). Two Icelandic vid execs target local pirate trade. *Variety*, p. 40.

Kindred, J. (1987, October 18). Life's tougher for Germany's video pirates. *Variety*, pp. 47, 65.

Knoll, M. (1986). Gray-market imports: Causes, consequences and responses. *Law & Policy in International Business, 18,* 172–173.

Landes, W., & Posner, R. (1981, March). Market power in antitrust cases. *Harvard Law Review, 94,* 937–996.

Lexecon Inc. (1986). The Economics of Gray-Market Imports.

Mankiw, N.G., & Whinston, M. (1986, Spring). Free entry and social inefficiency. *Rand Journal of Economics*, pp. 48–58.

Melanson, J. (1983, February 21). MPAA tries antipiracy revamp for regional and local emphasis. *Variety*, p. 45.

Mesce, D. (1987, March 24). Japanese digital recorders will offer quality copies. *Valley News*.

Miller, D. (1986). Restricting the gray market in trademarked goods: Per se legality. *Trademark Reporter, 76,* 375–377.

Nicolaidi, M. (1987, January 7). MPEA snoop sez NZ pirates abound. *Variety*, p. 130.

Nix, W. (1986). Buccaneers prey on the movie industry. *Security Management*, p. 35.

A no-win war in videocassettes. (1987, May 24). *Business Week*, p. 152.

Ogan, C. (1984, March). Media diversity and communications policy. *Telecommunications Policy*, p. 63.

On bluebeard's tapedeck. (1984, November 17). *The Economist*, p. 56.

Rosenfield, J. (1986, May 7). Fighting pirates where they live. *Variety*, p. 83.

Ruzicka,M. (1986, July 5). Europe fighting pirates who sell duplicates of rock music. *The Washington Post*.

Salop, S. (1979, May). Strategic entry deterrence. *American Economic Review*, pp. 440–449.

Schmalensee, R. (1978, Autumn). Entry deterrence in the ready-to-eat breakfast cereal industry. *Bell Journal of Economics*, pp. 305–327.

Shapiro, C. (1982, July). *Product differentiation and imperfect information: Policy perspectives* (Working Paper No. 70). Washington, DC: Bureau of Economics, Federal Trade Commission.

Spillman, S. (1984, November 12). Video piracy loss: $1 billion. *Advertising Age,* p. 105.

Stuart, J. (1986, October 29). Miffed antipiracy forum reports countries taking effective steps. *Variety,* pp. 5, 35.

Taping the pirates. (1986, April 12). *The Economist,* p. 71.

Telser, L. (1968, April). Some aspects of the economics of advertising. *Journal of Business,* pp. 77–84.

Valenti, back from orient, sez Japanese piracy is 'unbelievable'. (1987, October 22). *Variety,* p. 487.

Wentz, L. (1985, January 21). Pirate radio in Europe: Treason on high seas? *Advertising Age,* pp. 46, 48.

Wilson, C. (1978). The nature of equilibrium in markets with adverse selection. *Bell Journal of Economics.*

6

The Internationalization of the Television Program Market: Media Imperialism or International Division of Labor? The Case of the United Kingdom

Richard Collins

Internationalization of information markets is far from a new phenomenon. The communications industries we know as the mass media owe their existence to the economies of scale that different technologies of reproduction and distribution have brought to the marketing of information. To realize the potential economies of scale, markets must be extended in time or space, and preferably both.

Gutenberg's development of printing with movable type rapidly conjured into existence a European market for printed books stretching from Riga to Naples and beyond. But in recent years a pervasive alarm at the dissolution of national cultural and communication unities has taken television as its stimulus and "wall-to-wall Dallas" is now an accepted shorthand for the baleful results attributed to this process. Internationalization of television is nothing new, though a long-standing flow of television across national borders has been amplified by technological change. The "Coca-Cola" satellites "attacking our artistic and cultural integrity," as Jack Lang, the Minister of Culture of France put it (*Financial Times*, 1984) have been pre-echoed in the customary prominence in the prime time schedules of the

* The author wishes to acknowledge the assistance of Philip Hayward who prepared much of the statistical information presented here.

U.K. and other national television systems of imported programming. The British Broadcasting Corporation (BBC) used 35 Canadian television dramas in the mid-1950s in order to win back audiences it had lost to Independent Television (ITV), the newly introduced commerical channel and its 1984 screening of *The Thorn Birds* (a U.S. miniseries) was used by the Corporation to boost its ratings (the screening of the eighth and final episode achieved for the BBC its biggest audience in more than two years).

Within media and communication studies these processes of internationalization have been understood largely through the notion of media imperialism. Schiller's (1969) path-breaking *Mass Communications and American Empire* established an enormously influential paradigm that with few exceptions (see in particular, Lealand, 1984; Lee, 1980; Ravault, 1980, 1986) has provided the optic through which international flows of information have been understood by academics. Schiller's powerful thesis is hard to capture in a single citation, but its essence is contained herein:

> Free trade is the mechanism by which a powerful economy penetrates and dominates a weaker one, the "free flow of information," the designated objective incidentally of Unesco, is the channel through which life styles and value systems can be imposed on poor and vulnerable societies. (Schiller, 1969, pp. 8–9).

A distinctive feature of international information trade is its dual impact on the economic and cultural spheres. Thus if it could be established that economic welfare was maximized by a division of labor and international trade in television programs, this would not be sufficient to challenge the objections to such trade and specialization based on assessment of the cultural impact of consumption of foreign television.

The classical paradigm employed in trade theory is that of division of labor on the basis of comparative advantage (Schiller's argument is explicitly directed against this dominant paradigm). Aggregate welfare is maximized if producers A and B specialize in producing what each of them produces best, and trade with each other in order to secure supply of the whole range of products produced between them. The comparative advantage model is derived from just such trades in agricultural products in which static attributes of climate and soil fertility clearly promote specialization by producers in certain products and trade between them. The model is widely applied to trade in manufactured goods and services, but its application to secondary and tertiary production is often challenged on the grounds that the major factors of production required in these sectors are not static.

It has been established to the general satisfaction of the academic community that international flows in television program trades are unequal, dominated by exports from the United States and, some way behind, the

United Kingdom (Nordenstreng & Varis, 1974; Varis, 1985). I do endorse Chapman's (1987, p. 10) identification of the "overall paucity of what has been produced," but there seems to be no reason to doubt the preeminence of the world's two largest Anglophone states in the international program trade. From where does this preeminence derive? From a classic comparative advantage? What then are the factors exclusively or preeminently possessed by the U.K. and the U.S., and are they actually or potentially contestable by other producers? If so, under what conditions could their preeminence be successfully challenged?

Among the pertinent factors that contribute to the success of the U.S. and U.K. in the international trade in television programs are language (English is the most "internatinal" of world languages); the size and structure of domestic markets; the possession of a "critical mass" of creative personnel competent in acting, makeup, and videotape editing; an infrastructure of prop, set, and costume renters and makers; ready availability of financial services such as insurance; manufacturers of electronic and cinematographic equipment; and processing laboratories and electronic services such as video standard conversion and image manipulation. Some of these factors, such as language, could be defined as attributes of a classical comparative advantage; others, such as the availability of a pool of actors and efficient financial services, are probably better defined as competitive advantages. However, for most purposes such distinctions are more theological than real. In production centers such as New York, Los Angeles and London, factors required for production are present that to create elsewhere would require enormous and comprehensive investment.

Substantial investments have been applied in a variety of locations in order to establish national production industries. Such development policies often, but not necessarily, go hand in hand with import controls through mechanisms such as quotas. But the effect of quotas is to deny consumers foreign products that they would otherwise have consumed because of their superior price/performance characteristics relative to domestically produced products. Consumer interests are thus, at least in the short- and possibly in the long-term, subordinated to those of producers by a policy of import quotas. The economic rationale (and it is important to recognize that the economic rationale is not the only one) for such policies is that of establishing an infant industry which will, when mature, be able to compete internationally unprotected by subsidy, quota, or other protective measures, and make a return to investors whether directly, through taxation, or both. Such policies do not seem to have been particularly successful. Hoskins and McFadyen (1986) have described the operation of Canada's national television program promotion policy which principally consists of a subsidy of 49% of the costs of qualifying productions. They cite the judgment of the Government of Canada's Nielsen report (1986) that public support has "only a modest impact on income, tax revenue productivity and the balance of payments," and that "although the economic benefits may exist, they are unlikely to be as high as for other economic investments."

There are, then, two possible rationales for the subsidy policy: that there are positive externalities realized (i.e., noneconomic benefits); and protection of an infant industry which may, once up and running, be internationally competitive. However, the infant industry rationale is one that applies only to temporary subsidy. If long-term or permanent subsidy is maintained, it has to deliver positive externalities, the social or cultural benefits that would not otherwise be enjoyed, to justify subsidy.

In Canada, mobile capital does not seem to have been attracted to the putatively infant industry, which suggests the Nielsen judgement that returns are unlikely to be as high in television production as in other economic investments was justified. The positive externalities remain as the justification for state subsidy of television production in Canada, and here we suggest the case and experience of Canada is representative of other nations. It is important to make clear that the high profitability of Canadian broadcasters does not contradict this argument. These profits come from the sale of advertising time and not from program production and sale.

The lack of success in establishing competitive suppliers of television programming outside the United Kingdom and United States can be explained in a variety of ways. The U.S. and U.K. markets are the world's largest Anglophone markets, and each are resistant to penetration by imported television programs, in the United Kingdom that is because of regulation, and in the United States because of the perception of audiences by broadcasters and advertisers as uninterested in foreign programs. United States and United Kingdom producers are therefore able to recoup much if not all of their production costs in their home markets, and sell into foreign markets confident that however low the price secured from a program sale, the marginal cost of production (little more than the cost of an extra film print or videotape) will be amply exceeded. Nevertheless the rising cost of television programming is encouraging international coproductions to both spread costs and guarantee market access.

In economic terms, it is therefore a rational choice for broadcasters in importing countries to import at close to marginal cost foreign programming that enjoys acceptability with domestic audiences, rather than produce indigenous product. Since television programs are relatively imperishable and not exhausted in consumption, consumers around the world are potentially able to benefit from the low marginal cost of production of television programs and enjoy cheap high-budget product from existing dominant producers.

The United States and United Kingdom, though dominant, are not omnipotent; there are important niches in the international market where they have either no presence or a weak presence. Japan has been able to sucessfully occupy one such niche by producing computerized animations (mostly for children), and others exist. (A BBC source stated that there is a world undersupply of live action location-based dramas for children.) There is also a demand for programming in languages other than English that cannot be met by Anglophone producers, even in dubbed or subtitled form, that reflects the experience of regions and cultures other than those surrounding the North Atlantic. Mexico, for example, has been able to establish itself as an important regional and Spanish language producer in spite of its proximity to the United States.

Although aggregate economic welfare may be maximized by a trade regime that permits economies of scope and scale to be realized, and the average price of program products more and more closely approximate to marginal cost as markets are extended, the distribution of the maximized welfare may be profoundly unequal. If, for example, world television production were to be concentrated in New York or even in a variety of locations, it is quite possible for program supply to be circulated internationally at very low cost, but the benefits of such a regime to be preeminently experienced in New York. Jobs, revenue, and tax-generating power would tend to be decanted from the rest of the world into New York, and unless the other world locations from which television production had been decanted were able to specialize in the production of other products which could be successfully traded on "equal" terms of trade with New York, they would be disadvantaged and impoverished. (This is a calculus that is almost impossible to perform.) In theory, again assuming that economic criteria are the only relevant ones, everyone would be better off if, say, Canadians produced wheat and hydroelectricity, Jamaicans bananas, Brazilians coffee, and New Yorkers television, and then traded these products freely between themselves. But few producers would voluntarily stake their existence on a single product and the successful maintenance of international free trade, and there are significant intervening political and cultural variables that make such a regime supply fantastic.

I turn now to these variables that are as significant structuring features of the international trade in television programs as the economic factors considered above.

A particularly strong imperative that militates against the international organization of television production on a basis of comparative advantage and free trade is concern among non-Anglophones for the survival of their languages. This concern is particularly marked among, though not peculiar to, Francophones. A major initiative, La Francophonie, was launched by the Mitterand socialist government to consolidate the French language community around the world, although within the French language community there are complaints from the smaller nations that France has created a less than perfectly competitive regime. Quebecois television producers are unable to establish a dubbing industry in Montreal because it is only programs dubbed in France that are acceptable to French quota administrators. And the African film *Sarraounia* experienced curtailed exhibition in France for its allegedly anti-French qualities. But survival of national languages is a powerful reason adduced by governments for promoting (via subsidy, tax breaks, public sector institutions) indigenous production and restricting consumption of programs in other languages.

Finally there are cultural, moral, and religious criteria exercised for the promotion of indigenous production and restriction of consumption of foreign programs.

The cultural, moral, and religious alarm at the consumption of international television programming is a conservative alarm based on the assumption that the national cultural, religious, and moral order prior to exposure to nonnational television programming was superior and any change is for the worse. It seems very unlikely that the effect of foreign television will invariably be either negative or positive. At the macro level, maintenance of national political sovereignty and national identity is becoming increasingly precarious as the unities of economic and cultural production and consumption become increasingly transnational. It is an open question whether the reharmonization of political, economic, and cultural institutions (if to be sought at all) should be performed by a more insistent nationalization of the economic and cultural realms, or by an internationalization of the political. At the micro level there are very many cases in which the freedom, welfare, and contentment of individuals is sustained and extended by the contestation of the autority and hegemony of the nation-state and the national culture.

The threat to communications sovereignty latent since the beginning of the 20th century and slowly actualized in North America (Canadian subordination to U.S. broadcasting remains the classic, even though earliest, instance) has, with the triple impact of new distribution technologies, new ideologies of deregulation, and the accelerating demand for quantities of high-budget but low-cast software, become a matter of general concern. In Western Europe, national governments have lost confidence in their ability to maintain communications sovereignty buttressed by national newspaper and publishing industries and state control of broadcasting. Italy's experience, following the Tele-Biella judgement, of the national broadcasting monopoly's vanishing access to the Italian people in favor of unregulated private broadcasters distributing largely U.S. programming, is exemplary. Moreover, the critique of the loss of communications sovereignty customarily runs in harness with a qualitative judgment that the new order and its product is inferior to the old. The concept of cultural imperialism or media imperialism is dependent on qualitative and quantitative judgements. The conditions of quantitative subordination are economic and organizational, while the conditions of qualitative subordination are cultural and aesthetic.

It is an enduring European characteristic to hold up a mirror to U.S. chauvinism. In the United Kingdom, critical concern focuses on the proliferation of U.S.-style hamburger outlets, not on the proliferation of Turkish, Greek, and Lebanese kebab houses, or French, Italian, Indian, and Chinese restaurants. The productivity of U.S. cultural influences are very quickly forgotten; for example, the appropriation of its practices by modernist artists such as Brecht and Grosz, or the impact of Hollywood cinema on the Nouvelle Vague, the New German Cinema, and on Italian film-makers like Sergio Leone or, as has recently been claimed, Gianni Amelio.

The shift in film and television production (though as indicated above, a shift that is far from total) from an artisan mode of production where products are strongly marked by an authorial signature, whether of director or scriptwriter, to series production in which it hardly makes sense to ask who is the author of *Dallas* or *Coronation Street,* is customarily deplored as a particularly insidious form of cultural imperialism. Yet this seems no more cultural imperialism than the adoption in Britain of the electrical engineering manufacturing techniques of Halske and Siemens, Pascalian mathematics, or the astronomical theories of Copernicus and Galileo. U.S. television series production techniques have dominated television in Britain since the 1960s, coexisting with, and some would claim making possible, British television's substantial dominance of the U.K. audience ratings.

It is in this complex ensemble of political, cultural, and economic forces that the international trade in television programs is caught. None of the forces in play operate singly. The low marginal cost of production of television program products will tend to call into existence markets that are widely extended in time and space. Political and cultural forces for the preservation of national language and culture will tend to inhibit these kinds of extension. This ensemble of forces has been imperfectly understood largely in terms of two contradictory paradigms, those of media imperialism and of the international division of labor on the basis of comparative advantage. Neither paradigm is adequate; the comparative advantage paradigm is questionable in its economic analysis and for its neglect of political, linguistic, and cultural criteria. The media imperialism paradigm fails to recognize that imported programs may be important sources of diversity and quality in television program schedules, and is flawed in its thesis that "most countries are passive recipients of information" (Varis, 1984, p. 152). This contention is hard to reconcile with the evidence of Katz and Liebes (1985) that different national and ethnic groups make highly differentiated use of that quintessentially international program, *Dallas.*

Ravault (1980) has pointed out how imperfect are the linkages between cultural production and consumption, and trade, and other political economic forces. Ravault contrasts U.S. and U.K. success in international media markets with the decline in their political, economic, and military power, and observes that West Germany—among other states—successfully reconciles importation of information goods with increased power in other arenas.

The U.K.'s place in these processes is contradictory and little understood. The transnational cultural and economic unity that U.K. information producers have customarily inhabited is that of the international Anglophone (predominantly North Atlantic) community. But since the U.K.'s accession to the European Economic Community, the *political* unity it inhabits is increasingly European: a unity that is now (Commission of the European Communities, 1984) attempting to Europeanize the cultural and economic activities of the U.K. (and other member states) in the information sector. In a plethora of instances the UK is having to choose Atlantic or European solutions.

Although the empirical studies of Nordenstreng and Varis (1974) and Varis (1985) concluded "that there were two indisputable trends: (1) a one-way traffic from the big exporting countries to the rest of the world and (2) a predominance of entertainment material in the flow" (Varis, 1985, p. 53), Varis further recognized that there is considerable variety in the extent to which these trends were experienced:

> In all parts of the world there are countries which are heavily dependent on foreign imports in their programming but also countries with relatively low figures for imported material. (Varis, 1985, p. 53)

This is confirmed by Paterson, who observes of Brazil:

> The development of an indigenous television puts into question Schiller's thesis about the inevitability of traditional drama and folk music retreating before the likes of *Peyton Place* and *Bonanza*. (Paterson, 1982, p. 2)

There is, then, no stable interpretative paradigm available which can act as an initial guiding hypothesis. The evidence of international television program trades can only with selective appropriation be made to fit available paradigms of media imperialism or division of labor on the basis of comparative advantage. My view is that what relations exist are highly context-dependent and that market structures, rapidly changing in an international broadcasting order where new technologies and ideologies are exercising their power, are the most important determinants of international information flows.

The U.K. television program production industry has reached a stable modus vivendi with other forces in the international market place. This could not have been anticipated given the vulnerability of U.K. film producers to competition from the United States. The factors that give the U.S. movie majors dominance remain: a shared language, U.S. economic power and ability to amortize high production costs in the domestic market, and the fundamental *attractiveness* of U.S. product to audiences. The vertical integration of producers and distributors in television, the successful imposition of quota restrictions on imports, the limitation of distribution capacity (all functions of state regulation) have enforced a different regime in television. Finally, these conditions of existence for television program production in the U.K. are all changing as national communication sovereignty declines. Changes in the market structure of U.K. trade partners, notably the United States, mean that their producers are also vulnerable to competition in the new television order. The decline in advertising revenues and network audience share in the United States create conditions more favorable to import penetration and less favorable to high-budget domestic production than before.

BRITISH PROGRAM TRADES

The Organization for Economic Cooperation and Development (OECD) estimates that the volume of audio-visual production in OECD member states is about $26 billion, of which almost half is earned by United States firms. Of this total, no more than $1 billion is traded internationally, and of that, $400 million is television programs and videofilms. In 1980, $350 million of trade in telefilms emanated from the United States, with the United Kingdom the second biggest exporter, exporting $22 million in telefilms (OECD, 1986, pp. 23, 25).

However the Department of Trade & Industry (DTI) publication, *British Business,* states the overseas receipts of the BBC and ITV program contractors in 1980 to be £50 million (*British Business,* 1986, p. 42). Though to compare the DTI and OECD figures is not to compare precisely like with like, for the DTI figures embrace world trades denominated in sterling and the OECD only OECD trades in U.S. dollars; there is an uncomfortably large discrepancy between them, a discrepancy symptomatic of the uncertainty of the data available on these trades and the tradeable information sector generally. But though it is difficult to establish the volume of trades authoritatively, there is no reason to doubt the OECD's definition of U.S. domination of international markets and the United Kingdom's second place.

In a survey of services in the U.K. economy (Services in the UK Company, 1985, pp. 404–414), the Bank of England comments:

Earnings from film and television amounted to 2.8% of exports and 3.5% of imports of financial and "other" services in 1984 and showed a surplus of £131m. Real growth in this sector has been strong but somewhat erratic, in recent years. (p. 413)

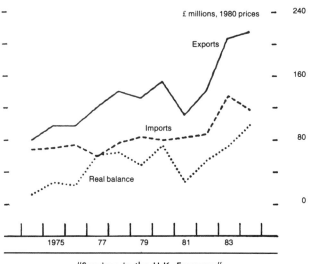

"Services in the U.K. Economy"
Source: *Bank of England Quarterly Bulletin*, 25(3), September, 1985, pp. 404–414.

Figure 6.1.   Films and Television: U.K. Service Earnings and Payments

The Bank displays the exports, imports and the real balance of trade. It is important to note that the *Bank of England Quarterly* does not disaggregate films and television. There are difficulties in doing so, as many programs produced and traded internationally for exhibition on television are recorded on film and may also be exhibited theatrically. Similarly, films may be distributed on videocassettes and be consumed through exhibition on a domestic television set whether the signal originates from a terrestial or satellite broadcast, cable, or a domestic videocassette recorder.

The last nine years (to 1986) were ones of increased volume of trade between the United Kingdom and the rest of the world in television programs. Both imports and exports of programs grew, though particularly in the last five years, imports tended to grow more rapidly than exports. In the period 1976–80 the average positive trade balance in television programs was 12 million pounds per year; since 1980 the positive balance of trade has declined. In 1985, a very strong positive balance of trade was reestablished (of £28m), but in 1986 this fell to £12m.

In the period 1968–76 receipts from the trade in television programs more than trebled, from £5m to £18m, and doubled, from £18m to £36m, between 1976 and 1977. Expenditure on overseas programming more than quadrupled between 1968 and 1976, from £4m to £18m, fell slightly in 1977, and then grew again at an increasing rate through the mid-1980s, falling off only briefly in 1985. Movements in the volume of trade are not regular either on a year-to-year basis or in terms of the geographical area in which the trading partner is located.

Table 1.   Transactions of the BBC and ITV Program Contractors, 1978/86: Analysis by Area *Receipts* **(millions of £)**

	EEC	Other W Europe	USA & CAN	Other Devlpd	Rest World	Total	USA & CAN Share	Balance of Trade (£M)*
1978	6	3	17	6	5	37	46%	15
1979	10	4	18	7	3	42	43%	14
1980	8	3	30	6	3	50	60%	19
1981	10	4	21	8	4	47	45%	10
1982	11	3	35	9	5	63	56%	8
1983	11	2	47	11	6	77	61%	8
1984	15	4	51	14	7	91	56%	1
1985	14	6	65	16	9	110	59%	28
1986	18	5	53	16	8	101	52%	12

* Receipts less expenditure

Figures taken from *British Business* dated 9-16-83, 10-5-84, 8-30-85–9-5-85, 9-19-86, 10-2-87. Other developed countries comprise Australia, New Zealand, Japan, and South Africa.

Table 2.   Transactions of the BBC and ITV Program Contractors: Analysis by Area (1978/86) *Expenditure* **(millions of £)**

	EEC	Other W Europe	USA & CAN	Other Devlpd World	Rest World	Total	USA & Canada Share
1978	4	2	12	1	3	22	55%
1979	6	2	15	1	4	28	54%
1980	5	4	18	1	3	31	58%
1981	11	2	19	1	4	37	51%
1982	9	4	36	1	5	55	65%
1983	12	4	47	1	5	69	68%
1984	16	3	64	2	5	90	71%
1985	13	4	56	4	5	82	68%
1986	15	5	57	5	7	89	64%

Figures taken from *British Business* dated 9-16-83, 10-5-84, 8-30-85–9-5-85, 9-19-86, 10-2-87. Other developed countries comprise: Australia, New Zealand, Japan, and South Africa.

However it is clear that North America, of which the United States is by far the most significant market component, is the most important single market, accounting for between 43% (1979) and 61% (1983) of the export market for British television programs, and between 43% (1977) and 71% (1984) of the imports of programming into the United Kingdom by value. The substantial improvement in the balance of trade in 1985 was principally due to increased receipts and decreased expenditure in North America. The shifting patterns of U.K. trade in television programs between 1978 and 1986 are shown in Tables 1 and 2.

BRITISH TELEVISION COMPANIES
AND FOREIGN COPRODUCTIONS

Direct program sales to overseas markets is not the only form of trading or production relationship between British television companies and overseas markets. There are a variety of coproductions concluded, either under coproduction treaties whereby the program or series produced counts as a domestic product in the home market of each coproduction partner, or in a less formal arrangement such as that between BBC's *Horizon* documentary program and the equivalent *Nova* series produced by WGBH in Boston for PBS in the United States. The arrangement is one in which the BBC and WGBH exchange a number of programs each year.

Co-producers' contributions to BBC program production are stated as follows:[1]

Year	1978/9	1979/80	1980/1	1981/2	1982/3	1983/4
	£5.5m	£2.9m	£2.7m	£4.6m	£4.6m	£5.9m

The production of Central TV's *Kennedy,* LWT's (London Weekend Television) *Dempsey and Makepeace* and Thames Television's *Reilly: Ace of Spies* were all done on the basis of a presale agreement with a U.S. client. *Reilly* had, for British television, a high production budget of £4.5m (11 episodes of 52 minutes, one of 75 minutes), or approximately £370,000 per program hour. This exceptional commitment, which required authorization by the main board of Thames Television, was made possible by a presale agreement with Mobil Oil of $100,000 per program hour. *Dempsey and Makepeace* was presold to the Chicago Tribune group for an estimated $100,000–200,000 per program hour (Stoddart, 1985, p. 38). An interview with Herb Schmerz (1985), the vice president of Mobil Oil responsible for Mobil's sponsorship of PBS television drama, established an average range of between $100,000 and $200,000 per program hour as the acquisition cost of "quality" television drama for exhibition on PBS.

The term "coproduction" describes a wide range of collaborative activities concerned with the finance and actual production of television material. Rarely do coproductions involve a fifty/fifty share of funding, production, and distribution responsibilities between partners on an equal basis. Most coproductions represent the collaboration of a project initiating company with a funding and/or facilities partner. In addition, the nature of such financial collaboration is such that there is increasingly a "blurring" between the boundaries of coproduction and presales activities.

---

[1] Source: *BBC Facts and Figures,* 1980–85, British Broadcasting Corporation, London, England.

Table 3. BBC Enterprises: Coproducers' Contributions
to Program Production/Foreign Program Sales
(Millions of £)

	Coproduction	Foreign Sales Contributions
78/79	5.5	7.6
79/80	2.9	8.5
80/81	2.7	9.7
81/82	4.6	15.7
82/83	4.6	12.4
83/84	5.9	17.4

Source: BBC *Facts and Figures* booklets, 1980 to 1985, British Broadcasting Corporation; London, England.
Note: Foreign sales figures include program presales income.

BBC Coproductions

The BBC has a long established tradition of coproduction activities, particularly with the (Anglophone) Commonwealth. Such coproductions have typically involved programs of the documentary/wildlife/travelogue/cultural/location historical drama variety. In such productions, the BBC has traditionally been the dominant partner in creative terms, and usually the sole beneficiary of subsequent international program sales.

For programs not simply requiring a specific foreign locale and/or on screen talent, coproduction partners are sought for purely financial purposes. Coproduction finance is sought firstly from BBC Enterprises, the business arm of the BBC, then by international shopping around. Byron Parkin, deputy managing director of BBC Enterprises, outlined the process as follows:

When programmes are offered to the controllers of BBC1 and BBC2, often they don't have sufficient money to take the more prestigious ones and so they tell the producers that the balance will have to be found from outside coproducing partners. The co-production department makes a list of all those programmes looking for co-production money and their first port of call is Enterprises. We say we'll put so much into that one and so on. After they've had our answer they go round the world trying to find the outstanding sums. For *The Living Planet* we put a substantial amount of money in and then we went out to try to pre-sell it. All of that pre-sale money comes back to us. On big productions pre-selling is very important and necessary to re-coup the large amounts of up-front money. It's a growing trend. (Wade, 1985, p. 45)

As Parkin describes the relationship, foreign coproduction partners are passive providers of finance to the BBC. Research interviews and Trade

Press reports do, however, indicate a growing resistance to this approach on the part of foreign television companies (particularly given the increasing range of players in this area)—Inta Janovskis (Director of Programme Development, Canadian Broadcasting Corporation) singling out the lack of production consultation and zero profit share in subsequent sales in particular as major shortcomings in BBC coproduction deals (Interview with Janovskis, Fall 1985). If this resistance becomes more pronounced, it seems likely that the BBC will look to more coproduction deals with nonproducing TV operations such as the American Worldwide Holding Corporation, a U.S. syndication company, where the "co-pro" arrangement is effectively a high price presale which gives the U.S. coproducer rights to U.S. syndication.

The area of high-budget drama production in particular has seen the BBC alter its traditional approach to coproductions. The case of *Tender is the Night* illustrates how the high production costs of prestige drama increasingly require the BBC to take major coproduction partners who have a significant role in both funding and creative decision making.

Channel 4/European Coproductions

Joint productions with European partners have been an established aspect of British Television coproduction activities for some time, but recent developments have led to increased activity of this kind. The significant factor has been the introduction of Channel Four with its specific cultural programming brief; the similarity of Channel Four's programming policies to other European broadcasters such as ZDF (Zweites Deutsches Fernsehen), with *Das Kleine Fernsehspiel,* has been an obvious incentive to coproduction.

Channel Four has actively pursued European coproductions since its introduction in 1982 (e.g., its £1m input into the C4/RTE/Astramead series, *The Price*). In addition to collaboration in television drama coproduction, a second area of coproduction is coming to assume increasing prominence, that of cultural, documentary, and television feature film coproductions involving a number of European partners. It should be noted, however, that only one or two of the partners involved in such multipartner coproductions usually control production decisions; the others characteristically provide "presale" type finance.

Justin Dukes (business manager of Channel Four) has emphasized the potential long-term importance of European coproductions to minimize the duplication of European productions addressing common European interests (e.g., cultural anniversaries, performance events, etc.); Dukes has predicted that up to 15 percent of future Channel Four production could derive from such arrangements, thus freeing around 40 percent of the national cost of a similar domestic production for other production activities (Interview with Dukes, Fall 1985).

Additional interest in the area of multipartner European coproduction has arisen from 1984 publication of the Commission of the European Communities Green Paper, *Television Without Frontiers* (1984), and the ensuing debates. The European Broadcasting Union canvassed a European production fund, a measure referred to in the Commission Green Paper. However, even given the acknowledged importance of such production activities, European broadcasters have largely rejected proposals for an EEC (European Economic Community) administered European coproduction fund of $20 million. The BBC comments are representative: "The BBC is sceptical about the usefulness of a fund but it all depends on what it is for. In principle the BBC would oppose any initiative which brought Government or EEC involvement in editorial decisions. Coproduction projects are already made in reasonable numbers in Europe and extra money alone is unlikely to significantly increase such coproductions. The BBC therefore would ask what purpose a fund might serve (House of Lords, 1985, p. 70).

This rejection follows lengthy discussions between representatives of European broadcasting companies, and demonstrates a reluctance to collaborate with a funding source which requires executive supervisory powers over editorial and production decisions.

ITV Coproductions

Though information on the annual income from Independent Television (ITV) coproduction deals is unavailable, trade press reports indicate that in addition to coproductions with European and Commonwealth partners, ITV companies are attempting to increase and diversify their coproduction activities with a range of U.S. partners. There has also been greater willingness to work with foreign partners in a genuinely collaborative manner, for example, the Yorkshire Television/Alan Landsburg coproduction of *Glory Boys* which was produced in separate versions for the U.K. and U.S. markets (*TV World,* 1985, pp. 12–14).

Coproduction deals encompass a wide range of financial arrangements and production responsibilities and such arrangments often overlap with "presales." The growing importance of such deals has led in some cases to the presale purchaser being able to dictate script modifications and approve casting and thereby produce ostensibly British domestic market programming tailored to the American market. A recent example of this is London Weekend Television's *Dempsey & Makepeace* presale deal with the Chicago Tribune group.

British television companies' production and presale of program material specifically developed by independent agents for American network transmission also blurs the coproduction/presale boundaries. Harlech Television (HTV) has been particularly active in this field, with a number of major deals with CBS and NBC. Deals such as that struck with CBS for the production of the television film *Arch of Triumph* have seen the U.S. partner supplying over 50 percent of the production budget through its presale license fee. This has resulted in allegations from within the industry of HTV simply acting as a "facilities house" for foreign production. (*Broadcast*, 1984, p. 48).

ITV company subsidiaries such as Central's Zenith have also involved themselves in similar activities, coproducing properties specifically for the U.S. market. For instance, Mary Tyler Moore Productions developed *Finnegan Begin Again,* starring Mary Tyler Moore, directed by Joan Micklin Silver, and shot entirely on location in the United States. These coproductions have been subsequently broadcast by the parent company in the United Kingdom. Subsidiaries of ITV companies such as Zenith and Euston Films have an advantage over ITV parent companies, as their residuals are calculated on the anomalous basis of them being film production companies rather than television producers and are consequently smaller. The question of residual payments to creative personnel following sale of a property in additional markets is an important influence on ITV company strategy, and has led to the anomolous situation of the BBC receiving a fee for the relay of its programs by cable in Belgium, and the ITV companies declining to accept a fee because of their consequential liability to pay residuals.

Program Format Sales

Thames Television has developed further methods of exploiting its intellectual property assets. The *Benny Hill Show,* a product that has enjoyed considerable longevity in Britain (and of which, therefore, there is an extensive archive) is re-edited into 22½-minute units and sold to the U.S. syndication market for stripping. New *Benny Hill Specials* produced in and for the United Kingdom are sold to Home Box Office for its satellite/cable pay TV services on an exclusive basis for 18 months. The rights then revert to Thames Television, and the shows are re-edited into a different time format and sold to the syndication market for stripping. The U.S. syndication market demands a high volume of programs so that a stable schedule can be constructed and audiences know, for example, that *M*A*S*H* will be screened at 7 p.m. on Thursday evenings. British programming is ordinarily not made in sufficient volume for stripping, and so however high the quality of individual programs or short series, their lack of volume makes them unattractive in the most important U.S. markets. Thus a series such as *Fawlty Towers* made in a dozen episodes is attractive only to PBS in the United States.

Thames has developed further successful strategies for exploiting its intellectual property in the U.S. television market by selling a series of "formats" to U.S. producers. The original British situation comedies such as

Keep It In The Family, Man About The House, Robin's Nest, and *George & Mildred,* have in this way been transmuted for the U.S. market into new sitcoms such as *Too Close For Comfort, Three's Company, Three's a Crowd,* and *The Ropers,* which have enjoyed considerable success. The success of the American format clones has provoked Thames to sell the British original versions of the sitcoms to U.S. broadcasters under the title, *The Thames Comedy Originals,* advertised as "156 half-hours for strong, cost effective stripping." Thames has also established a Californian production company, Grand Central Productions, as a 50/50 joint venture with Thames' long-standing U.S. distributor, D.L. Taffner. Grand Central Productions proposes to make programs for six principal U.S. buyers: Home Box Office, Showtime, syndicators, and the commercial networks ABC, CBS, and NBC. Thames' explicit equity stake in Grand Central Productions is a novel initiative in its North American operations which have customarily been through companies in which it takes no equity, but a share of profit.

The Profitability of Overseas Sales

Sales to overseas markets are likely to continue as an important element of British television companies' activities. The BBC is unable to continue its existing activities and levels of employment at the current levels of its license fee revenue, and is actively pursuing revenue-raising activities including publishing, the sale of information from its archive, and a more vigorous exploitation of its program stock by BBC Enterprises. The relationship between average and marginal costs in television program production is such that sales of programs to small overseas markets for low prices may still realize very high profits in relation to the costs incurred. A hypothetical example will clarify this argument. A program may be produced at a cost of £200,000. Much, if not all, of this cost of production will be defrayed from revenues accruing in the United Kingdom home market, whether from the sale of audiences to advertisers or from license fee receipts. The cost of printing an extra copy of a film or dubbing an additional copy of the program onto video tape is negligible compared with the first copy costs, against which virtually all production costs are allocated. Indeed, the customary practice of the ITV companies is to write off costs in the United Kingdom. The customary formula regularly used in Thames TV's Annual Report and Accounts is representative of the ITV companies' practice.

To the marginal cost of making a second film or videocassette for sale in additional markets must be added the costs of promotion, residual payments to actors and other personnel, marketing, and sales. These may be considerable, as distributors customarily take 30 percent of fees realized. In 1984, BBC Enterprises incurred the following costs:

Sales   £13,715,986
Distribution   £6,671,379
Administration   £4,379,609
Interest   £1,107,225
TOTAL   £25,834,199,
in effecting a turnover of £31,414,923,
and a pre-tax profit of £5,852,173[2]

However, it is likely that many of the costs incurred by BBC Enterprises do not vary proportionally with turnover, and profit will rise more than proportionally with each additional sale. Thus even markets in which low returns are realized may, once "first copy" costs have been defrayed in the home market, be highly profitable.

THE UNITED STATES MARKET

A consequence of the profitability of foreign sales of television programs and the relatively uncompetitive nature of the domestic market (in which there is a very indirect relationship between consumption and audience size on the one hand and revenues and profitability on the other) is a tendency to tailor programming to the requirements of overseas markets, and in particular to the requirements of the largest and potentially most rewarding market of the United States. This tendency is relatively satisfactorily controlled in the commercial sector by regulation, although whether it should be an aim of regulators to control it or deny British audiences Americanized programs for which a consistent liking has been demonstrated is another question. The Independent Broadcasting Authority (IBA) in 1981 declined to renew the franchise of Associated Television (ATV) to transmit programs and sell television advertising in the Midlands region of England. ATV had a long history of producing evidently "mid-Atlantic" programming such as the series *Baron, The Protectors,* and *Man in a Suitcase.* Nonetheless, the pull of the United States market remains a potent one; the predominance of high budget costume drama in British companies output is likely to be related to the evident PBS market for "quality" television of this order.

But there are characteristics of the British and American markets that are difficult to reconcile. The United States market, with the exception of PBS, demands a high volume of product for stripping. There are very few British programs that meet this requirement (*Dr. Who* and *Benny Hill* do and have been successfully sold to the U.S. syndication market), although ATV attempted to develop British product in volumes suitable for stripping with programs such as *The Prisoner* and *The Muppet Show.* Rather the program

---

[2] Source: BBC Enterprises Annual Report & Accounts. 1984 British Broadcasting Corporation, London, England.

form that is perhaps most successfully "amphibious" in both markets is the miniseries. Much of the drama output sold to PBS for screening under Mobil Oil's sponsorship as *Masterpiece Theatre* or *Mystery!* has been of this kind, and characteristically commands prices of between $100,000 and $200,000 per hour. Presale agreements with Mobil enabled Thames Television to proceed with its expensive *Rumple of the Bailey* and *Reilly: Ace of Spies* productions. *Reilly* cost £4.5m for 12-1/4 program hours, with revenue from the PBS presale accounting for perhaps 20 percent of its budget. The sale of Canadian Francophone rights, an audience of approximately eight million, realized $16,000 per hour for Thames. Such agreements have become of increasing importance to U.K. producers. Indeed Central Television's daughter company, Zenith, set up after the successful transnational miniseries production *Kennedy,* receives a maximum of 50% of its production budgets from the parent company. The requirements of the IBA and institutional amour-propre are such that few U.K. producers will admit to any relationship with coproduction partners which might compromise British autonomy and control, or to any tailoring of cast or productions to foreign markets. But the quantity of coproduction and joint ventures, and the importance of foreign markets, is such that it is unimaginable that the anticipated requirements of the most important market, the United Sates, has no impact on editorial or creative decisions.

The joint venture, coproduction phenomenon is a two-way street; a number of U.S. series owe their continued existence to their success in the U.K. market, and *TV World* testifies to the need of U.S. producers for foreign partners and the power of these coproducers:

> What were co-financing deals in years past are now becoming fully fledged international co-productions today. The U.S. and European partners involved are not only sharing production costs but more than that. There's a shared creative role in the project as well. At least for us its no longer a case of a major studio saying to a foreign partner "Give us your money but don't open your mouth." The foreigners want to be part of the editorial creative process and on that side they're playing a greater role than ever before. (Gershman, 1985, p. 12).

To be sure, the two-way street carries a disproportionally high volume of U.S. traffic, but the flow *is* two-way. No market in the world can now consistently support the cost and volume of production necessary to supply its domestic market. The United States' longstanding comparative advantage in audiovisual media production has been critically dependent on the size of its domestic market. The command of a high-income market of approximately 250 million people generally resistant to penetration by imports, has enabled U.S. film and television producers to invest very large sums in production budgets, recoup these investments in the home market, and then sell very high quality product at marginal cost in foreign markets.

Table 4.   Share of Viewing Hours by Television Provider.

Year	1975	1981	1986	1991
Networks	84	75	67	56
Independent and PBS	16	22	22	23
Pay		2	7	13
Non pay cable services		1	3	7

Grieve Horner & Associates, A study of the United States Market for Television Programs, Toronto 1981; p. 4.

Producers have customarily been able to recoup costs in the U.S. market by licensing a network for two screenings of an hour of programming. However, this equilibrium is being disturbed as the production costs of U.S. television series rise, and the ability of broadcasters to pay declines. Broadcasters' ability to pay is declining as advertising revenue declines and as competition, most importantly with the challenge to the three networks' hegemony by the "fourth network", Fox, and indepentent stations grouping into syndicate, becomes more effective. The networks' prime time share of the U.S. audience has declined to below 75%, from 90% at the beginning of the 1980s, and advertising revenues fell in 1985 by 2.6%. This means that a prime-time slot "that commanded over $100,000 two years ago is now selling for under $95,000 (*Financial Times,* 1986, p. 24). A representative example of production cost inflation is the U.S. series, *Miami Vice.* Each episode of *Miami Vice* costs $1.2m, of which $850,000 is covered by NBC's network licence fee (*Business Week,* 1985, p. 77).

NBC and the other U.S. television networks' ability to pay $850,000 in license fees is likely to continue to decline. As other terrestial broadcasters augment their audiences, share of advertising revenue, and ability to pay for programming at the expense of the networks, and as pay services (whether delivered by satellite, cable, or video) grow, the networks ability to pay high program license fees declines. Grieve Horner projects a trend of continuing network decline. As the long period of network oligopoly in the United States draws to a close, the market structure of the United States will approximate to a model of a plurality of middle-sized distributors, each disposing of license fees for programs lower than those affordable by ABC, CBS, and NBC in their heyday. This change in market structure is likely to create more opportunities for non-U.S. producers to sell into the U.S. market. If the attrition of the networks' share of audiences and revenues continues to be faster than growth in aggregate revenues, then the revenue pool will be shared more evenly among a greater number of players, with each player commanding fewer resources than do the biggest current players. The ability to pay for the production costs of an episode of *Miami Vice* will decline. But the ability of a greater number of players to pay intermediate prices for programming will rise. In this new regime, where very high-cost programming may no longer be afforded, and in which demand and ability to pay for low-to mid-cost programming increases, there may well be increased opportunities for sales to the U.S. by foreign producers. Increases in U.S. distribution capacity, through licensing of new terrestial broadcasters and satellite and cable-delivered pay television, and redistribution of advertising revenue among broadcasters, are likely to diminish the comparative advantage of a strong home market resistant to foreign products long enjoyed by U.S. film and television producers.

There are of course counterindications to this scenario: The merger of a network, ABC, with one of the principle independent groups, Capital Cities Communications (*Philadelphia Inquirer,* 1985, p. 1), to form the United States' largest broadcasting group suggests that other resolutions of this contradiction are possible.

Accordingly the phenomenon of *Kennedy,* a production by a British company with a British script made in the United States with United States actors and crew is likely to become more widely generalized.

For the future it may be anticipated that British producers will continue to successfully penetrate foreign television program markets. It is likely that they will do this in conjunction with foreign coproduction partners and that, particularly if successfully alliances are concluded with established producers for the U.S. networks, sales to the U.S. networks will become established. The agencies through which these productions are launched are likely to be daughter companies of the ITV companies and independent producers rather than the ITV companies themselves. Many of these independent production companies and daughter companies will be located outside the United Kingdom, as production and consumption of television programs becomes more and more international. It makes little sense to ask whether *Kennedy, Star Wars, Finnegan Begin Again,* or *Murder in Space* are British or American or Canadian productions, or, in another medium, to ask whether *The Economist* is British; or the Frankfurt or New York editions of *The Financial Times* are British. It will make less and less sense to ask that question about more and more television programs. Culture and cultural production are international phenomena, and the political institutions of the nation-state are highly imperfect tools through which to control or regulate these practices and activities.

REFERENCES

BBC Facts and Figures (Annual Report). (1980–85). London: British Broadcasting Corporation.
British Business. (1985, September 19). London: Department of Trade & Industry. p. 42.
Business Week. (1985, February 11). p. 77.

Chapman, C. (1987, January). Towards a geography of the tube: TV flows in Western Europe. *Intermedia, 15,* 10–21.

Commission of the European Communities (1984). *Television without Frontiers* (Green Paper on the establishment of the common market for broadcasting especially by satellite and cable. COM (84) 200 final). Brussels: Office for Official Publications of the European Communities.

Financial Times. (1984, April 30). p. 3.

Financial Times. (1986, September 12). p. 24.

Grieve Horner & Associates. (n.d.) *A study of the United States market for television programs.* Toronto.

Hoskins, C., & McFadyen, S. (1986). *Stimulation of national television program production. A Canadian success story?* London: International Television Studies Conference Paper.

House of Lords. (1985). *Report of the Select Committee on the European Communities Television without Frontiers* (HL 43). London: HMSO.

Katz, E., & Liebes, T. (1985). Mutual aid in the decoding of Dallas preliminary notes from a cross-cultural study. In P. Drummond & R. Paterson (Eds.), *Television in transition.* London: British Film Institute.

Lealand, G. (1984). *American TV programmes on British screens.* London: Broadcasting Research Unit.

Lee, C.C. (1980). *Media imperialism reconsidered.* Beverly Hills, CA: Sage Publishing.

Nielsen Report. (1986). *Economic growth culture and communications* (A study team report to the task force on program policy). Ottawa: Ministry of Supply & Services.

Nordenstreng, K., & Varis, T. (1974). *Television traffic: A one way street?* (Reports and papers on Mass Communication No. 70). Paris: Unesco.

OECD (Organisation for Economic Cooperation & Development). (1986, July). *OECD Observer Paris,* pp. 23, 25.

Paterson, R. (Ed.). (1982). *TV Globo Brazilian TV in Context.* London: British Film Institute.

Philadelphia Inquirer. (1985, March 19). p. 1.

Ravault, R. J. (1980). De l'explotiation des 'despotes culturels' par les telespectateurs. In A. Mear (Ed.), *Recherches Quebecoises sur la Television.* Montreal: Editions Albert St. Martin.

Ravault, R.J. (1986). Defense de l'indentite culturelle par les reseaux traditionnels de 'coerseduction'. *International Political Science Review, 7*(3).

Schiller, H. (1969). *Mass communications and American empire.* New York: A.M. Kelley.

Sunday Times. (1985, January 20). p. 38.

Services in the UK Economy. (1985, September). *Bank of England Quarterly Bulletin, 25*(3), 404–414.

TV World. (1985, August). pp. 12–14.

Varis, T. (1984). The international flow of television programs. *Journal of Communication, 34,* 152.

Varis, T. (1985). *International flow of television programmes* (Reports & Papers on Mass Communications, No. 100). Paris: Unesco.

Wade, G. (1985). *Film video and television.* London: Comedia.

7

Expanding Competition in the International Market —An Industry Perspective

Jack Valenti

Films and television programs are fragile creations. Perhaps that is why making a truly fine movie or television program is so very difficult to achieve. But it is the movie and television program that the customer wants. No family buys a delivery system, whether it be a movie theater, or a cable system, or a videocassette recorder. What the customer buys is a program—something exciting, something entertaining. Network television, VCRs, cable, direct broadcast satellite—these are conduits, transportation systems which convey the program to the customer. Often we, the industry, confuse conduit with program, but the customer is not confused. The customer knows precisely what is attractive and valuable.

An an individual who loves to read, who is infatuated with the simple English sentence, who admires so warmly and greatly a superior movie, I view with respect the ability of a movie to hold an audience entralled. To transport a viewer to a distant, strange and enchanting place for a couple of hours, to cause that viewer to cry, to laugh, to be held in suspense, to share romance and tragedy, is the most exciting of all the art forms.

That is why I believe that the quality of the movie-going experience is responsible for the ascending curve of movie attendance in most parts of the world. A movie must be one that people want to see. The theater must provision that movie goer with the best in accommodations. In short, the theater must provide the viewer with an epic viewing experience that cannot be duplicated in the living room or the den. In a darkened theater, when what is happening on the screen collides with an audience and sparks fly up, you have a hit.

147

Since the time of the ancient Greeks whose playwrights captivated audiences in the great amphitheaters, people have sought to be entertained. This is an ageless, unchanging human desire. It is as alive today as it was 2,500 years ago. In spite of the ferocious competition for the attention and favor of the viewer, the cinema flourishes. That is why the American cinema box office rose to an all-time high in 1987, with approximately $4 billion in box office receipts. Around 23 million people a week attend U.S. movie theaters. Obviously this cannot compare with the weekly attendance figures of 80 million before the appearance of television 40 years ago. But it is a monumental achievement today.

Generally speaking cinema attendance is up around the world, though there are some nations where there is no increase. But this is due usually to, first, the lack of attractive pictures produced by native producers, and second, the absence of a large number of first-class theaters.

Many exhibitors throughout the world have come to understand a simple equation: If you can fill the customer's needs by offering him or her a terrific viewing excitement, business will multiply. In the United States, there were 22,275 theater screens in 1987, an increase of 48% over the last 10 years. Most of these new halls are comfortable, clean, with large screens and four-track, six-track stereophonic sound, seating 250 to 700 people. As a result, when customers come to the theater, they are involved in a social experience that they find to be fun and wonderfully alive. We have seen the result of new "screen builds" in Great Britain. Some years ago, Britain was in the depths of a sour and draining loss of cinema attendance. With the new screens, however, there is a renaissance of cinema viewing in Great Britain. Wherever there is new building, or renovations of theaters, attendance rises.

But there is another reason also. The creative process is mysterious, strange, unfathomable. No government can order a great film to be made, or to coerce audience from attending a movie that people perceive to be good. Yet, the process is maddeningly imprecise. No one wakes up in the morning and says "today, I'm going to make a bad movie." Yet it happens. For between the idea and the finished print so much can go wrong and often does. Out of every 10 films produced by the major U.S. studios, only two ever recoup their total investment from theatrical exhibition in the United States. And six out of every 10 movies never retrieve their total investment in all markets in the world. That is a piece of humbling arithmetic, but it is a fact. Therefore a major cause of increased box office is the increased number of good movies in the marketplace. There are the kind of films that people want to see, and after watching, they tell their friends "you have got to see this movie, it's terrific." That is the best advertising.

But the industry does have long-term problems. The major pain we suffer is piracy. In the last 10 years, this contagion has surfaced in markets on every continent. It threatens the very fabric of our business. The MPAA has mounted a worldwide attack on piracy. We are spending many millions of dollars to combat it. We have deployed antipiracy forces in over 41 countries. We have allied ourselves with other producer countries, joining with them in their efforts to bring piracy under control. While we are making progress, I cannot warrant we will succeed in demolishing this monster. Like violent crime and drugs, the best we can hope to do is bring it down to acceptable limits. To that end we are determined we will succeed.

In Japan, it is estimated that U.S. films are losing some $200 million at retail value in the home video market due to piracy. This is the largest hemorrhaging we confront, except in the United States, which is the largest market in the world.

Internationally, we are fighting to stem piracy in the Philippines, in other nations in the Far East, in Latin America, and in western Europe. In the Middle east, piracy is almost out of control. We have a presence in Egypt, Kuwait, Jordan, Cyprus, and Turkey. Compounding the piracy problem is the lack of stern and effective copyright laws in too many countries. We are working closely with local producers and local lawyers to try to convince their governments it is in the best interest of that nation to refurbish copyright laws so that they work.

Next to piracy, our biggest problems are nontariff trade barriers. Through the most ingenious kind of trade hedgerows, some nations try to restrict the free entry of American visual material, under the theory that if the American movie can be suffocated or exiled, the local film industry will become healthy and robust. The fact the theory is spurious does not diminish its popularity.

Yet, if the American movie is popular in many nations, it is because local citizens make their own decisions about what movies they want to see. It is the local citizenry casting their votes, not the American film industry. Voltaire was right when he said he would put his reputation as a playwright in the hands of Parisians. If one of his play failed, it was probably a bad play. If it attracted Parisians to the theater, it was doubtless a very good play.

All the American industry wants is a chance to compete. We will put our future in the hands of the local movie-going public. Let Canadians, Italians, Koreans, Belgians make their own decisions about what they want to watch. Japanese cars are selling in the United States for no other reason than Americans like to drive them. I tell my U.S. automobile friends, "you want to increase sales, then make better cars and Americans will buy them." Simple as that. That is why we have tried to convince the American Congress that we only ask for fair treatment. We want the same access to foreign markets that foreign businessmen find so alluring in ours. New trade laws emerging in the United States should put heavy emphasis on fair trade, and that is all that we ask.

Other problems stem from the new technological discoveries, as well as the incompatibility of new systems with old ones. New technology will have a radical effect on how people will see entertainment in their home, and in the theater.

In the past 15 years, the direct broadcast satellite industry has sprung up. When satellites jostle with each other 23,000 miles above the earth, in geosynchronous orbit, there will be a traffic jam in the sky. Each of these satellites will have the capacity to rain down programs by the thousands at the speed of light. In time, when satellites are riding in the Ku Band, the home viewer can have a little dish in his attic or a smallish rectangular stem on the roof enabling the viewer to fetch from the sky any one of a thousand programming options.

In a few years, a system will evolve which will allow a single motion picture print to be hurled to individual theaters where, in marvelous fidelity to sight and sound, the movie will be exhibited to cinema audiences. Think of the savings in print costs this will allow. Digital technology is waiting just over the horizon. No longer will a camera be needed. A computer will record the scene and the finished print will be projected to a screen with a million little crystals, each one lighting up on command from the computer, to display a picture absolutely impeccable in quality.

High definition television is also waiting in the wings. Currently, there are no worldwide accepted standards. Right now meetings are being held all around the globe seeking a solution to this problem. HDTV creates a compatibility problem. Right now the Japanese system does not allow a current television set to project a picture in HDTV. The new set is not compatible with the current system. With some 180 million television sets in American homes, lack of compatibility exposes a tough dilemma. How to have HDTV enter the home and still use the family television set—that is the key riddle that must be solved.

Then there is cable. We have some quarrels with cable right now, only because cable is a monopoly in the neighborhood with government-granted privileges, giving it a competitive advantage over other delivery systems. We are suggesting that cable be treated like its competitors and be shorn of its artificial advantages. Competition is the one element in the marketplace that is valuable. We believe that competition must be preserved in every market, in every delivery system, in every country.

How this all will affect our future, I don't know. But I do know that the cinema will not die, it will prosper. This is because of the human condition. No one wants to be umbilically connected to an electronic box in the home every night. Human beings want to get out of the house frequently. They want to participate in a social experience. That is why the cinema is here to stay. Human desires are stronger and more enduring than any technology.

8

International Trade
in Television Programs:
Quota Policies
and Consumer Choice Revisited

Jean-Luc Renaud

The debate revolving around the international flow of television programs predates the communication deregulation era. In their 1974 pioneering survey, Nordenstreng and Varis (1974) documented the essentially unidirectional nature of this flow—from industrialized to developing countries—and the origin of the traded material—overwhelmingly American. Situated within the North-South context of the New World Information Order rhetorics, the ensuing "media imperialism" debate contributed little in way of understanding the mechanics of the international trade of television programs from the economic perspective.

The debate about trade in film and television programs is permeated by the unstated assumption that these programs are pure commodities whose production, distribution, exhibition and, ultimately, value are solely determined by market forces. This assumption is not necessarily shared by most recipients of (U.S.) television material worldwide. The clash over the nature of the audiovisual material and the ways in which media resources should be allocated is nowhere better illustrated than in Europe.

The historical view in "public broadcasting" countries according to which media production and consumption should be somewhat insulated from market forces—themselves judged to be poor mechanisms to guarantee optimal consumer welfare—is strongly challenged today by a new group of entrepreneurs. Thus, in tune with the liberal ideology of the time, the analysis of media industries is dominated by an economic discourse which seeks to exclude political and cultural concerns. This mode of analysis reflects the preoccupation of powerful sectors, especially in the United States, wishing to penetrate new "deregulated" television markets by fighting what they perceive to be protectionist measures.

From the outset, it should be pointed out that the economic analysis of broadcasting is dominated by Paretian welfare economics. This school of thought bases its definition of optimal social welfare on the outcome of individual, autonomous economic decisions expressible in terms of price. It assumes the homogeneity of commodities, the perfect divisibility of both commodities and factors of production, and that all production functions are continuous; it assumes a static economy with no uncertainty about the future and perfect knowledge of the present. These conditions, however, are met only in perfect competition. Collins, Garnham, and Locksley (1988) underline that, in the case of the audiovisual industry in particular, such a model of optimal resource allocation under market conditions is highly abstract and unrealistic.

In view of the media entrepreneurs' contention that the government has no business involving itself in what should be a competitive market for media products, it is imperative to revisit the assumptions underlying four major interrelated claims put forth in most of the economic thinking about the international media market.

First, media entrepreneurs claim that the worldwide domination of U.S. media products is the sole product of the free interplay of competitive market forces. Is the dominance of U.S. programs on foreign television screens really the result of competitive market forces? The trade of television products rather conforms to oligopolistic practices inherited from the internationalization of the motion picture industry, a process thoroughly documented by Guback (1969).

Whereas World War I had disrupted European film industries, the productive capacity of U.S. companies was burgeoning. In the decade up to 1923, the volume of U.S.'s film exportation quadrupled. From 1913 to 1925, film exports to Europe increased five times and to the rest of the world 10 times. The industry was characterized by a strong vertical integration, a condition which persisted until the Justice Department forced the studios to pull out of the exhibition circuits in 1949.

The Motion Picture Export Association—the umbrella organization for the Hollywood majors—was registered under the Webb-Pomerene Export Trade Act of 1918 which exempted the overseas operations of U.S. firms from provisions of the Sherman and Clayton antitrust acts regulating their domestic activities. In practical terms, the strength and associated harmful consequences of a cartel are essentially to decrease and, at worst, eliminate the negotiating power of its clients through monopolization of distribution of film and television material. A cartel finds its concrete expression in practices such as market allocation, price fixing, block booking, and information sharing, among other collusive strategies. Independent producers have recently been allowed to benefit from the Webb-Pomerene exemptions. The State Department has also been assisting in the internationalization of the U.S. film industry.

"The Motion Picture Industry—A Pattern of Control," a report prepared in 1941 by the Temporary National Economic Committee already pointed to the dangers of economic concentration in the film industry. More recently the Washington Task Force on the Motion Picture Industry noted in 1978 that the major producers/distributors were effectively limiting competition by maintaining tight control over the distribution of film, both by the failure to produce more films and by their failure to distribute more films produced by others.

Given the huge potential profit anticipated from national and world markets for audiovisual products, it is no surprise to witness oligopolistic consolidation. Cartels restrict output within the range where price exceeds marginal costs. Firms in a cartel arrangement will charge the highest possible price to maximize profit. Indeed, 265 films a year were produced in the 1970s down from 375 a year 20 years earlier. Proportionally, the number of films distributed by the large companies has decreased even more rapidly. Since 1920, eight majors have dominated the film industry, and now control 90% of the U.S. market and 70% of the world market. In this context, it is somewhat ironic for Jack Valenti, MPAA president, to quarrel about "a marketplace dominated by a handful of actors" as he mentioned the program acquisition practices of some MPAA's foreign clients.

The second claim of U.S. media companies regarding the international market relates specifically to import quotas. Given the popularity of U.S. television imports, it was argued that quotas in recipient countries deny consumers their rights of choice; these are protectionist measures that should disappear. In fact, the success of U.S. exports over indigenous production, or rather the presence of U.S. programs on foreign screens, has much less to do with any intrinsically superior appeal of commercial broadcasting over public broadcasting than with the unique features of the U.S. market. Audience preferences for programming produced in their own country or culture has been solidly documented (Chevaldonne, 1987; Straubhaar, 1983; Tunstall, 1977; de Sola Pool, 1966). Tracey has provided the most thoroughly researched empirical verification of this phenomenon to date (1988). So, why is there a systematic mismatch between expressed tastes and actual consumption?

In many cases, local product is simply not available. Television is an expensive business. The huge U.S. domestic market has so far enabled producers to recoup most of their costs, making programming available on international markets at a very cheap price. Smaller markets cannot benefit from the economies of scale which can be achieved in the U.S. market (Hoskins & Mirus, 1987). Because of these economies of scale, the actual consumption of American audiences can somewhat approximate expressed tastes, at least as defined by producers and distributors.

Quotas have been criticized on the grounds that they reduce the freedom of choice of the consumer. "If people watch *Dallas,* no restraints should be exercised," goes the common complaint. This assumes that audiences are segregated by television formats, and that people watching *Dallas* watch only similar shows. It remains that if *Dallas* receives, say, a forty ratings, sixty percent of viewing audience do not watch it. Empirical evidence recently collected by Ehrenberg (1986, p. 3) in the United Kingdom shows that viewers of all kinds make use of the wide range of different types of programs that are provided now:

> People do not just watch the most popular program all the time. Their full viewing needs and preferences are revealed by the other, lower-rating, programs which they also choose to watch. People spend almost 40 percent of their time on relatively more demanding programs, and this is equally so for different social classes, for heavy and light viewers, and for all the other population subgroups. The demand for range is there.

A similar pattern in television consumption was observed in Switzerland in an editorial in *Media Magazine* (1984). As the U.K. weekly *The Economist* put it succinctly: "Everybody is a minority for part of his viewing life."

Quota policies can be seen as fulfilling distributive aims. In an arena dominated by oligopolistic circuits of television programs distribution, quotas become a means, however imperfect, of improving the negotiating position of those nations that do not possess the natural attributes (market size and single language) of the United States. Far from distorting competition, quotas can conceivably be understood as aiming to restore competition if not in international market then at least in the domestic market. However, Lange and Renaud (1988) make it clear that quota policies are sensible only if accompanied by positive measures for promoting the audiovisual production, such as tax incentives, subsidies and liberal patronage and sponsorship rules.

The quota system is criticized for being paternalistic and inefficient: Popular programs subsidize the production of demanding programs. However, in broadcasting it is not the case of the many subsidizing the few. Instead, such a policy lets people choose to watch their individual selections of programs for substantial parts of their viewing time. Competition or market forces are not necessarily synonymous with the consumer interest. In an unregulated market, viewers would be deprived of a program altogether just because less than a majority might watch that program. Profit-maximizing broadcasters do have a direct economic incentive to respond to audience demand, but the nature of this incentive produces a pattern of output which is clearly suboptimal. The broadcaster wholesales audiences to advertisers, rather than programs to final consumers, on the basis of crude numbers unrelated to intensity of demand. Studies have shown that under competitive conditions such a relationship tends to maximize total audience but restrict the range of program choices (Hoskins & Mirus, 1987).

If, indeed, one could make the case that some audience segments subsidize the welfare of others, it would not be out of line with allocation of other public goods. Citizens without children subsidize others' education, highway construction is paid for by those without cars, and people pay for police, fire departments and public hospitals irrespective of their need for them. In any case, the empirical work conducted by Hoskins, Mirus, and Rozeboom (1986) provides very weak evidence that import quotas—if it is to work like import tariff—drive up the price of programming.

Regulation of broadcasting is also a matter of industrial and employment policy. As Collins (1988) put it:

One does not need to erect an argument against the quality or desirability of U.S. television programs on the cultural grounds of the wall-to-wall *Dallas* variety, in order to argue that free trade in general, but especially in the broadcasting sector, may not be in the national interest. (Collins, Garnham, & Locksley, 1988, p. 166)

The third claim focuses on the cultural preoccupations underlying quota policies. Critics of quotas claim that only an undisturbed marketplace can cater to cultural needs, thus denying the wisdom of public-sector intervention in the cultural industry. Those critics, U.S. distributors in particular, have found ideological, if not intellectual, comfort in the work of media diffisionists like Pool, for whom cultural protectionism is self-defeating in three ways: (a) one country loses the opportunity to learn, borrow, and adapt from other cultures; (b) commerce seeks to reflect world cultural tastes, subsequent cultural protections can be attributed to a painful process of men's emotional resistance to the change in value; and (c) cultural products, like other commercial commodities, must submit themselves to an open-market competition: "Any culture that can exist only with cultural protectionism policies are not worthy of protection" (de Sola Pool, 1974). This line of argument finds its economic legitimation in the following four-stage product life cycle theory: (a) innovation of products in the U.S. made possible by large domestic markets; (b) loss of monopoly position at home owing to competing firms, followed by growth through foreign export; (c) foreign companies exploit technology transfer to challenge U.S. companies, and (d) decline of U.S. firms, and rise of foreign industries which penetrate the U.S. market. Lee notes evidence which shows this theory is less than satisfactory. The product life cycle theory predicted that the American television program flow would lead to (a) establishment of local production facilities abroad, (b) co-production efforts with local film makers abroad, (c) local acculturation of imported television culture, and (d) erosion of the American television market and the rise of foreign-produced programs in the United States. This process, at least in its last stages, failed to materialize because the model ignores conditions of production and distribution of cultural goods (Lee, 1980).

One does not need to go outside the United States to find evidence that public intervention can come to the rescue of market forces to secure consumer welfare. In the United States, the government has passed measures based on assumptions, some of which are noneconomic in nature. When the government subsidizes education, highway construction, hospital, defense, social security, food stamps, and minority programs, the desirability of this intervention is hardly questioned. The establishment of the National Endowment for the Arts and Humanities points to the limit of market forces in the cultural industries. Tax breaks exist for the foreign exhibition of U.S. documentary films, while foreign artists who wish to perform in the United States must prove their star status in their home countries; a law apparently aimed at combating high unemployment in the domestic cultural industries.[1] The same concerns presided over the development of a federal shelter program to stimulate film production, which was terminated when the 1976 Tax Reform Act became law, but restored in 1978 by a program launched by the Small Business Administration to finance production by independent companies. The Informational Media Guarantee Program allows film companies to sell some of their soft currency earnings to the American government for dollars to help U.S. films to be exhibited in critical foreign areas. The Revenue Act of 1971 includes provisions for the establishment by a U.S. firm of a Domestic International Subsidiary Corporation, which, if 95 percent of its revenues are derived from foreign activities, can qualify for a tax break. The money saved can be used for development of export activities or production of export products (Guback, 1969).

There are nationality requirements for the ownership of U.S. media properties. The stringent regulation of horizontal integration of broadcast media and media cross-ownership has more to do with the protection of the Miltonian "marketplace of ideas" than with the Friedmanian Chicago School of Thought. The same consideration presides over special postal rates and tax breaks for the newspaper publishers. It is well understood in the United States that some cultural products which contribute to overall

---

[1] Difficulties in having the leading role in the British-imported *Les Miserables* performed by a British actress on Broadway is the latest example.

consumer welfare—and to which the consumer is entitled—cannot necessarily be governed effectively by market forces alone.

Protectionism is a word that has a pejorative ring, but we would do well to understand the many facets of such a policy. All countries, all industries, all companies, are concerned about the sanctity of their markets. Businesses naturally seek to safeguard and enlarge their markets and their earnings, but not all businesses do this in the same way. U.S. interests typically point to European governments and European industries as being protectionists. But U.S. interests are protectionists in their own right. The distinction is essentially this: European interests seek to protect their *domestic* markets; U.S. interests seek to protect their *foreign* markets. (Guback, 1986, p. 58)

The strategy to protect those foreign markets will intensify because of the very nature of television economics. The need for product innovation is not unique to cultural industries, but only in the cultural industry is extremely rapid product innovation a central condition of existence. Cost-inflation pressures stem from the incidence of Baumol's cost-disease model. Baumol argues that the basic commodity production process of the cultural industries—that of constantly producing prototypes—is inherently labor intensive. The possibilities for exploiting the productivity advantages of capital investment in labor-intensive technology in the production of a television program are strictly limited. Much capital investment is a form of nonprice competition which increases costs rather than being labor-intensive. The general real level of prices and wages in the economy is determined by increases in productivity in the capital intensive sectors. As a result, there is an inexorable tendency for the real costs of cultural production to rise (Baumol & Bowen, 1966, 1985). Entrepreneurs will be forced to exploit economies of scale in order to keep unit costs down in the face of these inflationary pressures. Since the domestic market is already saturated, the cost of production rises and so must the unit costs of consumption. This trend is exaggerated with the number of competing channels. In the United States the index of costs per program hour rose tremendously (Collins, Garnham, & Locksley, 1988). As Renaud and Litman show, access to foreign markets therefore becomes critical as revenues derived from them are increasingly important in the overall financial equation (Renaud & Litman, 1985).

An expanding European TV industry would offer additional markets to help U.S. companies recover their program production costs, which are increasing dramatically. Helping to finance this expansion of the European program market would be global marketers. (Guback, 1986, p. 54)

The fourth claim of proponents of commercial television eyeing Europe states that deregulated markets combined with new distribution technologies, particularly DBS, will best meet consumer needs by promoting an indigenous audiovisual industry. The promise of a greater variety of programming sources of increasing quality overlooks the microeconomics of cultural production which tend to develop towards oligopolistic structures, despite the impact of new technologies. Small groups will still dominate the market, strengthening the horizontal and vertical integration of international markets. Warner Brothers is a case in point. It is involved in cable, satellite, and video ventures abroad to maintain its distribution channels.

European entrepreneurs are quick to point out that the opening up of the continent to commercial competitive networks will lead to more indigenous production and, with satellite technology, to the creation of a European market. This market will foster the production of goods competitive with U.S. products, owing to economies of scale. But other economic arguments belie this claim. For one, the advertising market is wrongly assumed to be inexhaustible. Current limitation on competition stems from the finite supply of advertising financing rather than from spectrum scarcity.

So far, evidence shows that by 1987 competition between public and private stations, and among private stations, has generally led to increased use of imports at higher costs, compounded by decreasing revenues since the greater supply of advertising time brings down price. Colin Davis, President of MCA has estimated that program prices in France had escalated by up to 600% or more since the launch of the commercial TV networks there (*Variety,* 1988, p. 37). French producers complain that newly generated revenues have not been directed to the domestic production industry but to purchase imports. Italy is the counterexample used by Waterman (1988) to support the thesis that commercialization and liberalization leads to an increased capacity for domestic production. Indeed, Berlusconi's Reteilatia produces film and television material as the market generates greater financial resources. This in-house production is foremost a response to counter the spiraling costs of imports. It is not yet clear that this strategy will be permanent. Since this evolution threatens U.S. distributors' access to foreign markets especially in a period when revenues derived from those markets increasingly represent the difference between profit and loss, it is likely that the U.S. industry will counter-attack by setting a new price equilibrium whereby "buying American" is still economical for its traditional clients.

Proponents of commercialization of television in Europe are often keen to argue that commercial television is "free" to viewers, and therefore a fairer system than license fees paid by all, irrespective of preference or consumption. The attraction of advertising support over license fees is mainly the lure of the free lunch. But economists know that there is no such thing as a free lunch. Everyone pays for consumed goods whether directly or indirectly. It was calculated that British viewers pay the same amount for commercial and public channels. The counterargument, according to which advertising benefits overall economic performance, has never been supported with convincing evidence.[2] Most advertising is defensive in nature. Moreover, comparison with countries where there is less or no television advertising (e.g., Germany and Scandinavia) suggests that television advertising is not a sine qua non for efficient marketing. Hence it may be at least in part an extra cost, that is in as far as it is not merely a switch of money from other marketing budgets (Sturgess, 1985).

The question, then, becomes how to allocate viewer resources so as to maximize program offerings given the difficulty of establishing relations between price, quality, and audience satisfaction. In this respect commercial television does not have a natural superiority over a publicly financed system, to the contrary.

Proponents of a Europe-wide market via satellite fail to realize that any European country trying to sell to its neighbors faces essentially the same types of problems encountered in trying to penetrate the U.S. market, namely language barriers and cultural specificities. Even though Europeans are more used to dubbing or subtitling than their U.S. counterparts, the markets for satellite-delivered programs, linguistically defined, are bound to remain relatively small, making it difficult for satellite television producers to benefit from the economies of scale enjoyed in the United States. It is therefore not at all clear that, in the absence of a European market, satellite systems, developed in many instances through public financing, could become self-supporting when left to the rigor of the marketplace. Indeed, to date, all European satellite ventures are losing money, even the best established and the one with the most pan-European programming—Rupert Murdoch's Sky Channel. After all, the DBS systems in which many European entrepreneurs and governments place their hopes failed in the United States at a time when conditions seemed ripe.

As Tunstall (1986, p. 123) put it in his latest book:

Deregulation does not take communications out of politics. On the contrary, to deregulate communications is to move it out of the government bureaucracy of regulation and throw it into the twin marketplace of commerce and politics. The giant new communications field is a political field. Having fewer rules is not the same as having no rules at all. The significance of the rules that remain is all the greater.

REFERENCES

Baumol, H., & Baumol, W. (1985). L'avenir du theatre et le probleme des couts du spectacle vivant. In L'Economie du spectacle vivant et l'audiovisuel. Paris: La Documentation Francaise.

---

[2] Argument put forth by Galbraith, in particular, cited in Ehrenberg (1986).

Baumol, W., & Bowen, W.G. (1966). *Performing arts: The economic dilemma.* New York: 20th Century Fund.

Chevaldonne, F. (1987). Globalization and orientalism: The case of TV serials. *Media Culture and Society, 9,* pp. 137–148.

Collins, R., Garnham, N., & Locksley, G. (1988). *The economics of U.K. television.* London: Sage Publications.

The Economist. (1987, October 17). p. 18.

Ehrenberg, A.S.C. (1986, February). Advertisers or viewers paying? *ADMAP Monograph (London),* p. 3.

Exporting U.S. image. (1988, June). *Variety,* p. 37.

Guback, T. (1969). *The international film industry.* Bloomington: Indiana University Press.

Guback, T. (1985). Hollywood's international market. In T. Balio (Ed.), *The American film industry* (pp. 463–486). Madison: University of Wisconsin Press.

Guback, T. (1986). *The United States filmed entertainment industry.* Report prepared for the European Institute for the Media, University of Manchester.

Hoskins, C., & Mirus, R. (1987, May). *A study of the economic, social and cultural reasons for the significant international popularity of television fiction produced in the United States.* Unpublished manuscript, University of Alberta Faculty of Business, Canada.

Hoskins, C., Mirus, R., & Rozeboom, W. (1986, October). *The pricing of U.S. television program export.* Unpublished manuscript, University of Alberta Faculty of Business, Canada.

Lange, A., & Renaud, J.L. (1988). *The future of the European audiovisual industry.* Manchester: Haigh & Hochland.

Lee, C.C. (1980). *Media imperialism reconsidered: The homogenizing of television culture.* Beverly Hills: Sage Publications.

Les suisses et leur télévision. *Media Magazine, 3*(2), 13.

Nordenstreng, K., & Varis, T. (1974). *Television traffic: A one-way street?* (Reports and Papers on Mass Communication, No. 70). Paris: Unesco.

Renaud, J.L., & Litman, B.R. (1985, September). The changing dynamics of the overseas marketplace for television programming: The rise of international coproduction. *Telecommunications Policy, 9*(3), 245–261.

de Sola Pool, I. (1966, Spring). The changing flow of television. *Journal of Communication, 27*(2), 139–149.

de Sola Pool, I. (1974). Direct broadcasting satellites and the integrity of national culture. In *Control of the direct broadcast satellite: Values in conflict.* Palo Alto, CA: Aspen Institute, Program on Communication and Society.

Straubhaar, J.D. (1983, October 13). *Factors in the growth of television exports from Latin American countries and their implications for the theory of cultural industries and dependence.* Paper delivered at the Conference on Mass Media and Development, Northwestern University, Chicago.

Sturgess, B.T. (1985). International comparisons. *International Journal of Advertising, 4,* 232–247.

Tracey, M. (1988, March). Popular culture and the economics of global television. *InterMedia,* pp. 9–25.

Tunstall, J. (1977). *The media are American.* New York: Columbia University Press.
Tunstall, J. (1986). *Communications deregulation: The unleashing of America's communication industry.* Oxford: Basil Blackwell.
Waterman, D. (1988, June). World television trade: The economic effect of privatization and new technology. *Telecommunications Policy, 12*(3), 141–152.

9

A Taste of Money:
Popular Culture and the Economics
of Global Television

Michael Tracey

INTRODUCTION

One of the central images of modern political analysis, whether engaged in by allegedly detached social scientists or by political ideologues, is that of the export of culture. The idea is that the structures of relationships which have evolved in the modern world involve not just those of economic links, military liaisons, politically inspired coups d'etat, and economic domination, but also linkages of culture. The proposition is that though the export of cultural products from a relatively small number of countries to a much larger number of recipients, principally, but not only, in the form of television programs, one is witnessing the wholesale transfer of meaning, the generation and shaping of political consciousness with the effect, partially intended, of refashioning the world in the intellectual and political likeness of the exporter. The villain of the piece is usually held to be the United States, and this theme appears in the works of a number of key writers. Here one thinks of Herb Schiller (1969) and Cees Hamelink (1983), though the list of such theorists could be extended enormously.

The fact of the matter is that almost all of those writings are conceptually inadequate and methodologically untested. In fact, much of the discussion about the role of television in the construction of meaning within modern society rests on a sense of there being two underdeveloped worlds: the underdeveloped world defined by geography (Asia and Africa, Latin and South America), and the culturally and intellectually underdeveloped world of the captive populations of the developed societies. Astride these myriad minds, it is held, are the colossi of the superstates and their ideological arms, the cultural industries. What we have portrayed here is a vision of dominance, of cultural imposition, which curiously, at least to my way of thinking, contains much that has to be explored and worried over, but also much that provides the husk within which one finds the seeds of paranoia.

Recently there has been a reassertion of the theme of cultural dominance (as new distribution technologies seemed to make such dominance even more inevitable). In Britain, indeed throughout Europe, we have lived for some time with the widespread belief that two things were about to happen: one, that the sheer "space" for television was "about to expand enormously"; and two, this space would be filled with "wall-to-wall *Dallas*." It is a thesis which has been spoken of in countless conferences, seminars, books and pamphlets, and mouthed so often and loudly that it has been transformed from postulate to certain truth. It is a thesis which has shaped not just public debate, but the decisions of governments, corporate planners, media moguls, and would-be media moguls. And when the eyes of the interested observer have been raised to take in not only the terrain of the so-called first world, but also of the two-thirds world, the scenario has appeared even more powerful. The scenario involves smothering of indigenous cultures by a lava stream of international television spewing forth from the mouth of the Hollywood volcano, with the only applause at this spectacle being the loud clapping of the new media moguls, producers, and distributors of the images and sounds of the global village.

Having looked at the available evidence to support or contest this thesis, evidence which I admit is patchy and variable in the extreme, I am led to conclude that there is an urgent need to challenge some of the prevailing orthodoxies about the present and the future of television.

Hidden within the "inevitable dominance" thesis are, I suspect, two deeply questionable assumptions. The first assumption is of the power of television, and the view that it can override all other institutions that make up human society—can, as it were, imprint itself like a colossal seal on the soft wax of the global mind. This assumption is, of course, fed by the sheer ubiquity and visibility of television, and the fact that the other threads of influence within people's lives remain unalterably invisible. The second assumption is of the ubiquity and popularity of United States television. The significance of that phrase "wall-to-wall *Dallas*" lies precisely in the fact that it captures the vision of hell which is the waking nightmare of many a political and cultural global elite. Both assumptions, however, lack conceptual and empirical depth, and utterly misconceive the place of television within social influences, and what the populations of the world enjoy on television.

It is from within that framework of acute skepticism about the worth of the contemporary discussion of television of any kind that this chapter has been written. I was asked to look specifically at some of the noneconomic dimensions to the question of whether it is "inevitable" that the "rich countries" will dominate the global production and distribution of televisual product. I am not quite sure *how* "rich" is rich in this context, though I take it to mean to a considerable extent the suggestion that a country, not a million miles from these United States, is more likely to dominate world television markets than say Burkino Faso, or even that other third world country in the making, the United Kingdom.

My immediate response is that there is nothing inevitable, as distinct from likely or theoretically possible, about such domination. It is in any case wrong to see "rich countries," in television terms as coterminus with the United States and to a lesser extent the Anglo-European societies. Ample evidence exists of diverse flows of product, with quite complex hemispheric and regional influences, such as Brazil in South and Latin America, Egypt in the Middle East, between countries of the EEC, and also within the Eastern "bloc." I will also suggest that this plural structure of production and distribution is in its infancy, and will grow as the century proceeds and television markets evolve. This arterial structure of global television will be nurtured by the sheer force of local and national cultural tastes. I am not for one minute suggesting that there will not be much U.S. product whizzing round the globe in future decades. I am simply suggesting that there is historically an overemphasis on the ubiquity and presence of U.S. material, and a gross overestimation of its strategic strength.

In this chapter, I want to expand on the thread of these thoughts in the following manners:

1. By considering evidence of the existing availability of international television, and to a lesser extent video.
2. By pondering the evidence to support the argument that what will really make the difference in the future are the new media of satellite and cable.
3. By examining what we know of the ways in which the television audiences, in different societies, make choices about programming.
4. By assessing the kinds of responses which broadcasting institutions of the world will make, in the light of national policies, their own self-identity and their deeply felt need to survive.

OFFERINGS:
THE GLOBAL PATTERNS OF TELEVISION DISTRIBUTION

Just how dominant is television from "rich" countries at the present time? The most basic evidence is that contained in the research organized on behalf of Unesco by Tapio Varis (1984). Varis' study, which covers some 69 countries, updated a similar survey completed a decade before. Varis finds few overall changes since 1973 in the pattern of program flows, but indicates a trend toward greater regional exchanges along with the continued dominance of a few exporting countries. The 1972–73 study showed that there was, in effect, a "one-way flow" of television programs internationally, from the North Atlantic basin to the rest of the world, dominated by entertainment. In his updated study Varis used as a sample the two weeks for January 31 to February 13, 1983. His analysis is without doubt the best guide we have to the general distribution of television around the world, and has been used both rhetorically and analytically to support the proposition that flows of television are overwhelmingly unidirectional. Certainly he shows that overall, imported programs average one-third or more of total programming. My own reading of the Varis data, however, is that even in its necessarily limited nature it consists of something far more substantial and complex than the mere froth of argument and analysis which we have so far seen. He shows, for example, that in all parts of the world, while there are countries that are heavily dependent on foreign imports in their programming, there are those that are only slightly dependent.

In the Americas, the U.S. imports little—about 2% of its total television output—and mainly from the United Kingdom, Mexico, and Latin America, whereas in Canada the vast percentage of the imported material is from the United States. In Latin America, entertainment programming dominated all of the television studied, accounting for about 50% of total transmission time. Most of the imports were entertainment programs: 75% of the imported material is from the United States; 12% from Latin America; a few percent from Europe. In Western Europe, there are important differences between countries. Overall, 30% of television programs are imported, 44% of which are from the United States, with U.S. programs accounting for 10% of total transmission time in Europe in 1983, though much of that is outside prime time. Sixteen percent of imports of television into Europe are from the United Kingdom; Germany and France providing 5%–10%; Eastern Europe and USSR 3%.

According to Varis' data, 14% of entertainment programs are imported; and in Eastern Europe programs are imported from 26 countries, 43% from other Eastern European countries, and 57% from outside that area. Twenty-one percent come from the USSR. In Asia and the Pacific, 36% of all television is imported, but the variations are enormous between countries: For example, from 75% for Television New Zealand's (TVNZ) Channel 2 to 3% for a Calcutta station. The United States and United Kingdom are the main source of imported programs, along with Japan for children's programs, documentaries, and movies, and films from India, Hong Kong, and Taiwan. China produces almost all of its own television, with a little educational and news material from the United Kingdom.

In the Arab countries, the Varis study reports that 42% of television is imported, one third comes from other Arab states, and of 32% of non-Arabic imported programs France provides 13%, the United Kingdom, Japan, and Germany provide 5-7% each, the USSR less than 3% and other socialist countries about 1%. Of the Arabic countries, the most important source of imports is the United Arab Emirates (10% of imported programs), followed by Egypt (6%), Saudi Arabia (4%) and Kuwait (4%).

In Africa about 40% of programs are imported, though again there are wide differences in volume between individual countries. Of the imported material, 50% comes from the United States, 25% from Germany, and the rest from Western Europe. In South Africa, 30% of programs are imported: 54% from the United States, 30% from the United Kingdom, 9% from France, 5% from Austria, and 3% from Canada.

In both Western and Eastern Europe, according to the Varis study, more than 40% of imported programs originate within other countries in the region itself. In both regions the superpowers predominate: with the United States providing 40% of Western European, and the USSR 20% of East European imports. The most notable increase in regional exchange over the course of the 10 years of the two studies is, however, among the Arab states, with one-third of imports originating from within the region, and among Latin American countries, where the figure for regional exchange is said to be 10% and apparently growing.

I relate these details because they present a general picture of television flows which is not a one-way street—rather, a number of main thoroughfares, with a series of not unimportant smaller roads leading off of these. What is clear above all is that television as an international communication system is far more complex than is sometimes assumed, even when dealt with in the very general manner necessitated by the Unesco studies. We have at least to allow for flows within flows, patterns of distribution, which Varis' work hints at, that do not fit the familiar, simplistic model of the total domination of international television by the United States. Even at the simple level of just counting which programs are going where, that idea is simply not true. There are alternative sets of influences and movement within Latin America, within Europe, within Asia, within the Gulf states, and within the Pacific Basin. One cannot simply pretend that those do not exist, nor that they may not denote something rather more significant than a blip on the graph.

Even when one looks at the available evidence of programming for that most recent of televisual phenomenon, videocassettes, the patterns do not support the thesis of the total domination of video software by U.S. programming, though there does seem to be proportionately more of it than is the case for television (Alvarado, 1989).

At the end of 1983 there were an estimated 40 million viewers in the world, and the VCR enjoyed a growth rate much greater than that of the

TV. The Gulf States, for example, are an important area for the use of video-cassette recorders to watch television and films from other countries (Boyd, 1985). The penetration rate of VCRs in Saudi Arabis is about 85%; one study in 1981, which surveyed 120 people, they *all* had VCRs. In a survey in the Red Sea City of Jidda, 19% had two machines (Boyd, 1985).

There are basically two types of material available on videotape. In the first instance, there are large quantities of western television programs and feature films. At the time of Douglas Boyd's research, the latest episodes of *Hill Street Blues, St. Elsewhere,* and *The A-Team* were readily available, as well as such movies as *E.T.* and *Terms of Endearment.* All of it was pirated. Similarly, every evening's total BBC output is taped and flown out to the Middle East the following morning in a private plane. Pornography is also acquired from London, Paris, and Frankfurt. There is also extensive pirating of Arab television programs and films, particularly those from Egypt. As one observer noted: "In the tumultuous arena of Arab politics, the soaps are a soft-sell commercial for Egyptian values, and thereby a vehicle for Egyptian influence. They are a reminder to the Arabs than even when Egypt's political course is in disrepute, Egypt is still number one among the Arab States" (Viorst, 1984). The success and influence of Egyptian television follows in the wake of the success of its films which

> paved the way...by promoting the faces of its stars, the voices of its singers and the tales of its writers in every Arab city and town. Even more importantly, it spread a familiarity with Egypt's dialect. Thanks to the movies, the Arabic spoken by the Egyptians has come to dominate a language spoken in a hundred different ways in the Middle East. This dominance now virtually precludes any other Arab country from successfully establishing an entertainment industry of its own. An Egyptian TV producer observed: The rich markets for state TV are in Saudi Arabia and the Gulf and (Egyptian TV) will not produce anything that will alienate the Saudis. The Saudis only want things that could have been shown in the Middle Ages. Like all Arab governments, they want to promote the status quo. So that is what we give them. (Viorst, 1984)

In many Asian societies, governments are becoming worried that the use of VCRs is undermining development goals. For example, in Malaysia 75% of the viewers of VCR tapes are the Malaysian Chinese population. The government is trying to weld together a number of cultures through the use of a national language, Bahasa Malaysia, but the Chinese prefer Chinese language tapes from Hong Kong to the Bahasa Malaysia-dominated television service, a fact which is less than pleasing to the authorities. In 1982 the information minister, Abid Adam, expressed his fears that messages from the government were not reaching the people and that the loss of the television audience to video might "hamper government efforts to disseminate national aspirations and values and channel information to the people."

In a piece to the *Star,* a Malays daily newspaper, on June 21, 1983, Adam warned that videotapes could expose people to policies contrary to government policies and national culture, hurt television news and information, and hinder the government's efforts to foster racial harmony. The counter accusation, however, was one when an audience begins to flood away: The TV was boring. Equally, in Indonesia, the reaction to the impoverished character of the television service has been to turn more and more to VCRs: "Indonesian authorities are also concerned about Western video, constantly warning the public against 'cultural and political pollution' from abroad, particularly Communist propaganda from China" (Lent, 1985). In Islamic cultures the VCR is also playing havoc with traditional values and morals. Middle-class Indians also are now extensive viewers of programs using VCRs, including a good deal of U.S. material.

Writing about video in Asia, John Lent (1985) pointed out that in Singapore, 45% of the population watches less television produced by the Singapore Broadcasting Corporation now, preferring videocassettes, particularly Chinese language tapes for the predominantly Chinese population. What worries the Singaporean authorities in particular are the uncensored Western cassettes contrary to official guidelines on the portrayal of sex and violence, and the fact that people are reading less and watching more. The flight from government-dominated, worthy, development-oriented television to Western-dominated videocassettes also worries many Asian governments because of the frustration impact of Western-oriented video programs pushing modern and sophisticated lifestyles upon kampung (village) peoples who do not have the means of acquiring the paraphernalia of those lifestyles (Lent, 1985).

There is also evidence of the use of video to circumvent government restrictions on television viewing, both in terms of the amount of programming made available and the political and moral content of programs. I have already cited the examples of Malaysia, Indonesia, and Singapore. Georgette Wang, for example, showed in a recent study in Taiwan just how important is the sidestep function of video (Alvarado, 1987). By 1984 14.4% of households had VCRs, used extensively to watch programming banned on television, most notably from Japan, the United States, and Hong Kong. Similarly, the Saudi Arabian government was unable to stop the circulation within Saudi Arabia of the program *Death of a Princess,* pirated copies of which were available within 24 hours of the program's showing in Britain. In her study of video in Turkey, Christine Ogan comments: "Most of the content consumed is from pirated sources...The piracy situation has caused the legal film market to erode." She points out that the amount of programming available from the state-owned broadcasting system is extremely limited, no more than a few hours a week: "Such little programming schedule means that there has been little program choice, causing the video cassette industry to quickly fill the media gap.'' She estimates that there are 2.5 million VCRs in Turkey, with an estimated 3,000 to 5,000 video distribution outlets, offering 4,000 different foreign titles (Ogan, 1986). There is additional evidence from Latin America of video being used as a means of alternative communication in such places as Brazil, Chile, Peru, and Venezuela, though one would not wish to overstate this, however, since the overwhelming use of VCRs remains for the viewing of movies and not political tracts (Alvarado, 1987).

Consider the example of India, where Binod Agrawal writes:

> Video evokes multiple reactions in the broad cross-section of Indian society today. Among the urban rich, it is one of the focal points of drawing-room conversation, whereas among the youth of the same class, it evokes a sense of competition. It is a common scene to find young men and women hovering around video centers and libraries in the afternoons in search of pre-recorded video tapes of some classical cinema or a copy of the latest unreleased film. Quite often the talk about video turns into a serious discussion on the undesirable effects it has on the studies of students in all age groups and on the morality of the nation. Video has become a new craze, a fashion, and a new means of leisure time activity. Its easy operation, continuous supply of pre-recorded videocassettes, and above all, the uninterrupted import of videocassette recorders has taken the Indian men and women, whether urban or rural, by storm. It has become a phenomenon without any parallel. (Alvarado, 1987)

Agrawal's whole account pinpoints both the immediate and considerable implications for the film industry in India of this behavior, as well as the continuing elitist basis to the actual possession of video.

However, it remains extremely difficult to speak with any certainty of the patterns of distribution of programming on videocassettes. In the study which the Broadcasting Research Unit (BRU) in London completed for Unesco on the global distribution of video hardware and software, which brings together a formidable mass of new material, one is nevertheless left grasping for more systematic statistical data. Unfortunately, that will probably never be forthcoming because of the intractable, even dangerous, problems of gathering it. Nevertheless the sense that one has of the patterns of video software are that it is not dissimilar to that of TV: To wit, in some areas there is a heavy dependence on U.S. product, in other areas much less so, with considerable use of domestic product and non-U.S. sources. In Latin and South America, for example, the rule which seems to apply is that the hardware comes largely from Japan and the software largely from the U.S.

If, however, one looks to other areas, the pattern is far more complicated. Hong Kong, for example, has emerged as a significant production and distribution center for programming on video. Television Broadcasts International (TVBI) markets about 1000 hours of its 2,000–3,000 hours of productions annually to 25 countries with Chinese populations. The programming tends to be serialized drama, modern action, kung fu, variety shows, and comedies, all produced in different languages; Mandarin, English, Thai, and Vietnamese. Asia TV, based in Hong Kong, produces about 520 hours of drama on video. In addition, there are a host of film production companies in the colony, as well as an active distribution system. The copying house Esquire, for example, holds the rights to distribute approximately 2,000 Indian films worldwide, and serves the needs of the local Indian population as well. In Taiwan, as another example, there are about 7,500 video retail shops, with an average stock of 6000 tapes. These tapes can be categorized into five language groups: English (U.S.), Japanese, Mandarin, Cantonese (Hong Kong), and Fukienese (a local dialect). Far and away the most important of these are tapes from Japan, particularly Japanese detective series, love stories, and modern family drama, followed in popularity by Chinese martial arts movies and American horror movies (Alvarado, 1987).

The major industrial societies' use of video seems to involve a dependence on U.S. product. In Australia, 61% of video programming comes from the U.S., 16% from the U.K., 11.1% from Italy, and 3.7% from Australia. In Great Britain the rental market for videos in the English language market is dominated to a considerable extent by U.S. products. There is, however, another interesting aspect of the British video market, which is the importance of ethnic language videos. The Asian community is a phenomenally heavy user of video. A study quoted by Alvarado, for example, discovered in one area of London that one retail outlet for Asian films had a list of 30,000 titles and a membership of 5,000 people. Another study, found that the penetration of video in Gujarati homes is 74%, with an overwhelming tendency to use it to watch films from the subcontinent. There are apparently examples of some Asian women watching a hundred films *a week* (*Cable and Satellite Europe,* 1987). In Italy, 39.7% of films on video are from Italy, 44.7% from the U.S. In Spain the pattern is similar: 30% U.S., 25% Spain, 16% Italy, 10% Great Britain, and 19% from other countries.

Finally, in this examination of existing patterns of distribution of television and video programming, it is instructive to look at the program content of even those television services which, I suspect, are assumed by almost everyone to be dominated by American material. I admit here that I am only referring to Europe, but I do find it intriguing that the real picture of the program content is far more European than has perhaps been allowed. Table 1 describes the percentage of program material delivered by satellite-based services to cable systems which is produced in Europe and not in the United States.

What is the point I am making about the existing patterns of distribution of television, and to a lesser extent videocassettes by relating this mass of detail, which is, I admit, highly variable? My argument is a simple one: that

Table 1. Programming on Satellite Services (13-week sample)

	EEC Content %		Avg. Daily
	1986	1987	Output (hrs.)
THE ARTS CHANNEL	84	77	2.5
BRAVO	8	40	24
THE CHILDREN'S CHANNEL	62	63	10
HOME VIDEO CHANNEL	13	12	8
LIFESTYLE	55	37	4
PREMIERE	13	13	12
SCREEN SPORT	54	27	7
SKY CHANNEL	51	54	17
STAR CHANNEL	—	6.5	9
SUPER CHANNEL	—	88	24

Source: Cable TV Authority: Annual Report/Accounts 1986/7.

the structure of distribution is far more complex than has often been allowed for. One can see many nodal points for the future around which production has grown—principally in the major industrial societies other than the United States, but also to an increasing extent in other countries—which will simply not go away or readily wither under heat emanating from North America. Indeed, these centers will become ever more aggressive and successful in their efforts to compete with the United States on the international market. I have in mind here the increasing competitiveness on the international market of such major organizations as the British Broadcasting Corporation (BBC), Zweites Deutsche Ferensehen (ZDF), and Arbeitsgemeinschaft der offtenlich-rechtslichten Rundfunkkanstalten der Bundesrepublik (ARD), but also the rapidly growing power and wealth of production houses in such diverse places as Egypt, Brazil, Hong Kong, and Japan. In contemplating the future, it is useful to remember that television as a global institution is relatively new, a creation of the 1960s and 1970s, and that to this extent the potential competition to the United States is really only just up and running. In my view, what the existing and emerging patterns of consumption represent are not an American hegemony at all, if taken to mean a total domination, but a complex and evolving structure, which has hidden within the central fact of television: on the whole, national audiences and audiences defined by some singular demography, prefer *their own programming.*

CHALICES:
THE NEW TECHNOLOGY AND GLOBAL TELEVISION

Of course, whatever qualifications I am placing on contemporary patterns, there may be enough evidence for someone to argue that if new delivery systems are in place, they can overwhelm all potential opposition. Table 2

Table 2. Number of Households in Europe Able to Receive a Given Channel

CHANNEL	Austria	Belgium	Denmark	Finland	France	Germany	Ireland	Luxem-borug	Nether-lands	Norway	Sweden	Switzer-land	UK	TOTAL
3SAT	310,000					2,075,000						334,000		2,719,000
FILMNET		35,000		5,000					60,000	3,000	3,000			106,000
RAI		2,500,000						50,000				1,025,000		3,575,000
RTL-PLUS	270,000	40,000				2,046,000		100,000						2,456,000
SAT 1	360,000					2,075,000								2,435,000
SKY	293,708	963,420	103,410	281,963	37,931	2,023,212	238,971	76,227	3,156,658	279,695	256,222	1,200,239	200,549	9,112,277
SUPER CHANNEL	302,000	538,000	82,000	258,000	33,000	2,072,000	255,000	81,000	2,935,000	223,000	244,000	777,000	137,000	7,940,000
TELECLUB						700						45,000		45,700
TV5	16,293	1,049,589	43,773	77,873	67,012	1,038,000		71,373	1,655,177	62,698	156,739	406,712		4,645,239
WORLDNET	150	310,000	9,474	41,896	250	635,000	37,000	67,500	104,500	71,000	152,712	837	31,214	1,461,533
NRK										750,000				750,000
INTELSAT 27.5 WEST														
CHILDREN'S CHANNEL							225,000				1,500		100,000	327,000
CNN					2,281						141,956			144,237
ARTS							40,000		350,000		1,000		12,000	403,000
PREMIERE													40,000	40,000
LIFESTYLE							238,000				1,250		86,804	326,094
SCREEN SPORT				1,000			238,000				1,500		76,324	316,824
BR 3						1,569,000								1,569,000
EINS PLUS						2,075,000								2,075,000
EUREKA						1,533,000								1,533,000
MUSICBOX						2,075,000								2,075,000
WRD 3						1,185,000								1,185,000
CANAL J					10,000									10,000
LA CINQ					10,000									10,000
M6					10,000									10,000

Source: Cable and Satellite Europe, June, 1987.

allows us to examine the evidence, in particular from Europe, where there i certainly no arguing with the sheer *physical* availability of new channels. All very impressive, but the available objective evidence of the consider able and continuing losses incurred by cable and satellite services throughou Europe point to the difficulties of developing new television markets. Ther remains, however, a basic belief within the advertising industry that satellit television funded by advertisements will succeed. The optimism is borne or occasional flashes of success, even if at the moment these are as rare as th flowering of cacti in the desert.

The problem with the evidence employed is that it tends to be drawn onl: from cabled homes, which in Europe remain a tiny minority, and therefor provide a very uncertain basis on which to begin to make a judgment. Fo example, in Germany, the average daily television viewing in April 1987 wa 134 minutes. This was divided: ARD 57 minutes; ZDF 54 minutes; th regional network 14 minutes; all other channels including SAT 1 and RTI plus, 9 minutes. There is no question that if the programming packages pu together to be delivered by new media systems—cable, communicatior satellites, DBS—could restructure the television audience in key market: such as Europe, then there is vast wealth to be tapped in terms of the poten tial revenue.

Advertising on television within Europe is defined by three main zones

1. Those countries in Northern Europe where there has traditionally bee1 no national TV advertising—Norway, Sweden, Denmark
2. Those countries where there has been some advertising, but where i has been heavily circumscribed, such as Germany, France, Belgium Holland, Switzerland, Austria, and Finland
3. Those countries where advertising is generally accepted, such as Italy Portugal, Spain, Greece, Ireland, and the United Kingdom.

It was recently calculated that the total current advertising within Europe is about $6 billion, and that if television advertising were "set free" in coun tries within the first two zones, the figure could be closer to $8.4 billior (*Broadcast,* 1987). According to research commissioned by Sky Channe from Saatchi & Saatchi, expenditure on television advertising in Europe wa to be 58% by 1990, from $4.7 billion in 1985 (0.17% of GDP) to $7.4 billior in 1990 (0.24% of GDP). Patrick Cox of Sky argued that the figure could b 0.3% of GDP, or $12 billion (Sturgess, 1985). Cox's argument assumes tha the total amount of viewing will increase, particularly on the new advertis ing supported channels: "The problem we've had as a channel is that we ar selling a very sophisticated product—pan-European advertising—when th national advertising markets don't really exist." Presumably the same kin of argument could be made about other parts of the world: that the wealtl there and all that is needed is the correct programming strategy, to be carried by the new distribution technologies, and thus is provided the key to unlock the door to the treasury.

As indicated at the beginning of this paper, anticipation of the future, with fear and loathing rubbing up against hoping and dreaming, has rested on the assumption that the new technologies will be successful, and that U.S. product will be at the heart of the package they deliver. Certainly there are some interesting clues that such programming, used on new outlets, can occasionally gather the treasure. In one particular instance, new television services, using considerble amounts of U.S. material, have had spectacular success in restructuring the audience and generating advertising revenue. The example to which I am referring is that of Italy, where the rise of the television stations following the 1976 Constitutional Court's decision to allow unregulated local private broadcasting, led to a dramatic increase in advertising revenue, from 33 billion lire in 1970 to 198 billion lire in 1983, a growth of over 500%. Almost three quarters of this growth occurred between 1976 and 1983. Total advertising expenditure in Italy increased from 566 billion in 1970 to 2,666 billion lire in 1983; and as a percentage of GDP, from 0.42 to 0.50. That latter figure masks a decline from 1970 to 1976 from 0.42% of GDP to 0.30% in 1976. The new private television stations therefore had the effect of restoring the percentage of GDP to what it had been and then adding some, largely by drawing off revenue from other media and generating new sources of revenue (Sturgess, 1985; de Sola Pool, 1976).

I am led to conclude, however, that this example will not provide the model, and that *at best* television services, new or old, dominated by imported, specifically American television, are in for a very rough ride, precisely because they will find it increasingly difficult, politically and culturally, to unlock the advertising wealth which undoubtedly exists.

An interesting and salutary tale which is relevant here occurred on August 8, 1987, when the board of Superchannel, the 24-hour pan-European satellite service run by the British commercial television companies, met in crisis. *The Sunday Times* headline reported simply, if a little obviously, "ITV fights to stay in orbit." Launched in January 1987, Superchannel offered to European cable systems "the best of British programming" provided from the massive archives of the BBC and the ITV companies. In March, its joint managing director Richard Hooper was still cooing optimistically about the future, the fruits that the new channel would offer, and the kind of audience that would be picking them. He told a meeting in Copenhagen, "We at Superchannel strongly believe that there is a market for pan-European television that sits alongside and enriches national television, increases choice." The character of that market, he made clear in a later article: "Superchannel is an entertainment channel but is seeking out the 25 year-old to 45 year-old upwardly mobile family audience.'' At the beginning of the year, neverthe-less, everyone—the channel, its rivals, ad agencies—agreed that only time would tell if a diet of essentially U.K. programming would draw the crowds and particularly those all important, highly valued Euro-yuppies. The mood, however, was optimistic—how could it not be—here was a station offering the best product from what the British had been touting for years as the best television system in the world.

However, the experience of the Murdoch rival, Sky Channel, had made it quite clear that starting a satellite channel to Europe was, at least in the first years, a good way of losing money. Sky in fact lost approximately £5.6 million in the year prior to the start of Superchannel, and the Swedish-owned channel *Filmnet* lost £ *8 million* in the first nine months of 1986.

The picture presented at the crisis meeting of Superchannel in August, however, was of a channel which, while it could be received in more than 8 million homes in 15 countries with an average audience of 1 million, was simply not generating enough advertising revenue to survive. The roots of the crisis were varied; for instance, there had been enormous and damaging difficulties in making agreements with all the relevant parties for the use of British material. Critically, though, the advertising simply was not there in the necessary quantities. The projected operating costs for the 1988 years was £21 million, up £2 million from the previous year. The revenue from advertising was projected at £7 million, with the shareholders expected to make up the shortfall. It was this discrepancy between revenue and expendi-ture, amplified by increasing doubts as to whether there would ever suffi-cient market for satellite delivered services, which led to the crisis meeting of Superchannel's board. The board's response was to cut costs, shed staff, and completely reappraise their programming strategy with the aim of introducing more mass appeal programs into peak time slots. There were those in the industry who remained less than convinced that the channel would see another summer, and their doubts were shown to be correct when in 1988 the major investors in Superchannel sold, at enormous loss, their controlling interest in an Italian company.

Much of the analysis of Superchannel's problems point to the institu-tional trip-wires being placed in front of it—by European governments, European cable operators, and the trade unions—as being the real basis for its fall. Certainly these were real problems which should not be underesti-mated, but it is interesting, however, to speculate as to what would have happened had the channel been given a straight run at the European tele-vision audience. In my view, it would almost certainly have been in exactly the same failure.

The basis of my conclusion is relatively straightforward: the Channel and its backers were using an expensive means of throwing a uniform program schedule mainly at audiences whose singular characteristic was that they were different from each other in their needs and expectations, moods and manners, histories and cultures.

The assumptions behind Superchannel are by now fairly commonplace; in the satellite and cable fields, new markets are there to be developed on the wave of the future: deregulated, nonpublic service television. What is becoming very clear is that the missionaries of the new age have, in fact, little grasp of the social dynamics of the European television audience, even though such understanding is quite clearly necessary to the design of the television architecture of the future European audience. Indeed, as I have suggested, it is in the very use of the singular noun "audience" that much of the problems lie, since the structural weakness of pan-European television is the logical assumption it must make about there being a pan-European *audience,* rather than *audiences.* Superchannel's error was to put together a naive equation: British television has masses of high quality television; this appeals to yuppies; there are lots of yuppies throughout Europe; they have lots of disposable income; advertisers like that; therefore deliver those programs and presto! you have yourself an income. This grossly overemphasized social commonalities, underestimated the forces of national cultures as powerful definers of national cultural taste (even among yuppies), and ignored the fact that not all those yuppies reside at the end of a cable system. It is an error, not unique to Superchannel, rooted in the hubris so redolent of the so-called third age of broadcasting, the paucity of market research, and the beguilement with the Gucci technologies of satellite delivery. The result was the absence of any proper attempt to grasp the more prosaic, but just as important, sociology of reception.

There is no decent model, both comprehensive and comparative, empirically and conceptually adequate for the television markets of the future. However, clues do exist, scattered around, providing insight into the likelihood, or not, of imported television being successful, or even acceptable, and into that mysterious question of what audiences of the future will require for their enlightenment and pleasure. To explain why I am saying this, in effect placing a question mark against the assumptions underlying the conventional wisdom, I need to examine the nitty gritty of *how* television audiences already make their decisions, and some of the reasons *why* they make those decisions.

CHOICE:
PUBLIC ATTITUDES TOWARD GLOBAL TELEVISION

The whole debate about international television, whether taking place inside the boardrooms of multinational corporations, at market research companies, or in the conspiratorial mind of the academic left tends to be loaded with assumptions about cultural influences, about meanings and the shaping of consciousness, and even about the sheer amounts of television flows. Yet each equally holds those views in the abstract, outside of any grasp of their place within the individual biographies of the myriad members of more than a 100 television societies. I must agree with the following observation by the late Ithiel de Sola Pool (1976):

> There is, in fact, remarkably little research of any kind on international communication. There is a great deal of essay writing about it. But by research I mean studies in which data is collected to establish or refute some general proposition...The two topics regarding international communication that have been most extensively studied, and very badly, I must say, are the balance in the flow of communication among countries, and the cultural biases in what flows. These are topics on which there have been a few empirical studies, though by far the great bulk of that literature consists of polemical essays unenlightened by facts.

Well, what do the facts tell us? Let's begin with that most famous son of the television age, J.R. Ewing and his "wall-to-wall *Dallas*." Since its launch in 1978 and its export to many foreign countries, *Dallas* has become the exemplar of the global influence of American television, the apparent embodiment of the theory of cultural imperialism, a metaphor for an entire argument, and the very essence of discussions about international program trade. Slick, polished, dramatic, sexy, wealthy, cheap to buy in and so, so popular. At a Unesco meeting in Mexico in July, 1982, the then French Minister of Culture, Jack Lang, identified *Dallas* as a threat to the national culture of France. Lang called for a crusade "against financial and intellectual imperialism that no longer grabs territory, or rarely, but grabs consciousness, ways of thinking, ways of living (Cantor & Cantor, forthcoming).

Lang's words are familiar. What has been almost totally ignored, however, in the debate around *Dallas* is the relationship between the program and the various audiences who, for whatever reasons or circumstances, actually sit down and watch it. Any exploration at that level, no matter how cursory, provides some important qualifications to the argument of its dominant influence. For example, one discovers that in most countries, *Dallas* is not as popular as home-produced soaps. It is completely ignored in countries as diverse as Brazil and Japan, which nevertheless have well established and highly popular domestic dramas as part of their main television program output. In Britain, whence came the "wall-to-wall" phrase with the solitary exception of the "who shot JR" episode, the program never came anywhere near competing with such long-standing, popular dramas as *Corporation St.* and *Crossroads*. In Japan, *Dallas* was introduced in October of 1981, went to a 10% share, and then to a 3% share by December.

This is compared, for example, with the popularity of *Oshin,* a locally produced, six-day-a-week, 15-minute serial drama of a woman triumphing over
hardship. *Oshin* had an audience share of 57%, once recording the highest
share ever in the history of Japanese television, 63% (Cantor and Cantor,
forthcoming). In explaining the difference, two academic observers make
an extremely interesting observation:

> In contrast to *Oshin,* the suspense in *Dallas* arises from greed, self-interest, ly-
> ing and manipulation—behavior that might be considered objectionable and
> shameful in a culture that prizes loyalty, self-sacrifice and honoring one's obli-
> gation. Thus, it is possible that shows which do not conform to particular
> basic values in a culture might be rejected by that culture. (Cantor & Cantor,
> forthcoming)

In New Zealand, other kinds of imported programming from other countries are also more popular than *Dallas* and its ilk (Lealand, 1983).
    It is simply untrue that imported television programs, from the United
States or other metropolitan countries, always have a dominant presence
within the indigenous television culture. Certainly they do not always attract
larger audiences than homemade programs, nor do they always threaten
national production. In Brazil, for example, the sixth biggest television
market in the world, the level of imported television material fell by 32%
between 1973 and 1982, largely due to the activities of TV Globo, which
captures between 60% and 80% of the television audience. Between 5:30
p.m. and 11 p.m., 84% of the channel's programs are in-house productions.
In August 1983, the top 10 programs were all Globo productions, including
three telenovelas. As Richard Paterson points out, in Brazil one sees "a television devoted to national culture. TV Globo has fully utilized the possibilities created by these circumstances to develop a different sort of television.
The development of an indigenous television puts into question the thesis
about the inevitability of traditional drama and folk music retreating before
the likes of *Peyton Place* and *Bonanza* (Paterson, 1982). In fact, TV Globo
now produces more programs than any other channel in the world, and
reaches 99.9% of television households in Brazil. In 1986, it had the most
popular telenovela ever, *Roques Santeriro* (Roques the Saint), which at
times had a 90% of the audience. Globo exports to more than 100 countries,
including China, the USSR, and Germany. Its production *Isaura, the Slave
Girl,* was something of an international success. Other networks in Brazil,
such as TV Manchete and TV Bandeirantes, are beginning to compete with
Globo with their own productions. *Dallas,* by the way, in 1982 occupied
69th position in the Brazilian ratings, and 109th in Mexico.
    Elsewhere in Latin America there is much U.S. product to be found, but
one also finds the ubiquitous telenovelas which are, according to one recent

account "a fixed ad schedule-topping 'feature'" (Petch, 1987). In Central America, one new angle on U.S. influence is the growth of the Hispanic SIN-TV network. Its programs *Noticiero SIN* and *Mundo Latino* have been well received in Guatemala, Honduras, El Salvador, and Costa Rica. In Guatemala, however, schedules are dominated by such soaps as *De Pura Sangre* and *Viviv un Poco* from Mexico, and *Topacio* from Argentina. In Honduras, programming is dominated by a combination of U.S. imports and Latin American telenovelas. In Mexico, the popular channel, Channel 2, consists of family entertainment, sports, news, and hours each day of local telenovela. In Colombia, with three television networks, a "significant proportion of TV content is produced locally" (Petch, 1987). An analysis of programs during one week on the two commercial channels found 54% of programming produced domestically. Of the 46% of imported television, 14.6% were soap operas from Brazil, Mexico, and Venezuela; 18.7% were children's programs from Latin America and the U.S. Prime time was dominated by national soap operas such as *Tuyo es mi Corazon* and *Amandote*. In Venezuela, 55% of the programming is produced domestically, and while U.S. and Brazilian soaps are popular, "they do not compete for the prime time spots filled by local productions such as *Cristal* and *Los Donatti*" (Petch, 1987). Both of these programs have been exported to countries throughout the region and the United States. In 1985, *Cristal* had a higher audience share than *Dynasty* in Miami. In Ecuador, 65% of programming is imported from Latin America and the United States. In Paraguay, imports from the United States amount to 70% of programs, whereas in Peru the government has demanded 60% of domestic production. Presently, 65% of programs are imported, of which 46% are from the United States. The 35% domestically-produced television is remarkable, particularly since before 1980 there was virtually none at all.

Another illustration of how indigenous populations do not respond to imported material in stereotypical ways can be seen in South Africa. There TV1 carries such imports as *Dallas* and *The A-Team,* with indigenous programming on TV2 and TV3. In December 1983, Bophusthatswana Television, broadcasting from the Bop capital of Mmabatho, began to broadcast in English, but with increasing amounts of material of a local nature in Setswana. More and more of the black population of South Africa turned to Bop TV. Indeed, such had been its success that President Mpepha of the tiny republic of Venda has announced that he wants his own television service, Radio Television Thohoyandau. In Kenya, the most popular programs are locally produced programs such as *Vitimbi* in Kiswahili and social dramas such as *Fedhena.*

In Singapore, the government's Singapore Broadcasting Corporation runs three channels, broadcasting in English, Mandarin, Tamil, and Malay. Sixty percent of the programs are English language, the bulk of which are

nported, but Chinese programs, particularly from Hong Kong, are con-
stently the most popular. The Malaysian station TV3 had proven to be
articularly successful by transmitting in Cantonese for the Chinese popula-
on in Malaysia and Singapore. In Thailand the most popular programs are
hai movies, though as one commentator recently observed, "Chinese
lays are the new rage of Thai television with series from Hong Kong's TVB
nd ATV leading the rating charts" (Marshall, 1987). Japanese television
as also proven to be very successful in Thailand, while local Thai producers
oncentrate more and more on musical variety game shows and comedies,
hich are very popular with country housewives. In Ireland, which imports
5% of its total output, and where the BBC and ITV are already available
) most of the population, the most popular programs for many years have
een *The Late, Late Show* on Saturdays, hosted by Gay Byrne, followed by
1e home produced drama series *The Riordans, Brackens,* and *Glenroe.* In
ountries such as New Zealand and Sweden, where enormous problems facing
1e local broadcasting services necessitate importation of foreign television,
ome grown programs nevertheless compete in terms of popularity. In New
ealand, in fact, there is evidence that the bulk of the population actively
islikes the American television they see on their screens (Lealand, 1983). In
imbabwe, in 1982, locally produced programs such as *The Mukadda Family*
ad much higher ratings than the imported *Dallas, Dynasty* and *Falcon
rest.* One author writing about television in Bangladesh observed:

> Imported programmes are popular, but do not dominate BTV. In the 1980s
> some would say that the *Incredible Hulk* does sit uneasily between *Shilpo-O-
> Shahilya* [a series on art and literature] and *Jalsa* [a program on classical
> music]. *Dallas, Charlie's Angles* and *CHIPS* are cheaper for BTV to transmit
> than any local dramas—but local productions challenges them in a way few
> outsiders would believe possible. (Marshall, 1987)

And so one could go on. This is not to say that imported programs are not
n important part of the total content of many countries broadcasting, nor
ndeed that they are not, in some cases, very popular. It is merely to observe
hat even a limited glance at the available evidence indicated that the role of
elevision in any society is far more complex than is often allowed for. As
ar as we can tell, audiences do discriminate, and do tend to prefer home-
roduced television rather than slavishly pursuing imported programs.

There is another very interesting clue to the truth of this argument from
n example which at first might appear to support the opposite case, that
national cultures are cracking under the pressure from new transnational
programming and program forms. The classic example of a major European
tation setting out to produce a European *Dallas* was ZDF's production of
Schwardzewaldklinik (Black Forest Clinic). First shown in Germany in
October 1985, it was an immediate and massive success, with an opening

audience share of 60%. By January 1986, it was reaching 28 million viewer
per episode, about 65% of the audience. An obvious and plausible analysi
was that it had all the ingredients which seemed to characterize successfu
American television, the kind of television which maybe the new satellit
and cable services could successfully exploit: drama, family, romance
power, sex, intrigue. Another way of looking at its success, however, is t
see how it tapped into certain key themes lying half-dormant within th
modern German mind. The German sociologist, Michael Hoffman, in a
excellent analysis of this program, links its success not to its apparent trans
national ingredients, but to the creative genre of:

> *Heimatfilm,* films aboout localities and landscapes, which evoke in a large seg-
> ment of the population a strong feeling of belonging, even of identification.
> The need for "Heimat," sense of peace and home, for a personal, concrete
> environment is deeply embedded in the phenomenon which Elisas Canetti called
> the German symbol for the mass of people: the forest as the archtypical shelter.
> Expressed in terms of human relations it means the sense of community (a)
> tradition. . .reflected in the classic German (Sociological distinction) between
> Gesellschaft and Geminschaft i.e. between society and community. (Hoffman,
> 1987)

Hoffman points to the way in which the central, archetypical images of
culture are carried within an oral tradition and then sealed within th
physical artifacts of the print and visual media. The economics of produc
tion ensure that the images so captured have the most resonance wit
popular consciousness. There is a very plausible thesis, then, that the root
of the success of programming such as *Schwardzwaldklinik* lie deep withi
antiquity. When the gloves are really off in the emerging collision betwee
national and transnational television forces that basic observation will be o
far more than academic interest.

What I am suggesting is that one must approach the question of futur
television markets from a slightly different angle than that of econometric
and market research. One can only really understand the role and use o
television if one understands not how it is imposed on societies, since that i
simply not how the process works, but rather how it taps into and feeds of
the rhythms, moods, and moralities that are present. The case which Hoff
man makes, about the importance of deeply embedded cultural themes, coul
easily be echoed in Britain. There the most powerful television, certainly
drama, is the highly successful and long-running *Coronation St.,* and mor
recently *Eastenders.* There is also a long tradition of single drama. N
American program, not even *Dallas,* has come close to competing in popu
larity and critical success with these programs. And in this way, I am sug
gesting, British is far from unique.

The real clue as to what European audiences prefer is rather simple to portray. Table 3 is a list of the top 20 programs in France, Germany, and Britain in April 1987 (Eurodience, 1987). The significant feature of these listings of popular programs is just how little imported television, including J.S. programming, there is. There are also other more impressionistic but qually interesting clues scattered across European television. In Finland, a number of new channels are available through cable, along with the Finnish advertiser-supported MTV, but two-thirds of all viewing time is of programs from the public service Yielsradio [YLE]. In the year 1981–82, 60.5% of programming was produced in Finland, with individual figures of 63.3% or YLE and 48.4% for MTV. Of the 39.5% of programming from abroad 26.1% came from the United States, 19.6% from Great Britain, and 11.3% from Sweden. The rest of the foreign television came from 26 other counries—from Eurovision, Intervision, Nordvision, and from coproductions. Another interesting fact of Finnish television life is that TV3 (OKA), jointly set up by YLE, MTV, and the electronics company Nokia, is watched by more people in the Helsinki area than all satellite and cable channels put together. In Portugal, RTP produces 60% of it as own programming. Last year, the top program was the RTP soap opera *Palavras Cruzades,* and considerable success was also had with two Brazilian soaps from TV Globo: *Vereada Tropical* and *Corpo a Corpo.*

Table 3. Top 20 Programs in France, the U.K. and Germany.

	Channel	Day of Month	PM (time shown)	% Share of Viewing
op 20 France				
1 LA FEMME DE MON POTE	Film	TF1	5	20:31	38.8
Comedy 1st broadcast in 1986.					
2 LE GENDARME SE MARIE	Film	TF1	12	20:38	36.7
Comedy previous broadcast in 1981.					
3 LOTO SPORTIF		TF1	13	20:32	36.2
4 SUBWAY	Film	TF1	13	20:42	33.2
Comedy drama 1st broadcast in 1986.					
5 IL N'YEN A QU'UNE	Show	TF1	15	20:42	31.7
6 LOTO		TF1	15	20:34	31.6
7 MAGNUM FORCE*	Film	A2	21	20:35	31.6
Thriller.					
8 100 000 DOLLARS AU SOLEIL*	Film	TF1	26	20:36	31.3
Aventure comedy.					
9 LE TOMBEUR	Theatre	A2	29	20:33	30.7
Comedy.					
10 LOTO SPORTIF		TF1	6	20:31	30.2
11 LE CHEMIN DES ECOLIERS	Film	TF1	6	20:40	29.7
Comedy Drama previous broadcast in 1980.					

(continued)

Table 3. Continued

		Channel	Day of Month	PM (time shown)	% Share of Viewing
12 GRAND PUBLIC: SIM	Show	TF1	24	20:33	28.7
A live variety show based on entertainment star.					
13 TIRAGE DU LOTO		TF1	1	20:33	28
14 FOOTBALL: FRANCE-ISLANDE		TF1	29	19:55	27.8
15 CHAMPS-ELYSEES	Show	A2	25	20:32	26.2
Every Saturday night, well-established show.					
16 LA GRANDE EVASION*	Film	TF1	19	20:39	26
Adventure					
17 GRAND PUBLIC: S. STALLONE*	Show	TF1	3	20:37	25
18 L'HEURE SIMENON	TV Film	TF1	1	20:40	24.8
A new series of adaptions of Georges Simenon:					
19 UN ELEPH CA TROMPE ENORM	Film	A2	14	20:33	24.4
Comedy					
20 NOUS IRONS TOUS AU PARADIS	Film	A2	28	20:32	24.3
Comedy					

Top 20 UK

		Channel	Day of Month	PM (time shown)	% Share of Viewing
1 EASTENDERS [twice weekly]	UK Serial	BBC1		19:30	36.7/47.6
Twice weekly with rebroadcast.					
2 CORNATION STREET [twice weekly]	UK Serial	ITV		19:30	24.8/32.2
Produced by Granada, on air since 1960, twice weekly.					
3 LIVE FROM THE PALLADIUM	Show	ITV	5	19:45	29.7
One from a series of shows broadcasting during six weeks.					
4 DON'T WAIT UP	Series	BBC1	6	20:30	29.4
Comedy series.					
5 EVERY DECREASING CIRCLES	Show	BBC1	13	20:30	28.5
Comedy show.					
6 LIVE FROM THE PALLADIUM	Show	ITV	12	19:45	27.4
7 BERGERAC	UK Serial	BBC1	4	20:35	26.8
Detective serial.					
8 JUST GOOD FRIENDS	Serial	BBC1	12	21:25	26.3
Comedy serial.					
9 BOB SAYS OPPORTUNITY KNOCKS	Show	BBC1	4	19:50	26
10 THIS IS YOUR LIFE	Show	ITV	8	21:00	25.9
Based on the life of a entertainment star.					
11 WORLD CHAMPION	Boxing	BBC1	18	21:50	25.6
12 ONLY FOOLS AND HORSES	Series	BBC1	12	21:25	25.4
Comedy show broadcast on Christmas.					
13 BERGERAC		BBC1	11	20:35	25.3
14 CLIVE JAMES ON TV	Show	ITV	5	22:00	25.2
Comedy show.					
15 THE MIRROR CRACK'D*	Film	BBC1	18	19:45	25.1
Thriller.					
16 BOY SAYS OPPORTUNITY KNOCKS	Show	BBC1	11	19:40	25
17 NEWS, SPORT AND WEATHER		BBC1	18	21:35	24.9

Table 3. Continued

	Channel		Day of Month	PM (time shown)	% Share of Viewing
18 THIS IS YOUR LIFE	Show	ITV	1	19:00	24.2
19 ONE BY ONE	UK Series	BBC1	4	19:05	24
20 CLIVE JAMES ON TV	Show	ITV	19	21:00	23.9
Top 20 W.G.					
1 WETTEN, DASS	Game + Show	ZDF	4	20:16	40.4
"What are the odds".					
2 SPION ZWISCHEN ZWEIFRONTEN	Film	ARD	12	20:17	37.7
A spy between two fronts.					
3 VERSCHOLLEN IN PAZIFIK	TVD	ARD	5	20:35	36.8
4 LANDTAGSWAHL IN HESSEN		ARD	5	21:21	36.4
5 BEN HUR*	Film	ZDF	26	20:16	34.8
6 DAS ERBE DER GULDENBURGS	WG Serial	ZDF	4	19:32	31.4
7 EUROPAPOKAL		ARD	8	20:11	31.1
European football cup.					
8 EUROPAPOKAL		ZDF	22	21:59	30
Bayern/Madrid.					
9 DIE VERFLIXTE 7	Game + Show	ARD	11	20:16	28.9
"The silly 7"					
10 DAS ERBE DER GULDENBURGS		ZDF	11	19:30	28.6
11 TATORT	Series	ARD	20	20:17	28.2
WG series based on crime thrillers adaptions.					
12 EUROPAPOKAL		ZDF	22	20:04	28
Munchen Gladbach/Dundee					
13 DAS ERBE DER GULDENBURGS		ZDF	25	19:21	27.4
14 WAS BIN ICH	Game	ARD	14	20:17	27
"What am I?"					
15 EIN FALL FUR ZWEI	Series	ZDF	10	20:15	26.8
"A case for two".					
16 EUROPAPOKAL		ARD	8	22:04	26.5
Dundee/M'Bach.					
17 DERRICK*	Series	ZDF	24	20:15	26
18 DER GROSSE PREIS	Game	ZDF	9	19:30	25.8
"The big prize".					
19 DER DENVER CIAN DYNASTIE*	US Serial	ZDF	15	21:00	25.7
20 DIE WILSHEIMER	WG Serial	ARD	13	20:17	24.3

The point of this Cook's tour, then, is actually quite simple: To say that a rather more discrete, subtle, and empirical approach is necessary to the sociocultural experience of television, before we can begin to understand the actual experience of the flow of international television and therefore the notion of the likely dominance of U.S. television. And when we do experience how choices have been made about programming on terrestrial systems, the preference is clear.

Table 4. Average Hours TV Watched Per Week

	Netherlands	Switzerland	FRG	Belgium
Nov 1984 (4–64 yrs)	16.4	11.6	—	—
March 1986 (13–34 yrs)	20.9	13.4	17.8	24.2

Source: ESMAR 1987.

Table 5. Viewing Behavior

Total Available Channels	Loyalty to Channels (4 weeks)			
	Belgium 23	Germany 22	Netherlands 23	Switzerland 19
% WATCHING				
1 channel only	0.4	0.8	—	1.0
2 channels	1.6	1.2	10.1	2.2
3 channels	3.3	2.9	13.7	4.1
4 channels	4.8	4.2	18.7	8.0
5 channels	16.8	12.6	20.9	10.4
6 channels	25.4	17.0	15.3	17.3
7 channels	23.0	21.3	8.4	21.3
8 channels	8.7	16.9	6.8	13.3
9 channels	7.3	5.8	3.3	9.9
10 channels	6.2	8.8	2.4	5.2
11 channels	0.7	6.4	0.4	4.6
12+channels	1.8	3.1	—	2.6
Major channel share	38.1	24.8	56.0	24.9
Average watched	6.6	7.7	5.0	6.9

Source: Dent et al., ESOMAR, 1987.

What are the choices which people make in multichannel environments? Is there evidence here which will provide a clue to the question of whether or not the future of television lies with imported television from rich societies, particularly from the United States?

In a detailed, empirical study, shown in Tables 4 and 5, Dent, Winkfield, and Lloyd looked at the use of television in a multichannel environment (Dent, Winkfield, & Lloyd, 1987). The countries studied were Netherlands, Belgium, Switzerland, and FRG, and the sample was drawn exclusively from cabled households. Theoretically, the number of channels available at the time of the study in late 1986 were: FRG 3 domestic, 15 other terrestrial, 8 satellite/cable, a total of 26; Netherlands 2 domestic, 15 other terrestrial, 5 satellite/cable, a total of 26. In an earlier study in November 1984, they calculated the average amount of viewing in cabled homes in the four countries, and then recalculated in March of 1986. Allowing for the differences in the sample base, the authors find that of viewing in cable homes has increased. The most interesting part of their research is where they look at viewer loyalty. They comment; "Only a tiny minority are 100% loyal to one channel only, with significant numbers watching as many as 19 or more channels...findings which endorse the argument that audiences are fragmenting; viewers are exercising their choice and enlarging their viewing repertoire to cover many different channels in a variety of languages." However even within the fragmented structure of viewing in cabled homes, there still tends to be a preference for viewing one or two channels. For example, in the Netherlands the viewing of Nederland 1 and 2 accounts for 75% of viewing in cabled homes. In Germany, the viewing of ARD and ZDF amounts to 46% if viewing in cable homes, compared with 15.2% for SAT 1, 9.8% for Music Box, 9.7% for RTL plus, 5.6% for Sky, 2.6% for 3 Sat, and 11.1% for other channels.

Dent, Winkfield, and Lloyd's main conclusion, however, is that greater choice increases the television audience in terms of the total number of hours viewed. The German experience *seems* to suggest that the more television people watch in total, the more different channels they watch. Sky and Music Box hold strong minority audiences and are watched at different times of day, for different periods of time, and have a higher share on the second set: "In short, people in cabled homes are using the new opportunities to watch TV at times, or in places, where they did not previously watch." The authors also add: "Minority audiences are responding to the programmes designed for them, as has happened in the UK with C4. It appears that more could be done in this area, and furthermore that audiences will exercise their freedom of choice in a discriminatory way" (Dent et al., 1987).

The tantalizing thesis which emerges, and which remains hovering in front of the eyes of some media entrepreneurs, is that increasing choice leads to less loyalty, and to fragmentation defined not by demographics but "life-style" variables. These definable target groups and specific minorities then provide the basis for new markets.

In Britain there is some research on cable viewing patterns which seems to confirm the general thrust of this analysis. There were 1,190,000 homes passed by cable, and 193,173 homes subscribing to cable program services in Britain as of July, 1987 (Annual reports, 1986/87). Cable households in the United Kingdom tend to be larger (3.56 people), more likely to have a VCR (50%), and/or more than one TV (54%), and spend more time watching television (5.6 hrs. per day) than the national average. They are also overwhelmingly CDE rather than AB. In November, 1986, 28% of viewing time in cabled homes was spent watching cable programs as opposed to broadcast television, up 7 percent from the previous year. Particularly inter-

Table 6. Satellite Share of Weekly Viewing Hours as Percentage

	Scandanavia	Belgium	Germany	Netherlands	Switzerland
Domestic Channels	73	23	64	83	46
Satellite Channels					
Sky	20	1	2		
Superchannel 7	7	—	1	2	1
TV5	—	1	—	—	—
RA II	—	1	—	—	4
3 Sat	—	—	1	—	—
1 Plus	—	—	2	—	—
Musicbox	—	—	2	—	—
Teleclub	—	—	—	—	1
RTL Plus	—	—	13	—	—
Sat 1	—	—	14	—	—
Spill-in Channels					
i.e., other terrestrial		69	1	9	46

Source: PETAR/Dawson Media International, September 1987.

esting, although given the social composition not surprising, was the fact that there was considerably more viewing of cable than of Channel Four or BBC2, the "minority" channels within the Public service system (Annual report, 1986/87).

A study of cable viewing patterns by the Pan-European Television Audience Research [PETAR] (1982) company was conducted in 12 countries, involving 10,000 viewing diaries placed in selected homes. The survey focused only on households connected to cable services, on the grounds that "these represent the likely future scenario for broadcasters and narrowcasters alike." In so far as I understand what that latter statement is saying, it strikes me as begging several extremely large questions, particularly as there is no evidence whatsoever that, on a European scale, cabled homes will be the norm even by the next century.

The research pinpoints in some detail the share of total viewing held by satellite services in cabled homes. In the September 1987 edition of *Media International,* Charles Dawson of Young and Rubicam presented some of the results which appear in Table 6. It is important to remember that these figures are for viewing in cable homes, *not* television homes. What the PETAR research did not mention was the figure for the percentage of television homes on cable systems, and yet that figure is crucial in judging the worth of the conclusions being drawn.

In Belgium, the Netherlands, and Switzerland—the countries with a high penetration of cabled homes—satellite-delivered services are a minimal part of the viewing diet. It is difficult to see how the figures, even viewed with the most committed eye, can justify the statement by Dawson that "evidence

Table 7.   Cabled Homes in Europe in Relation to the PETAR Sample

	Scandanavia	Belgium	Germany	Netherlands	Switzerland
Households	7.25m	3.72m	25.30m	5.50m	2.50m
Homes Connected	1.79m	3.10m	2.30m	3.10m	1.40m
Penetration	24.7%	83%	9%	56%	56%

Source: PETAR/Dawson *Media International*, September 1987.

is growing that, when offered an increased choice of channel, European viewers vigorously exercise that choice.'' They might by straws in the wind, but the straw is truly tiny and the wind extremely limp. The fact remains, however, as these figures demonstrate that even in cabled homes with an existing disposition to at least try new services, audiences are not massively exercising their choice, at least not to an extent which would make the new services viable.

One has, therefore, to be very careful with all these figures since while, on one level, they point to a certain disposition to use the new services, the homes surveyed are only a small minority of those in a position to take out a subscription for new television services. (In Britain about 10%, and an even tinier minority of all homes, one out of 160.) For this reason a study by Wim Bekkers (1987) of the Audience Research department of the Netherlands Broadcasting Foundation (NOS) is particularly interesting since it looks at patterns of viewing of all homes in a multichannel environment, a much more useful sample base for any examination in the long-term strategic question in the development of new television markets than that utilized by PETAR.

Bekkers rehearses the argument of the expansion of the amount of domestic, other terrestrial, and satellite-delivered services to establish the incontestable argument that the amount of television available has increased dramatically in recent years and continues to do so. For example, the number of foreign stations available in the Netherlands has increased from 4 in 1973 to a dozen or more today. Around 60% of homes are connected to a cable system, and 15% to jointly shared satellite dishes. The average television home in the Netherlands can receive 6 foreign channels, and 30% of homes had a VCR as of 1986. Another factor which might make the Netherlands a particularly favorable market for new channels is that 80% of the Dutch speak German either well or reasonably well, and 75% speak English moderately well. The Netherlands therefore provide, if not an ideal, certainly a good context within which to examine in the potential for new services to create new markets.

Bekkers points out one of the main stable factors in Dutch viewing habits —indeed, in my view, of almost all national viewing habits—that ''whatever is made in the Netherlands is always very popular: Dutch products always

**Table 8. Netherlands Viewing Time Within
Sky Reception Area, March 1985, 1986, 12+**

	1985 (%)	1986
Sky	9	5
Music Box	1	1
Europa TV	—	1
BRT1	4	3
BRT2	2	3
ARD	3	3
ZDF	3	2
	22	16
Nederland 1	55	59
Nederland 2	24	25

Source: Wim Bekkers, ESOMAR, 1987.

draw more viewers than similar products from abroad.'' When German and Belgium television were available in the 1970s, interest in them was in the region of no more than 1–4%. Nevertheless, by the 1980s when Netherlands television was awash with potential choices for the viewer, Bekkers' research reveals a fascinating picture of considerable resistance among the Dutch public to exercising such choice. In 1980, 89% of television viewing went to the domestic channels, and 11% to foreign stations. Bekkers then looked at the patterns of viewing within the Sky Channel reception area. His findings are reflected in Table 8.

Bekkers points out that while the amount of viewing is increasing as the total amount of television increases, the extra viewing is not going to the new channels, but rather to the traditional domestic channels. For example, in March 1985, audiences in the Netherlands averaged 129 minutes daily viewing; 105 minutes went to Ned 1 and 2, and 24 minutes to other channels. While the average viewing time had increased one year later to 140 minutes, Ned 1 and 2 maintained their popularity with viewers tuning in on average 119 minutes per day, while viewing of other channels dropped to 21 minutes.

The strength of Bekker's study is that it challenges one of the central myths of world television: that new services offering bought-in television, particularly from the United States, are not only ubiquitous but immensely popular with the audiences of the world. Not so. The strengths of national cultures, the power of language and tradition, and the force that flows, still, within national boundaries, have been grossly underestimated by those who have sought to establish, in this case, Pan-European markets. Hence the qualifications one has to set against the apparent potential advertising revenue which waits to be harnessed, because as will become clear it is difficult to see how new satellite and cable-delivered services could sustain program schedules which are able to seriously dent that disposition, to cast the eye inwards rather than outwards.

While it is therefore objectively true that potential growth in advertising revenue exists, it is equally true that such potential is national rather than transnational. Toby Syfret (1987) of J. Walter Thompson, writing from within the very different world of a major advertising organization, nevertheless nods in the direction of this conclusion:

> It is questionable whether budgets for transnational and pan-European TV campaigns would exceed 5% of total potential expenditure during the next few years if current restrictions on the supply of commercial airtime were to be lifted. It is not possible in any case that they would exceed 10% of the potential. By implication...even if reception were no problem and everyone in Europe had immediate access to satellite TV, centres of broadcasting strength would remain national. They would not shift, as has often been supposed, to transnational "superstations."

What Syret is correctly suggesting is that the real battle for the future of the new television services and their attendant markets will, in all probability, not lie in the creation of new transnational markets, through the production of what Jeremy Isaacs, the first chief executive of Channel Four, called "Euro pudding," but in the reconstruction of national markets currently and traditionally dominated by public service broadcasting organization. The fact remains therefore that, even if the problem of reception is solved—for example, by the creation of extensive broadband cable networks or the ready availability of satellite dishes (the latter being more likely than the former)—the new television services will still have to produce programs of a quality, range, and national character on the continuing basis and at enormous expense if the status quo is to be broken and new markets created. It follows that if new markets are to be successfully created they will not only *not* be dominated by American product, but sociologically and culturally they *cannot* be so dominated. The initial floundering of the new television services which we have witnessed recently is largely rooted in this simple problem—simple, that is, to identify, but not to resolve. If, in the first instance, the new marketeers are marching down a road laden solely or even predominantly with U.S. product, or with product which is essentially "transnational" in nature, they are marching to oblivion.

I am not saying that U.S. television product will not be used by most television systems. Indeed, in some instances there will be a good deal of such programming, and some of it will even be successful. I am saying that U.S. product alone could not last the course, especially if the new markets are to be created through the use of enormously expensive delivery systems such as cable and satellite. The really powerful productive forces within television are and will continue to be national. Where it is used, U.S. television will be as a kind of televisual polyfilla, plugging the gaps in the schedule but with no seminal influence on the structure of the audience and therefore on the economics of future television.

When one undertakes this Cook's tour of world television the impression one is left with is not of uniformity of a single cultural voice and the immersion of all others but of the increasing assertion of cultural diversity on the part of national audiences. As I grubbed around for evidence, however, one dimension which slowly emerged was of the responses not just of the public but of the established media institutions who are increasingly making strategic decisions to kill off precisely those vehicles of the new media which, it has been alleged, will dump their product across the surface of the globe. I am, of course, making the assumption that the only way in which there will be further proliferation of U.S. product will be through the recreation of the individual global television markets on the back of the development of satellite and cable technologies. It could be that the proliferation will take place through the transformation of the existing terrestrial television systems as they shift and maneuver in response to the challenges of that cliche, the third age of broadcasting.

THE OLD ONES:
THE STRATEGIC RESPONSE OF ESTABLISHED BROADCASTERS

In examining the potential for new markets, one needs to allow for the activities of those who already dominate the television markets of many parts of the world, and certainly of the major industrial societies. The whole development of television within Europe, for example, has been based on the principle of public service broadcasting. In examining the future of television markets, and particularly in assessing the likely success of services established outside that tradition, one should not underestimate the strength of those public service traditions, the power of the expectations which have been created among national audiences, or the ability of public service institutions to defend their corner. I am not suggesting that these institutions are inviolable, nor indeed that they are not capable of supreme acts of folly, and of strategic and tactical error. I am merely emphasizing that historically, their power has flowed from their being deeply embedded in national soil. In 1986, the BRU published the results of its own research (Morrison, 1987) into what the British public wanted for the future of television. The context was the campaign then underway for the BBC to be made to take advertising. What the research showed was that while there was support at one level for the BBC being made to take advertising, it was highly qualified support. The public would not be happy, for example, with such arrangements if the programming subsequently offered was considered inferior to that which was previously available. Of the 54% who agreed to advertisements, only 29% said they would still accept them if it meant less choice of programs, a number representing only 16% of the total audience for television. However 75% of those wanting advertisement on the BBC still wanted them if it meant that while the total range of programming available was reduced, they had more of their favorite programs. The group represents 40% of the potential audience. What people would object to is greater scheduling of American programming: 65% of those who favored ads on the BBC changed their mind if it would mean more American programming on British TV. Those who would be prepared to accept the trade-off of ads on the BBC and lower license fees, but more U.S. television, amounted to only 14% of the population. This pattern—of the British television audience being extremely wary of anything which changes or affects adversely the kind of public service television to which they are accustomed —repeats itself across the whole of the research.

It would be wrong, however, to place too much emphasis on the protective significance of public attitudes, but public broadcasters possess another immediate advantage even as they appear to be under siege: their budgetary advantage over all new services. In Britain, the annual program budget for British Satellite Broadcasting, the new DBS service, will be £100 million. In its first years, operations were planned for 1989–90 but were actually up in 1990–91. The joint revenue of the BBC and the ITV companies by then were between £2–3 billion. In Germany, the operating budget for SAT1 was about $75 million and for RTL Plus $35 million—again, contrasting with the hundreds of million of Dms at the disposal of ARD and ZDF.

Basic wealth may not be everything, but in the words of Michael Caine, "I've been rich, and I've been poor, and believe me, rich is better." Their basic wealth clearly gives the large existing stations a considerable head start in developing the television markets of the future, and public service broadcasters throughout Europe are moving to close off their markets from the "predators" of the new services. In Finland for example, TV3 (OKA) was created by YLE, MTV, and Nokia precisely in response to the threat from new media and to advertising revenue. Its programming—film, sports, entertainments, serials, and childrens' programs—anticipates precisely the kind of programming which the new television services will have to offer if they are to prosper. One commentator noted: "At MTV, desperate attempts to recapture audiences and reverse the trend of diminishing advertising revenues have resulted in an unprecedented rush of production quickies: low comedy and quiz shows abound" (World Broadcasting Information, 1987).

In Germany, ARD and ZDF are ever more eager to pursue mass audiences and to kill off their potential competitors at birth. Friedrich Nowotty, *Intendant* of WDR, observed: "If public service broadcasting does not survive the battle for rating, there will be no minority and high quality news and in-

formation programming in the future.'' This is what I would call the temporary barbarism strategy, in which the theology of public service, with all
its worthy ambitions, is abandoned at least momentarily, and more populist
tactics employed in program strategies. A simple index of this is the increase
in the number of movies shown on the two systems, from 437 in 1980 to 660
in 1984. Recently ARD spent Dm 460 million on 2,700 movies. One commentator observed:

> Both ARD and ZDF have been trying to make their programmes more attrac-
> tive to a large audience, partly to avoid conservative criticism and to prove
> that there is no need for commercial television, partly to get higher ratings and
> thus showing that their programmes are well accepted by the audience...On
> the other hand both systems have replaced a considerable portion of foreign
> material by German production in the early evening entertainment programmes
> that are the background for advertising. They particularly made strong efforts
> in producing popular serials with plots and protagonists that are more familiar
> to the German audience than those of the foreign productions. In general the
> programmes for framing the commercials are selected more carefully to attract
> those audience segments particularly middle-aged and younger people, in
> whom the advertisers are interested. (Schultz, 1986)

In Norway, the appearance of satellite television led to a reexamination of
the role of television and the balance of policy between the potential defensive capacities of national television and the cultural threat imposed by
"foreign" satellite-delivered television. The research department of NRK
(Norsk Rikrkringkoisting) the Norwegian public service broadcasting organization, set out "to develop a type of research which could serve public
broadcasting in a new setting of international commercial competition. In
order to do so, we had to find out what would be the new obligations for
public broadcasting...(and) the new competitive environment" (Lund &
Rolland, 1987). The process of change and challenge to the public service
broadcasters began in 1981 with the election of a conservative government
which set out to break the NRK monopoly. The response from within the
NRK has been to articulate the virtues and superiority of domestically produced programming: "The general opinion is that Norway must adapt her-
self to the realities of the satellite age. The answers to the challenge from
abroad is to have more and better national television."

In March 1987, the President of Radiotelevision Italiana [RAI], Manca,
said that they would need to stress the fact that RAI is "an entrepreneur"
by searching for all opportunities to have joint initiatives with private television to compete with the big multinational companies which operate on
the world scene. It was a statement he echoed a few days later when he called
for cooperation between public and private television to develop DBS services

with an Italian flavor (BBC World Broadcasting Information, 1987). In Spain, while the Council of Ministers gave the go-ahead for three independent television channels, they insisted that each should carry at least 40% domestic productions. In another interesting development, it was decided in May 1987, that the Television Espenela TVE2 studio in Barcelona would opt out from the state network for three hours a day from Monday to Friday and offer programs in Catalan, including language courses, children and young people's programs, quiz shows, and news programs.

In other instances the existing large terrestrial systems are being privatized and set in competition with the remaining public service institutions, effectively carving up the television markets before the new services have sufficient time to develop. In Britain there is also much talk of the government using spectrum fees for the allocation of the franchise for the commercial ITV systems, of its "privatising" Channel Four, as well as its introducing a fifth, local television system. In France in 1987 the government privatised TF1, the main national channel, in the midst of a string of developments of new television channels. This left only Antenne 2 and FR3 in the pubic sector, both admittedly under siege. In June 1987, in an effort to further nurture the newly privatized TF1, Prime Minister Chirac announced that he felt it only right that only the private sector should be allowed to carry advertising revenue. TF1 was expected in 1987 to take about 50% of the 7.6 billion francs spent on television advertising. With nearly 2 billion spent on the other two public channels, and the fact that all its commercial rivals do not reach the whole of France, the position of TF1 will be greatly strengthened, particularly in its efforts to fulfill the ambition of its first chairman, Patrick le Lay, to invest heavily in French productions.

Indeed it is precisely these kind of responses which have led some commentators to question the future survival of public service broadcasting. This is not because the institutions as such will be destroyed by new competition, but because they will successfully fight off the competitors and by in so doing change into something closer to the main principles of public service. This is not to say that they will simply offer a diet of imported television, rather that they will bleed the vigor from these national systems and replace them with a domestically produced television which is altogether too bland and "nice." They will, in turn, also seek to sell that product on the international market, adding one more complexity to the pattern of distribution of television product.

It is, however, not just the broadcasters of the major industrial societies who are responding. In New Zealand, the English-born director general of the New Zealand Broadcasting Corporation, Julian Mounter, has increasingly encouraged the production of programs domestically. As one commentator stated:

Mounter has insisted on new directions which many critical New Zealanders have been urging on television: More Programmes for and about Maoris and Pacific islanders, more programmes on the arts, industry and science, more New Zealand drama hours and more money, a jump in local production to 50% of prime time in the next couple of years...(Mounter argues it is time) to reflect our culture, encourage what is good about New Zealand and perpetuate the differences between New Zealand and the rest of the World. (Duncan, 1987)

It is important to emphasize that this policy is not born outside of any grasp of real problems which will be faced in seeking to realize it. Nor is it born of idealistic musings, though national pride should never be discounted. Rather it follows logically from the fact that Mounter has seen the research and knows that New Zealand-produced television is more popular than imported television.

In Africa, there are interesting numbers of agreements to coproduced and exchange programs. For example, in February at the 10th Pan-Africa Cinema Festival of Ouagadouga in Burkina Faso, a number of countries agreed to set up the exchange programs, including Benin, Burkina Faso, Guinea, Mali, Niger, Senegal, Togo, Tunisia, and Zaire. In May, Egypt and Madagascar agreed to exchange radio and television programs. Straws in the wind or meaningless acts? At this stage, it is almost impossible to know, though one must remember that all of these countries are relative newcomers to the television scene, and it could just be that what we are witnessing in these tiny events and agreements is the planting of the seed of something much more long-term and substantial. Writing about the situation in Australian television, one producer commented: "People were worried that Australian producers would end up making mid-Pacific product, but now there is a real concentration on legitimate Australian production for the international market" (Broadcast, 1987).

CONCLUSION

I do not want to linger over these concluding thoughts, since they have been fairly explicit throughout the whole paper. It does seem to me, however, important to make one related point, which is that it is extraordinary, given the amounts of money spent on so-called market research, that the level of understanding of the audience remains so limited and at times utterly confused. There is clearly a crying need, intellectually as well as commercially, to have a much more substantial grasp of what one might call the biography of viewing, and to see and grasp the minima as well as the maxima the lives of the television audience. One of the more important developments in

European communications research is the growth of ethnographic studies of television audience, seeing them as richly complex groups of individuals, rather than abstract statistics with skins. It is a development to be wholly welcomed. To offer a few final thoughts:

1. There has been a widespread belief that U.S. television has traditionally been ubiquitous and popular: This is not true.
2. There is a conviction that the new distribution technologies will readily pour their wares over the populations of the world: This is also not true.
3. There is a belief that the production of television products will become concentrated in a small number of centers, particularly in the United States: Once again, not true.
4. There are assumptions that international television product is the cultural avenue to the global village, whatever that is: Again, this is not true.

Instead, the reality is that U.S. television was never as popular, or even widespread as was assumed. National populations basically prefer national programming and the new distribution technologies are in for a very rough ride, as national governments and broadcasters are and will continue to fight back. In fact, the reality of the future of television is that it will not be a seamless robe woven in Hollywood, but a patchwork quilt, with some patches larger than others, but marked by variety and size, and dyed in many, many colors.

REFERENCES

Alvarado, M. (1989). *Global video*. London: BRU/Unesco/John Libbey.

Annual Reports and Accounts. (1986/87). Cable TV Authority (CTA).

Bekkers, W. (1987). The Dutch Public Broadcasting services in a multi-channel environment. In ESOMAR (Eds.), *The application of research to broadcasting decisions* (pp. 169–188). London: European Society of Market Research (ESOMAR).

Boyd, D. (1985). VCRs in developing countries: An Arab case study. *Media Development, 32*(1), 5–7.

Broadcast. (1987, April 16). p. 22.

Broadcast. (1987, May 6). p. 15.

Cable and Satellite Europe. (1987, January). p. 10.

Cantor, M., & Cantor, J. (forthcoming). Unpublished manuscript. London: Sage Publications.

Dent, T., Winkfield, N., & Lloyd, S. (1987). TV Usages in a multichannel environment. In ESOMAR (Eds.), *The application of research to broadcasting decisions* (pp. 141–168). London: European Society of Market Research (ESOMAR).

Duncan, J. (1987). In R. Patterson (Ed.), *International TV & Video Guide 1987* (pp. 136–140). London: Tantivy Press.

Eurodience, No. 1. (1987, July/August). Paris: Mediametrie/Institut National Audiovisuel.

Hamelink, C. (1983). *Cultural autonomy in global communications.* New York: Longman.

Hoffman, M. (1987). *Schwardzwaldlelinik.* Unpublished manuscript.

Lealand, G. (1983). *American programme on British screens.* London: Broadcasting Research Unit.

Lent, J. (1985). Video in Asia: Frivolity, frustration and futility. *Media Development, 32*(1), 8–10.

Lund, G., & Rolland, A. (1987). What happened in Norway when satellite TV arrived: The consequences for research. In ESOMAR (Ed.), *The application of research to broadcasting decisions* (pp. 189–194). London: European Society of Market Research (ESOMAR).

Marshall, F. (1987). Asia and the Pacific. In R. Paterson (Ed.), *International TV & Video Guide 1987* (pp. 120–134). London: Tantivy Press.

Morrison, D. (1987). *Invisible citizens: British public opinion and the future of broadcasting.* London: BRU/Libbey.

Ogan, C. (1986, October). *Media imperialism, video cassette piracy and the case of Turkey.* Unpublished paper, School of Journalism, Indiana University, Bloomington, IN.

Paterson, R. (1982). *Brazilian TV in context.* London: BFI.

PETAR. (1987, September). *Media International,* p. 12.

Petch, T. (1987). In R. Patterson (Ed.), *International TV & Video Guide 1987* (pp. 56–63). London: Tantivy Press.

Report on Radio Finland: Transcript published by the BBC in their weekly publication. (1987, April 4). *World Broadcasting Information.*

Report on RAI Radio. (1987, March 19). *BBC World Broadcasting Information.*

Schiller, H. (1969). *Mass communications and American Empire.* New York: Kelly.

Schultz, W. (1986). *Public service broadcasting in the Federal Republic of Germany.* Unpublished manuscript.

de Sola Pool, I. (1976). *The new structure of international communication: The role of research.* Leicester, England: International Association for Mass Communication Research.

Sturgess, B. (1985). *Report by SRW forecasting.* London: BBC.

Syfret, T. (1987, February). *Cable and Satellite Europe.*

Varis, T. (1984). The international flow of television programs. *Journal of Communication, 24*(1), 143–152.

Viorst, M. (1984,, January/February). TV that rules the Arab world. *Channels.*

Author Index

Subject Index

A

American Worldwide Holding Corporation, 138; see also BBC coproduction, British television

Advertising, 174-175; see also Television programming
in United States, 64-67

Anglophone, 128, 129, 132, 137

Association of Advertising Companies (UPA), 36

Associated Television (ATV), 142

B

Bank of England, 133-134

British Satellite Broadcasting (BBC), 192-196; see also British television

British television, 136-142
BBC, 137-138, 172
Channel Four, 138-139, 195
companies, 136
ITV, see Independent television
profitability of overseas sales, 141-142
Thames Televsion, 136, 140-141

C

Cultural identity, see National culture

D

Domestic Opportunity Advantage (DOA), 14

Distribution, see also Trade flows
films, 16, 157-158
television, 165-172
videocassette, 169-171

E

European Broadcasting Union (EBU), 45

F

Filmmaking, 148

Francophones, 129

G

Gray market, 86, 87
and consumer welfare, 97-100, 112-114, 119
economic analyses of, 88-91
fringe, 91-97
"linear" model of, 96, 99, 101, 102, 108-109, 110, 111, 112, 119, 120, 121
and producer welfare, 114-118

Global television
and advertising, 175-177
and public attitude, 177-192
Superchannel, 175-177

H

High definition television (HDTV), 150

I

Independent Television (ITV), 139-140, 193; see also British television

International Broadcast Authority (IBA), 3, 142, 143

Internationalization, 125ff

Iron law of television, 41-43, 58

Italian Motion Picture Association (ANICA), 36

M

Media Americanization, 44, 46, 48, 52-56

Media integration, 55-56

Motion Picture Association of America (MPAA), 76, 83, 84, 153

Motion Picture Export Association (MPEA), 72, 152